T0311754

Quality Service Management

Providing clear guidance for anyone servicing internal or external customers, this book offers a framework for analyzing and managing quality using a comprehensive closed-loop approach.

This book cuts through the complexities of the mantra "better, cheaper, faster" (BCF) and offers procedures for the evaluation of customer needs, the determination of performance metrics, and the design of effective customer satisfaction surveys. It details basic statistical techniques and packages the framework, procedures, and methods into a management construct that includes external quality certification systems and internal performance management systems. Importantly, the book also describes how these systems can be implemented in a virtual workplace.

This quality management book will be essential to service-oriented firms (financial, government, healthcare, hospitality, etc.), as well as any firm with internal customer service processes such as human resource management, purchasing, and accounting. Professionals at all levels, corporate trainers, and students will welcome this book's common set of principles and tools, accompanied by many case studies that illustrate how they are applied in various environments.

John Maleyeff is an educator, practitioner, and researcher who specializes in helping organizations analyze, optimize, and improve the delivery of goods and services. He is Associate Professor of Practice at Boston University's Metropolitan College, where he teaches courses in business process analysis, supply chain operations, and quality management. He was previously Associate Dean for Academic Affairs and Professor of Practice for the Education of Working Professionals portfolio at Rensselaer Polytechnic Institute. He has also held full-time positions at the U.S. Department of Defense, RCA's David Sarnoff Research Laboratory, and the LEGO Group A/S (while residing in Billund, Denmark). He has travelled extensively while teaching and researching international operations, especially in Western Europe and China. He has consulted with corporations in the areas of decision support, quality assurance, statistical analysis, computer simulation, and capacity planning. In these projects, he helped hospitals, municipalities, service firms, and manufacturers by creating decision tools that use data to make effective decisions in the presence of uncertainty. He has also developed training programs for practitioners, covering process improvement and statistical methods for quality analysis. These experiences have enabled him to leverage his knowledge and experiences to the benefit of his professionally oriented university students. A native of Philadelphia, Pennsylvania, he holds an undergraduate degree in Mathematics from East Stroudsburg University, and M.S. and Ph.D. degrees in Industrial Engineering & Operations Research from the University of Massachusetts. He is the author of *Service Science: The Analysis and Improvement of Business Processes* (Routledge imprint of Taylor & Francis, 2020). He has also authored a definitive guide to applying process improvement methods in government (Improving Service Delivery in Government with Lean Six Sigma, IBM Center for The Business of Government). He has presented his research at numerous conferences and has published extensively including in quality-oriented journals such as *Management Decision, Health Informatics Journal, Quality Engineering, Journal of Service Science and Management, Journal of Healthcare Risk Management, International Journal of Lean Six Sigma, International Journal of Educational Management, The TQM Journal, Journal for Healthcare Quality*, and *Benchmarking: An International Journal.*

Quality Service Management

A Guide to Improving Business Processes

John Maleyeff

Routledge
Taylor & Francis Group

NEW YORK AND LONDON

Cover image: (Getty Images) simon2579

First published 2022
by Routledge
605 Third Avenue, New York, NY 10158

and by Routledge
4 Park Square, Milton Park, Abingdon, Oxon, OX14 4RN

Routledge is an imprint of the Taylor & Francis Group, an informa business

© 2022 John Maleyeff

The right of John Maleyeff to be identified as author of this work has been asserted in accordance with sections 77 and 78 of the Copyright, Designs and Patents Act 1988.

All rights reserved. No part of this book may be reprinted or reproduced or utilised in any form or by any electronic, mechanical, or other means, now known or hereafter invented, including photocopying and recording, or in any information storage or retrieval system, without permission in writing from the publishers.

Trademark notice: Product or corporate names may be trademarks or registered trademarks, and are used only for identification and explanation without intent to infringe.

Library of Congress Cataloging-in-Publication Data
Names: Maleyeff, John, 1955– author.
Title: Quality service management : a guide to improving
business processes / John Maleyeff.
Description: New York, NY : Routledge, 2022. |
Includes bibliographical references and index.
Identifiers: LCCN 2021057253 | ISBN 9781032057545 (hardback) |
ISBN 9781032057514 (paperback) | ISBN 9781003199014 (ebook)
Subjects: LCSH: Reengineering (Management) | Management–Evaluation.
Classification: LCC HD58.87 .M364 2022 |
DDC 658.4/063–dc23/eng/20211208
LC record available at https://lccn.loc.gov/2021057253

ISBN: 9781032057545 (hbk)
ISBN: 9781032057514 (pbk)
ISBN: 9781003199014 (ebk)

DOI: 10.4324/9781003199014

Typeset in Bembo
by Newgen Publishing UK

Access the Support Material: www.routledge.com/9781032057514

To Frank C. Kaminsky, who taught me the right things to do and reminded me to do things right.

Contents

Figures

Tables

Preface

Every process manager seeks to meet their customers' needs in a prompt and cost-effective manner. Most firms have implemented controls to manage costs by creating budgets and periodically reporting cost variances from targets. Many firms ensure prompt service by using Lean methods to eliminate the time spent on activities that add no value for customers. This book concerns the desire of a process manager to deliver superior quality to their customers. It will focus on core services delivered to external customers as well as business processes that serve internal customers.

Several challenges compromise a process manager's ability to consistently ensure high-quality service delivery. First, customers have needs that are dynamic and multidimensional. A process manager can be ignorant of how each customer perceives the value they receive. Second, quality tends to be evaluated using metrics that are easily measured. These metrics can ignore more nuanced or difficult-to-measure customer needs. Third, process outcomes vary randomly even when the service delivery process is unchanged. Many managers do not account for variation when making decisions. Fourth, incentive structures built into many performance management systems motivate actions that conflict with high-quality service goals. Even well-intentioned workers can transition from serving customers to "serving the numbers."

The aim of this book is to provide a concise but comprehensive treatment of quality management as applied to processes that deliver services. These processes will be referred to as business processes regardless of whether their customer is internal or external. Readers will be exposed to the foundational principles that underlie the creation and management of an effective "quality system" that ensures value creation across all customer needs. The book describes fundamental qualitative and quantitative quality analysis techniques and provides guidance on how these techniques are applied in diverse service settings. It discusses the need for an organizational infrastructure to ensure that all incentives are aligned throughout an organization. Finally, it describes how quality improvement activities can be managed effectively when a project team is globally dispersed and culturally diverse.

The book will be useful for practitioners or soon-to-be practitioners within any organization. Some readers will apply the book's coverage to service delivery as a core focus of their firm, such as employees in hospitality, medical, government, and other service firms. Many readers will apply the book's coverage as a process manager with either internal or external customers, such as those engaged in accounting, human resources, information technology, business analytics, planning, call centers, and many other internal functions. Although these jobs concern service delivery, this group of readers may be employed by firm that manufactures products.

The book's intended audience includes individuals found in all levels within a firm, from entry level (including interns) to the firm's leadership. This group includes: (1) skilled workers in medium or large organizations who perform a specific service such as engineers, accountants, human resource professionals, and business intelligence analysts; (2) entrepreneurs in startup or small organizations who have a broad range of responsibilities; and (3) front-line service providers who are self-employed or work in established firms. The book may be especially helpful to new workers who can impress supervisors by showing their appreciation of how work processes can be improved.

With its integrated, closed-loop approach, the book provides an effective introduction to the field of service quality management. It discusses historical perspectives while maintaining a contemporary focus. The book will be useful for readers who seek a broad management focus as well as those who will implement specific quality analysis routines. A high-level executive will be shown how critical information can remain hidden behind simplistic dashboard displays. A mid-level manager will understand the essence of statistical approaches and how best to explain their application to their less technically sophisticated peers. Entry-level workers will learn how customer needs are determined and how to measure and analyze performance to support their superiors' decision making.

A significant portion of the book concerns process analysis, in particular the analysis of performance data. Data visualizations and subsequent interpretations represent an important skill for a process manager or quality analyst. Statistical methods are required because process outcomes are subject to variations. That is, a process generates outcome data that will vary randomly even when the process is unchanged. Readers will be exposed to statistical concepts that form the basis of performance data analysis. The analysis tools require only basic mathematical expertise, and instructions are provided to implement them in consistent ways. Many examples are provided to help readers overcome the challenges associated with the accurate interpretation of statistical calculations and data visualizations.

Topical coverage is integrated across chapters and readers are reminded of relationships among topics as they progress through the book. Many chapters include comprehensive case study examples to illustrate the methodologies addressed. Quantitative methods are presented in simple terms assuming that readers have a basic numeracy ability, although applications are implemented using a set of Excel templates. The book's companion web site provides these templates along with videos that demonstrate their use. The web site also includes practical exercises with solutions that reinforce quantitative methodologies and add nuance to the book's coverage.

This book would be very informative to undergraduate and full- or part-time graduate students who seek practical knowledge of service quality management. Its target audience includes entry-level and experienced professionals. Coverage applies within many academic disciplines found in business schools, hospitality departments, industrial management programs, engineering management departments, public health schools, and other practice-oriented disciplines. It can also be used as a textbook in courses such as service operations management or quality management, or courses focused on process improvements such as Lean management, Six Sigma, or Total Quality Management (TQM). It will be useful as a supplement for corporate and professional trainers.

The book is designed to help readers understand how to identify customer needs, find ways to measure quality, understand how to analyze performance data, and how to manage (or participate in) a quality improvement project. With the proliferation of process improvement programs, such as Lean Six Sigma (LSS), employers seek professionals who can both do their job and play a role in improving how their work is done. The book's coverage is consistent with many Six Sigma certification requirements.

The book includes a chapter devoted to the management of globally dispersed project teams that interact for quality improvement. These remote meeting environments became commonplace during the COVID-19 pandemic and will continue to become necessary due to other natural or manmade disruptions. It has also become common for organizations to employ groups of workers who perform similar tasks while located in geographically dispersed locations. Guidelines are provided that include helping remote project teams develop a sense of comradery, while participating effectively on quality improvement projects.

This book's high-level learning objective is to provide practitioners (who are directly or indirectly responsible for quality) with a highly relevant collection of concepts, methods, and procedures to ensure that customer needs are met now and in the future. A more precise list of learning objectives for service providers, their managers, and the firm's leadership is provided here (each learning objective corresponds to a chapter in the book):

1 To define quality and its determinants from both the service provider and the customer's perspective.
2 To appreciate process thinking that forms the foundation of contemporary quality management and to appreciate how process thinking may conflict with incentive systems.
3 To identify the needs of customers as a set of performance dimensions that are dynamic and evolving.
4 To define performance metrics and data collection plans so that quality is measured in unbiased and precise ways.

5   To create customer satisfaction surveys that motivate participation and ensure that results correspond precisely to customers' emotions.

6   To apply intuitive qualitative quality analysis tools that are focused on process learning and root cause identification.

7   To apply quantitative quality analysis tools using statistical summaries and data visualizations that inform rather than confuse or mislead.

8   To understand probability models at a conceptual level, to apply them properly, and explain their use to others.

9   To implement control charts that determine if a process has changed with visual guidance for root cause discovery.

10 To evaluate process quality to determine if performance is consistent with internal targets or external benchmarks.

11 To make sustainable improvements to a business process using Lean methods and innovative approaches.

12 To create a quality improvement system based on LSS that requires a supportive organizational infrastructure to ensure long-term success.

13 To manage quality improvement projects using a formal DMAIC structure that ensures consistency across the firm and over time.

14 To implement a comprehensive quality system that conforms with process thinking and meets contemporary standards.

15 To create a remote quality improvement system for projects with geographically dispersed and culturally diverse teams.

This book recognizes that quality management consists of a set of management principles and a collection of statistical techniques that are implemented by people. A quality system will not be effective unless these three elements – principles, techniques, and people – are integrated effectively. The book's approach ensures that these three elements are addressed at every stage of quality management – quality system design, quality assurance, and quality improvement.

Acknowledgments

I have been fortunate to learn from many extraordinary individuals during my quality management journey. Frank C. Kaminsky exposed me to the teachings of W. Edwards Deming, whose philosophies inform many pages of this book. He also taught me that every process is a random number generator whose behavior an analyst should seek to uncover. The late Robert D. Davis taught me to keep my work practical and to respect everyone I encounter in a workplace. Bob's influence on my approach to work and life will never be forgotten. I am grateful for the opportunity to work with colleagues who helped me gain perspective about statistics and quality. They include the late Poul Dalsgaard, David Rainey, Edward Arnheiter, the late Venkat Venkateswaran, and the late J. Byron Nelson. Special thanks to Danielle Song and Yuzhen Liang, who assisted me by developing many of the book's practical examples and by confirming the accuracy of quantitative calculations and visualizations. Finally, I thank Meredith Norwich at Taylor & Francis for her support during my belated book-writing career.

1   Introduction to service quality management

Introduction

The management of quality constitutes a complete system including a philosophy, a framework, and a set of methodologies for analysis and improvement. This system should support decision making at leadership, management, and operational levels. Its intent is to evaluate performance, maintain customer satisfaction, identify the root causes of quality-related problems, operate an improvement methodology that maintains quality as defined by constantly evolving customer needs. A quality management system is unique in its integration of decision-making processes, analysis methodologies, and the psychology of how humans behave in the context of the incentive systems within which they work.

This chapter introduces two definitions of quality, one evaluated objectively from the firm's perspective and the other evaluated subjectively by the customer. It lists and describes the contributions of five key leaders whose teachings underlie the book's content: Walter Shewhart, Joseph Juran, W. Edwards Deming, Kaoru Ishikawa, and Leonard Berry. It describes a process thinking approach that seeks to address quality at its source rather than relying on inspections. The state of contemporary quality management is discussed with a focus on Six Sigma and its define-measure-analyze-improve-control (DMAIC) construct. The focus is on both core processes that provide services to external customers and business processes that provide services to internal customers.

Definition of quality

The scope of service quality management encompasses all business processes that work together to create the firm's products and services, including supporting processes that serve the needs of internal customers in service or manufacturing firms. Quality is defined from two perspectives, and the quality system would include mechanisms for measuring quality with respect to both perspectives. They are:

DOI: 10.4324/9781003199014-1

Provider perspective: Quality is defined as the degree to which process output meets its specified performance standard. This standard is either externally imposed (e.g., by contracts, established criteria, or government regulations) or internally imposed (e.g., by leadership dictates, competitor performance, or improvement targets). The measurement of quality based on this definition is accomplished using an inspection system that should provide unbiased and precise performance data.

Customer perspective: Quality is defined as the degree to which a service satisfies customers. Customer satisfaction is influenced by their individual expectations, which are based on service provider information as well as customers' related experiences. Quality derived from this definition is subjective but important to monitor as customer needs evolve. The main mechanism for measuring quality based on this definition is a customer satisfaction survey that should be provide unbiased and precise data.

Both perspectives should be considered equally important to a process manager. The provider perspective provides more timely and comprehensive information. The customer perspective can suffer from delays and can be less comprehensive, although it is more relevant to the firm's success. Together, these perspectives provide all the information needed to measure quality while maintaining close contact with customers to ensure that their evolving needs are met.

Consider a troubleshooting call center where the firm targets a maximum hold time of 10 minutes. Accordingly, a relevant performance metric is the percentage of calls with a 10-minute or less hold time, which constitutes the provider perspective. Many customers, however, may consider a 10-minute wait to be unacceptable, which constitutes the customer perspective. In this case, customer surveys will show dissatisfaction with the hold time, even when the internal 10-minute standard is reliably met. Good performance to the internal standard coexists with poor customer satisfaction. An effective quality analysis approach would encompass both perspectives and clearly delineate this conflict.

Performance dimensions

Both perspectives of quality should be applied to the way customers define the value of the service they receive. This robust value definition should be based on the entirety of how a customer evaluates quality. It should avoid the potential for measuring quality based on narrowly focused contractual agreements or easy-to-collect performance metrics. Consider an insurance firm that outsources claims processing. The service provider may be flawless in processing claims accurately, but they may be inconsistent at processing claims quickly because they may ask many questions when claims have unusual requirements. The client firm likely defines value based on factors such as accuracy, timeliness, and competency, among others.

Performance dimensions (also called discriminators or drivers) are categories that span all of the ways in which a customer evaluates service quality. The list of performance dimensions should be tailored to customers of the business process under study. A banking customer who applies for a mortgage may be concerned with six performance dimensions: (1) a convenient application process; (2) an accurate analysis; (3) a fast decision; (4) knowledgeable service providers; (5) courteous interactions; and (6) information security. The need to establish performance dimensions extends to business-to-business services where contractual agreements exist. Although a contract may be narrowly focused (e.g., on cost and delivery), a sustainable relationship may depend on other factors that make the relationship fruitful for both parties.

Historical evolution and influencers

The industrial revolution and interchangeable parts manufacturing (circa 1800) created a need for companies to control the quality of manufactured items. The first quality departments focused almost entirely on postproduction inspections with the intent to separate good items from bad items. When inspecting 100% of products was not practical (financially or practically), a random sample of items was inspected. The first formal quality control sampling plans were developed by Harold Dodge (1893–1976) during World War II. These plans, called acceptance sampling, required the inspection of a specified number of items from each batch of manufactured items. On the basis of the inspection results, the entire batch was either accepted and sent to customers or rejected and returned to the manufacturer.

The Dodge approach has also been applied to services, albeit less formally and not as commonly. For example, a natural tendency of many service process managers is to review (i.e., inspect) process output prior to delivery to customer. Consider the following examples: (1) product designs are reviewed by the engineering manager before delivery to the manufacturing department; (2) architectural projects proposals are reviewed by a partner before submission to the client; (3) in-hospital patient pharmaceutical plans are reviewed by the lead pharmacist before initiation; and (4) analytical calculations are checked for accuracy by a senior technical expert before presentation. Some form of sampling may be employed, although often sampling is subjective based on perceptions, such as when the work of first-year employees is checked.

It has become clear that assuring quality with inspections, reviews, or checks has many drawbacks, including: (1) they place the responsibility for quality in the hands of inspectors who were often not process experts; (2) they add time to the service; (3) they use valuable resources inefficiently; (4) they do not identify many noncompliant characteristics; and (5) they are ineffective at facilitating improvements. The last drawback is important to highlight – inspectors focus on identifying nonconformances (i.e., errors) rather than carefully recording their occurrences. This approach precludes the creation of data sets that can be analyzed for root causes of poor quality.

In summary, a system of service QA based on inspections is ineffective. The goal of a process manager should be to maintain quality levels that satisfy customers. This goal is achieved by understanding customer needs, designing a superior process, collecting relevant performance data, identifying (and removing) the root cause of problems, and making improvements when conditions warrant. Inspections whose intent is to separate good from bad are ineffective at helping the process manager achieve these goals. A better approach is described later in this chapter, based on the foundational philosophies and methodologies introduced by five key leaders in quality management.

Walter Shewhart's influence

Walter Shewhart (1891–1967) was a scientist at Western Electric and an important quality management pioneer. His most important contribution was the development of methodologies for statistical quality control that used performance data to improve quality. These methods are included in *Economic Control of Quality of Manufactured Product* (Shewhart, 1931). Shewhart's intent was to analyze quality-related data so that evidence was preserved that would be helpful for root cause analysis (RCA). His methods aim to develop a detailed understanding of a process's behavior in the context of the statistical variations expected in its outcomes. Shewhart's most important contribution was the development of statistical control charts. These graphical representations, covered extensively in this book, are designed to apply a process thinking approach to quality analysis. Control charts have statistical underpinnings that form a set of decision rules that remove the subjectivity from their interpretation.

Shewhart's second contribution was the creation of a quality improvement framework called the Shewhart cycle or plan-do-check-act (PDCA). A similar approach is called plan-do-study-act (PDSA). Although PDCA is often called the Deming Cycle, Deming credits Shewhart with the development of the approach. PDCA provides an important foundation that has spawned many current process improvement approaches, most notably the Six Sigma DMAIC framework detailed later in this book.

W. Edwards Deming's influence

W. Edwards Deming (1900–93) is the most important figure in the history of quality management. In 1950, at the invitation of the Japanese Union of Scientists and Engineers, Dr. Deming introduced his philosophy of management to Japanese industrialists. Deming's teachings became popular in the United States (U.S.) after a 1980 NBC television broadcast *If Japan Can … Why Can't We*, which introduced Deming and his philosophies to a U.S. audience. Through the 1980s, Deming was a sought-after conference speaker and corporate consultant. His teachings emphasized management's responsibility for creating a process thinking quality system. He pleaded with managers to stop blaming employees for quality problems, which he explained were caused mainly by the system within which the employees worked. Deming railed against many traditional management ideas, such as the misconception that improving quality would increase costs (he emphasized that if quality improved, costs would decrease).

Although he was educated as a statistician, Deming was highly critical of acceptance sampling. In his landmark book *Out of the Crisis* (Deming, 1986), Deming listed his 14 Points for Management. Among them, he stated: "Cease dependence on inspection to achieve quality. Eliminate the need for inspection on a mass basis by building quality into the product in the first place." He taught that acceptance sampling, with its goal of separating good from bad, was ineffective principally because it was not designed to find the root cause of poor quality. Deming advocated the use of Shewhart's statistical control charts, which shifted quality analysis from a passive to an active endeavor that sought to understand and improve processes.

Deming's Deadly Diseases of Management addresses what he saw as problems with traditional methods of management (Deming, 1986, p. 97). The five deadly diseases are as follows:

1 Lack of constancy of purpose to plan product and service that will have a market and keep the company in business and provide jobs.
2 Emphasis on short-term profits: short-term thinking, fed by fear of unfriendly takeover and push from bankers and owners for dividends.
3 Evaluation of performance, merit rating, or annual review.
4 Mobility of management; job hoping.
5 Management using only visible figures, with little or no consideration of figures that are unknown or unknowable.

Joseph Juran's influence

Joseph Juran (1904–2008) was influential in creating the profession of quality management. He promoted quality-related training and education of managers, and he advocated for a new role of the quality department. Its role would be changed to include responsibility for the development and implementation of quality systems. Juran's trilogy (quality planning, quality control, and quality improvement) helped to promote a professional emphasis on the field of quality by shifting the emphasis from inspections to a more broad focus on quality improvement. Juran, along with Deming, was among the American business leaders sent to Japan after World War II to consult with Japanese business leaders. After his retirement from Western Electric, Juran became a sought-after consultant and highly regarded author. Juran's *Quality Control Handbook* is among the most important works in the field of quality management (Juran, 2010).

Juran (and others) also quantified the cost of quality (COQ), which includes four categories: (1) prevention costs (e.g., planning and training for quality); (2) appraisal costs (e.g., performing inspections and auditing); (3) internal failure costs (e.g., correcting defects or mistakes found within the firm); and (4) external failure costs (e.g., correcting defects or mistakes identified by customers). Some practitioners refer to the latter two categories as the cost of poor quality (COPQ). Some organizations routinely collect data on internal failures (often called turnbacks) and external failures (often called escapes). Juran was active in promoting a concept called quality circles based on Kaoru Ishikawa's work in Japan, which (along with the Shewhart cycle) has influenced more recent quality improvement systems.

Kaoru Ishikawa's influence

Kaoru Ishikawa (1915–89) was a leader in the implementation of new quality theories in Japan during the years after 1945, including those espoused by Deming and Juran. He was a practicing engineer until he became a university professor in 1947. He stressed that managers should involve employees in the business as essential resource, and that quality should be defined from the customer's perspective. Workers should be cognizant of the business's objectives and possess full confidence in the tools they employ to assure quality. The organization should implement a systematic long-term approach that facilitates full cooperation across functions within the firm.

Ishikawa was the inventor of quality circles, where workers implement analysis tools based on training provided by their managers. He believed that a few basic tools would solve most quality-related problems. He invented or encouraged the use of several of the basic quality tools discussed later in the book and included in *Guide to Quality Control* (Ishikawa, 1982). In particular, he advocated the use of fishbone diagram (also called the cause-and-effect or Ishikawa diagram), check sheets, control charts, and Pareto charts.

Ishikawa also emphasized the importance of internal customers. He believed that specialization of skills within a firm had the potential to compromise the involvement of employees across the organization. He stressed that internal processes need to be monitored to ensure that they contribute to the overall quality of goods and services sold to customers. As such, the methods included in this book are equally relevant to services delivered to either external or internal customers.

Leonard Berry's influence

Leonard L. Berry (1942–) is a university educator and leader in the field of service and healthcare quality. He is known for his authorship of *Discovering the Soul of Service* (Berry, 1999), which includes a study of successful service businesses. The aim of this study was to identify the drivers that assured long-term success. Although successful companies cover a wide range of businesses, they are similar in many ways. Many of the drivers of success are associated with quality (such as executional excellence) while others focus on human relationships (such as building trust-based relationships and investment in employee success).

Berry also worked with other academicians to develop a tool, called the SERVQUAL survey, for evaluating service quality (Parasuraman et al., 1985). The SERVQUAL survey consists of 22 questions that cover 5 performance dimensions: tangibles, reliability, responsiveness, assurance, and empathy. Each of the questions is asked in pairs, with the first question addressing the customer's perception of quality and the second question addressing their performance expectation. The coverage of performance dimensions later in this book was motivated by this work but includes dimensions that span a more robust range of customer needs that are customized for each process.

Contemporary quality management

The discipline of quality management encompasses all organizational activities associated with the design of quality systems, the implementation of these systems, and the improvement of both quality and the quality system. A quality system would include the following:

> *Quality Control:* The statistical methods that collect, analyze, and interpret quality-related information to determine if processes are creating products and services that are consistent with expected performance, based on performance metrics and customer satisfaction surveys.

> *Quality Assurance:* The procedures that an organization employs to ensure that products and services have quality levels that meet the needs of customers, including determining performance metrics and targets, and developing customer satisfaction surveys.

> *Quality Management:* The creation and maintenance of a quality system that integrates quality assurance and quality control, and ensures that the organization empowers everyone to participate in quality improvement activities.

Service quality management should implement a closed-loop and robust process thinking approach that recognizes the important contributions of its founders.

> The Shewhart influence will ensure that the analysis of outcome data will account for expected variations while including mechanisms for identifying root cause. The quality system will include control charting and a structured quality improvement framework.

> The Deming influence will appreciate that performance is dictated primarily by the system within which a process and its workers operate. A quality system will avoid creating incentives that ignore variation or

assume that an individual is solely responsive for the quality of process output.

The Juran influence will assign the quality department responsibility for maintaining the quality system and training workers so that the Shewhart and Deming approaches can take root. A quality system will be cognizant of both visible and hidden costs that result from poor quality.

The Ishikawa influence will verify that employees and their managers work in concert to ensure that process output meets the needs of customers. A quality system will include cooperative team efforts to improve quality using basic qualitative and quantitative tools.

The Berry influence will create an organizational culture that possesses features common to high quality entities, including seeking extraordinary performance and nurturing an effective workforce. A quality system will identify the totality of customer needs listed as a set of performance dimensions.

The first quality systems that incorporated Deming's philosophy along with Juran's trilogy, the Shewhart techniques, and other process thinking precepts was TQM. Initiated in the early 1980s, TQM moved the responsibility for ensuring quality from the quality department and to each process manager. Quality control transitioned from inspections to control charts. Producers and service providers monitored the quality of process output, with the quality department maintaining the system within which the required activities were undertaken. Variants of quality circles and the Shewhart cycle formed the basis of quality improvement.

TQM was effective for many organizations, especially those that created a comprehensive management infrastructure allowing the requisite culture to take root. But sustained TQM implementation faced a variety of challenges in many firms. At the operational level, weak or decentralized coordination led to inconsistencies in approaches across functions. Communication across business units and departments was ineffective and employee training was often inconsistent. More importantly, leadership sometimes failed to appreciate the legacy performance incentives that compromised TQM's effectiveness.

Six Sigma

Six Sigma was initiated by Bill Smith (1929–93), an engineer at Motorola Corporation. Smith noticed that product returns were increasing even while manufacturing processes remained stable. It became evident to Smith that a decrease in product quality had resulted from the increased complexity of products, rather than deficiencies in manufacturing capabilities. Compared to simpler products, complex products have many more opportunities for defect (OFD), defined as the number of ways for a product to be defective. Although a set of good manufacturing processes may be sufficient for a simple product, superior manufacturing processes are necessary when products are more complex.

For example, let's assume that a process generates a defective outcome 0.1% of the time (one per 1,000 outcomes). For a final product that consists of 100 such outcomes (100 OFDs), the final products would average 0.1 defect, whereas for a final product that consists of 1,000 OFDs, the final products would average 1.0 defect. Hence, as products become more complex (and all other factors remain unchanged), the final product quality will decrease as the number of OFDs increases. At one time, the Ford Motor Company estimated that an automobile contained about 18,000 OFD.

During the period when Smith was studying the Motorola dilemma, the generally accepted conformance target was 99.7% (so-called 3-Sigma quality). Smith saw the need to create stricter quality goals, and the 6-Sigma quality metric was created. A process producing an outcome with 6-Sigma quality generates 3.4 defects per million opportunities (DPMO). Readers will note how this final product goal compares to the traditional goal of 99.7% OFD conformance.

Although the 6-Sigma metric was based specifically on process characteristics found at Motorola, it became widely adopted as a quality standard. Over time, Six Sigma developed as a comprehensive quality system to replace TQM. As a quality system, Six Sigma includes a formal project-based framework for process improvement (called DMAIC) and a highly structured training regimen based on certifying individuals as belts (green belt, black belt, etc.). Today, Six Sigma places less emphasis on the 6-Sigma quality metric and tends to emphasize quantifiable financial success. The latter focus is one with which Deming would likely disagree, although many aspects of the Deming philosophy can be found in the principles and tools of Six Sigma.

DMAIC

Many practitioners consider the Six Sigma's project management framework to be its main strength. Known as DMAIC, it refers to five stages of improvement project execution: Define, Measure, Analyze, Improve, and Control. With DMAIC, improvement projects follow similar steps across an organization and common tools are employed during each step. By using a standard approach, project execution requires less direct supervision and objectivity is maintained when applying analysis methodologies. The five stages of DMAIC are defined here:

> *Define*: Describe the problem, the project's purpose, the process boundaries, key stakeholders, and customers. Finalize the project team, list relevant metrics, indicate important risk factors, and develop a project plan. The result is a concise problem statement, objective, and project charter.

Measure: Gather information on the current process, develop a process map, describe process inputs and outputs, collect data and summarize using statistical methods, and confirm accuracy of measurement systems. The result is a description of the current process focusing on the problem at hand.

Analyze: Evaluate process maps and associated data to identify wasteful activities and instances of unacceptable quality, identify root causes of problems, and confirm findings using statistical methods. The result is a thorough evaluation of the current process with a focus on where improvements should be targeted.

Improve: Use available methods to list potential corrective actions, choose improvement ideas, develop the revised approach (including benefits, costs, risks), and evaluate alterative interventions. The result is a set of improvement recommendations and their justification.

Control: Design a plan for ensuring that the predicted improvements are sustained by developing training courses, data collection routines, quality tracking mechanisms, and statistical analysis procedures. The result is a plan for confirming and sustaining the improvements.

Lean management

Quality management has elements in common with Lean production, a term originally used to describe the Toyota Production System (TPS) developed by Taiichi Ohno (1912–90) and Shigeo Shingo (1909–90) at Toyota Motor Manufacturing in Japan. Lean production is characterized by the elimination of time spent on wasteful activities so that only items in demand by customers are produced, thereby eliminating costly inventory and streamlining the production lead time. The concepts that underlie Lean production are routinely applied to services, healthcare, and other businesses. It is now common to use the term Lean management, or simply Lean, when referring to approaches that are based on the TPS.

The TPS is firmly grounded in respect for people. The workers who are directly involved in delivering a service have the best understanding of customer needs and the best ideas on how to improve the service they deliver. As a clear application of the respect for people concept, Toyota issues a guarantee to workers that no layoffs will result from a process improvement project. Studies in North America have shown that organizations that have long-term success implementing effective process improvement also state this guarantee.

To improve quality in a Lean setting, many organizations employ a methodology called kaizen (loosely translated from Japanese as change for the better). A kaizen project (or kaizen event) would typically consist of a dedicated 1–5-day effort. The project team would include managers and employees, with a facilitator (often referred to as a sensei). With top management support (and often direct involvement), the project team analyzes the current process, identifies wasteful activities, and removes as much waste as reasonably possible. With kaizen, a quick good solution is valued over an optimal solution that may take more time to determine.

Lean and Six Sigma have many features in common and many organizations have implemented an LSS program that combines elements of both systems. LSS implementations often employ a DMAIC framework with standard training denoted by green and black belts. LSS service organizations often emphasize Lean methods because they require little mathematical knowledge and can have substantial impacts on service process quality. Examples include 5S (maintaining an organized workspace), poka yoke (mistake-proofing a task), and standard work.

Many organizations operate quality systems that differ from Lean and/or Six Sigma, although they also have many elements in common. The quality improvement system developed by the Institute for Healthcare Improvement (IHI) is called the IHI-QI system. Both IHI-QI and Six Sigma include a formal project framework for improving quality. They are both heavily grounded in the Deming philosophy of management and Lean. Maureen Bisognano (CEO, IHI) has been quoted as stating "Everyone in healthcare should have two jobs: to do the work and to improve how the work is done." IHI advocates that leaders in healthcare need to promote a system that encourages, educates, and empowers healthcare practitioners to take part in quality improvement efforts.

References

Berry, L.L. (1999). *Discovering the Soul of a Service*. New York: Free Press.

Deming, W.E. (1986). *Out of the Crisis*. Cambridge, MA: MIT Center for Advanced Engineering Study.

Ishikawa, K. (1982). *Guide to Quality Control*. Tokyo: Asian Productivity Organization.

Juran, J.M. (2010). *Juran's Quality Handbook* (6/e). New York: McGraw-Hill.

Parasuraman, A., Zeithaml, V.A., and Berry, L.L. (1985). A conceptual model of service quality and its implications for future research. *Journal of Marketing 49*(4), 41–50.

Shewhart, W.A. (1931). *Economic Control of Quality of Manufactured Product*. New York: Van Nostrand.

2 Process thinking in service quality management

Introduction

Contemporary quality systems are based on a philosophy known as process thinking. This philosophy seeks to control quality at its source, while abandoning outdated attempts to inspect quality into a product or service. It is based on the premise that good processes generate good outcomes. Its implementation is complicated by the presence of random variation because outcomes of a process will vary even when the process remains unchanged.

This chapter begins by defining a business process, including its nuanced characteristics and customer types. It introduces a descriptive mechanism known as SIPOC. A discussion follows that details the concept of random variation and its impacts on decision making. An example is provided that compares process thinking to an outcome-focused approach that ignores variation. Deming's system of profound knowledge, a foundational principle of process thinking and contemporary quality management is then described using a comprehensive example.

The business process

All organizations provide external customers with products or services by operating a system of interconnected business processes. Each of these business processes has suppliers and customers, most of whom are internal. Every business process transforms inputs to outputs, and its customers judge the quality of process outputs based on their needs. When effective, this system of business processes works in concert so that the quality of goods or services provided to external customers is consistent with their needs. A single firm will operate a wide variety of business processes, and many of these processes operate in a similar fashion across firms.

Some service processes are fundamental to the operation of the firm by serving external customers with core needs. They are found in hotels, hospitals, and government offices, among many others. Other service processes serve a firm's external customers with supplemental services, such as repairs and troubleshooting. Some of these firms may, in fact, be a manufacturing business. The customers of both core and supplemental services

DOI: 10.4324/9781003199014-2

may be consumers or other businesses. Most business processes exist within every firm. They support internal customers so that its external customers are served effectively, and costs are managed. The three main types of business processes are described in more detail in subsequent sections.

Core business processes

The nature of a core business process will depend on its sector within the global economy. In the United States, major industries include natural resources and mining, manufacturing, healthcare, education, and services. Many types of core business processes exist within each sector. For example, financial processes involve investing and tax preparation, manufacturing processes include machining and assembly, education includes instruction and evaluation, restaurants include food preparation and table service, and hospitals include urgent care and surgery. Core processes serve different sets of external customers, although everyone is a customer of firms across numerous sectors.

Core process can exist within firms classified as for-profit, nonprofit, government, and charitable, among others. Performance data collected from a process will possess commonality across sectors. Although processes within a sector appear unique, there are opportunities to apply improvement ideas to processes across sectors. Quality system structures are robust and therefore they will look similar across sectors even when the process types are dissimilar. Practitioners should learn from successful applications found in sectors other than their own. This book will include examples of core processes in all nonmanufacturing sectors to illustrate how its concepts and techniques are universally applied.

Supplemental processes

Customers of every industry sector are also provided with products or services that supplement the core offering of each firm. For example, an airline serves food to a passenger and a utility company offers troubleshooting to a homeowner. Some firms use supplemental services to obtain a competitive advantage, such as a producer who helps customers choose the best product for their needs. A firm can earn a negative reputation by ignoring the value of these supplemental services to customers. Examples include a call center with long hold times or a web site with confusing information.

Similar supplemental processes are common across business sectors. Many firms provide customers with similar services that include instructional materials, bill paying applications, informational websites, comfortable facilities, and troubleshooting help desks. Hence, performance data will likely possess common metrics and improvement ideas will often apply across sectors. Performance data across sectors should be analyzed in similar ways. Enlightened process managers will recognize these commonalities and thereby learn from more successful firms. For example, a hospital administrator can better serve patients and their visitors by studying how successful hotels operate patient check-in, check-out, and other hospitality services.

Administrative and support processes

A myriad of business processes that serve internal customers can be found within every firm in every industry sector. The finance department creates pro forma financial statements, performs cost analyses, and manages the firm's investment portfolio. The human resource management department recruits and interviews potential employees, maintains the talent management system, and negotiates employee contracts. The information technology (IT) function writes code for the firm's applications, maintains employee hardware and software, and offers a troubleshooting help desk. The sales and marketing function maintains the firm's social media presence, surveys customers, and identifies new marketing strategies. The purchasing department identifies new suppliers, evaluates supplier management structures, and manages purchase orders. The sustainability function develops business continuity plans, evaluates risks, and assists with energy conservation. Many other examples can be stated.

The myriad of support processes constitutes a web of interconnections. Their customers are usually internal because they exist completely within the firm's organizational structure. Internal customers include decision makers within the firm, as well as others who need these services to work effectively. Managing quality can be a challenge because their effectiveness as well as their inefficiencies are often hidden. For example, their costs are aggregated into indirect costs or overhead categories and quality is not easily measured. Although budgets exist, the overall cost impacts are filtered throughout the firm and hence are impossible to quantify precisely. These services are not ignored in the pages that follow. In fact, they are embraced as opportunities to significantly impact a firm's long-term outlook.

Process description

Every business process transforms inputs to outputs. Sometimes the transformations are physical, such as when a plastic molding process converts plastic granulate to a LEGO brick. Other times, information is transformed, such as when an analyst converts a set of numbers to a useful visualization so that their internal customer can make an informed decision. Every business process generates outcomes that can be used to determine how well it meets customers' needs. The importance of thoroughly understanding each business process motivates a common descriptive method, called SIPOC.

SIPOC

The five critical components of any business process are: suppliers, inputs, process, outputs, and customers, which is called SIPOC. Each component of SIPOC is described here.

Suppliers provide inputs that are used to initiate the process. Suppliers may be external (e.g., a regulator supplying updated rules to an audit process) or internal (e.g., a manager supplying job descriptions to a hiring process). Suppliers can also be customers, such as a help desk caller supplying a problem description to a technician.

Inputs are provided by suppliers. They can be tangible (e.g., a sick patient, an item to be stored, a taxi customer) or intangible (e.g., a patient's description of pain, storage requirements for an item, or a taxi destination). Intangible inputs are usually referred to as information. The information is considered intangible even when it has a visible manifestation, such as a written problem statement.

Process refers to the activities that transform inputs to outputs. The collection of activities can be described effectively using a process map or flowchart. Improvements are usually accomplished by changing the way activities are performed. Performance data inform improvement projects by highlighting those activities that are compromising the process's ability to meet customer needs.

Outputs are provided to customers. Tangible outputs generally appear differently after being transformed, although exceptions exist (e.g., a child should appear the same at the end of a school day). Intangible service outputs usually take the form of information, even when presented in a physical form (e.g., a blueprint is valued for the information it contains).

Customers are the entities receiving the service outputs. Service customers usually have three main goals. They want the service to solve their problem; they want their problem solved inexpensively; and they want their problem solved quickly. As such, they often evaluate performance as consisting of three goals, referred to as better, cheaper, and faster (BCF).

Process performance

A process manager is responsible for ensuring that customers' BCF goals are met. The most visible of these performance categories is cost (i.e., the cheaper goal). Through budget variance reports that compare money spent to money allocated, process managers are incentivized to maintain acceptable cost levels. They may strive to keep all resources (including workers) busy so that service delivery costs are minimized. Costs are somewhat visible to many customers because they affect its price. Because most internal customers pay no fee for service, a process manager needs to be cognizant of how their focus on cost minimization can affect the better and faster BCF goals for these customers.

The second most visible performance category is speed (i.e., the faster BCF goal). Unfortunately, many process managers compensate for anticipated delays and inefficiencies by quoting long service times to customers (e.g., for programming support, design changes, or web site updates). Although managers may be satisfied when due dates are met, customers' perception of performance will usually be poor (i.e., they are not fooled). Lean methods are used in many firms to increase speed by reducing time spent on non-value-added activities. Lean methods are addressed only briefly in this book; a primer is available for readers interested in additional details (Maleyeff, 2021).

The third and least visible performance category is quality (i.e., the better BCF goal). Measuring performance relative to this goal is extremely complex when compared to the cheaper and faster goals because: (1) a consistent definition of quality may not exist across customers; (2) customers' definition of quality will evolve over time; (3) there are many dimensions across which customers define quality; and (4) process outcome data that form the basis of quality analysis will vary randomly. This book addresses these challenges by providing methodologies devoted to quality analysis and improvement.

Outcomes and variation

In quality management, the term outcome is used to denote a characterization of process output. Outcomes associated with most manufacturing processes include physical characteristics, such as dimensions, strength, and texture. Service outcomes are more nuanced, but they possess commonality across process types. Time is always an important process outcome that characterizes its ability to provide the service in a prompt manner. This outcome is typically expressed as waiting time or turnaround time (i.e., waiting plus service). At least one outcome should exist for every multidimensional need of a service customer.

Outcome data are analyzed periodically, with timeframes that correspond to the nature of the process and the number of customers. A considerable challenge is introduced by random variation, which affects all process outcome data. A decision maker (or a system that supports a decision maker) must be able to distinguish between outcome variation from a process that has not changed from outcome variation from a process that has changed. As stated by the consultant and educator Frank C. Kaminsky, "the data change even when the process remains the same."

Practitioners can learn to appreciate how outcomes derived from an unchanged business process vary randomly by using a manual simulation or a computerized random number generator. Consider the following simulation using decks of ordinary playing cards. Each deck contains 52 cards with four suits in equal proportion – hearts, spades, clubs, and diamonds. They are used to represent a process during a single week. Each card represents process output. The card's suit will represent the outcome, with clubs considered undesirable (hearts, diamonds, and spades represent desirable outcomes). After a card is drawn, it is replaced, the desk shuffled, and another card is drawn. The generation of outcomes continues until 20 cards are selected, representing 20 customers during one week of operation. This procedure of drawing 20 cards at random is repeated for 24 decks so that 24 weeks of process outcome data are generated.

The simulation is generic and can be described as mimicking different types of processes and outcomes. For example, a club can be described as representing a late project, an unhappy customer, an unsuccessful treatment, or a denied loan. In Excel, the suits can be simulated using the function rand between (1, 4). This function generates a random integer between 1 and 4 inclusive, and the value 4 would represent the undesirable outcome. In both the manual and electronic simulations, we know that the process is unchanged and that it generates undesirable outcomes with a likelihood of exactly 25%.

The following data were generated by the simulation (starting in week 1 and ending in week 24): **7, 3, 4, 5, 6, 2, 4, 9, 2, 4, 2, 7, 2, 4, 5, 7, 4, 3, 5, 3, 5, 1, 6, and 4**. In week 1, for example, 7 of the 20 cards were clubs, a proportion of 35%. As one would expect, the proportion of clubs dealt per day varied, even though the process had not changed. A process manager would need to appreciate that variation will exist in these outcomes in order to successfully use these data to make a decision regarding performance. This is true about the simulation and it is true about data collected from any business process.

Process thinking

The concept of process thinking forms the core tenant of contemporary quality management. Process thinking recognizes that process performance results from numerous influences, and most of those influences cannot be controlled by service provider. These influences form sources of variation that cause outcomes to vary, even when the process remains unchanged. Process thinking replaces a system of rewards and punishments with a statistical analysis approach that seeks to understand the process. It endeavors to discover if a process has changed, if it is acceptable, and how it can be improved.

The understanding of process thinking is compromised by subtleties that can confuse first-time learners. Although inspections are not used to separate good from bad outcomes, inspection data remain the source of the information for implementing process thinking. The difference is found in the motivation for analyzing outcome data and the analysis methodologies that are employed. Process thinking is proactive and forward looking. Its application is best discussed by contrasting it with an alternative known as management by objective (MBO).

Comparison with MBO

MBO sets target performance levels for key process outcomes and rewards organizational entities (departments, managers, or workers) when the targets are met. These targets are based on peer organization comparison, prior performance levels, or stretch goals that seek to motivate workers to achieve superior performance. W. Edwards Deming considered MBO to be a flawed "management by numbers" scheme. He described its flaws as antithetical to process thinking by using an interactive exercise called the red bead game (Deming, 1986, pp. 346–54). In this section, the concepts illustrated with the red bead game are replicated using the playing card simulation.

In the playing card simulation, 20 cards were drawn at random over a simulated 24-week period. The number of clubs drawn, by week, were: **7, 3, 4, 5, 6, 2, 4, 9, 2, 4, 2, 7, 2, 4, 5, 7, 4, 3, 5, 3, 5, 1, 6, and 4.** To use the MBO approach, there needs to be a target for undesirable outcomes (i.e., clubs); we will assume that the management sets a target of no more than 4 clubs per week. This target corresponds to a 20% or lower proportion of clubs. The performance target was met during many of the weeks (e.g., weeks 2, 3, 6, etc.) and it was not met during other weeks (e.g., weeks 1, 4, 5, etc.). With MBO, a bonus may be forthcoming for the process manager in weeks during which the 4-club target was met. Readers are reminded that the likelihood that this process generates a club is 25% (an average of 5 clubs per week).

The simulated process is not acceptable because its 25% likelihood of clubs exceeds the target of 20% or fewer clubs. If this were a real process, many potential factors would exist for its being unacceptable, and a few of these factors would be directly controlled by the service provider or the process manager. These factors include supplier quality, worker education and training, technology support, customer expectations, and many other internal and external factors. In fact, the 20% target set by management may simply be unattainable under the current conditions. No system of rewards and punishments targeted at the process manager or service provider will change this fact.

The simulation highlights a dilemma for decision makers. The target of 20% or fewer clubs was met in many weeks by pure chance. In those weeks, the *data* met the target although the *process* was not acceptable. This circumstance exemplifies the concept that the data changed even though the process remained unchanged. As an example, in week 8 the number of clubs was 9 (45%) while in week 9 the number of clubs was 2 (10%). In both weeks 8 and 9, the *likelihood* of a club was exactly 25%. Meeting or not meeting the goal during a given week is meaningless without a statistical method that accounts for variation.

The problems posed by MBO in quality management are also present in other approaches that appear more benign. Consider the dashboards that many firms use to inform managers and executives of key performance indicators (KPIs). These dashboards often include a set of color-coded icons or dials that compare each key outcome to its target. The color green indicates that the target was achieved and the color red indicates that the target was not achieved. Sometimes yellow is used when the target is almost achieved. Dashboards are appealing but cannot be used to better understand processes because they do not account for variation. That is, the color may change even when the process remains the same (also, the color may not change when the process has in fact changed).

Dashboards and other MBO-like systems often lead to dysfunction as entities seek to "manage the numbers." The actions these methods can motivate range from subtle manipulations to outright fraud. This practice generates useless data, even if other more appropriate analysis approaches are employed. A quality system based on MBO (or a similar approach) does little to improve quality and usually causes managers to focus on meeting numerical goals while ignoring customer needs. Deming referred to the change in focus as moving from serving customers to serving the numbers.

Deming's system of profound knowledge

Deming described process thinking as the integration of mathematics, decision making, and human behavior. He recognized the importance of this integration by introducing his system of profound knowledge (Deming, 1993, pp. 92–115), which has four underpinnings: (1) appreciation for a system; (2) knowledge about variation; (3) theory of knowledge; and (4) psychology. They are detailed in the sections that follow.

Appreciation for a system

A business includes external suppliers and customers, along with a myriad of internal supplier-customer relationships that span the entire firm. This system comprises a system of interconnected processes. Each process consists of a sequence of activities, with rules, procedures, and incentives enforced by its process manager. All these activities impact the firm's long-term performance, often in ways that are difficult to predict when studying each activity independently. Changing one activity for the better can have detrimental effects on the system. In fact, systems with high levels of process complexity face an especially difficult task when coordinating activities for the common good.

The concept of a system is well understood in some settings, such as sports teams or orchestras. Although the intent of a soccer team is to score more goals than their opponent, the general manager would not consider rewarding players based primarily on the number of goals the player scored. The general manager understands that this incentive can lead to decreases in the team's overall performance by reducing cooperation among teammates. This same phenomenon will exist in a firm albeit not as obviously. For example, reducing operating costs for a training department may result in a bonus for its manager, but this decrease may have negative system-wide effects if employee skill levels are compromised.

Knowledge about variation

Deming once stated, "Understanding variation is the key to success in quality and business." Management needs to appreciate the existence of variation and create decision rules accordingly, so that MBO and other violations of process thinking principles are avoided. Shewhart (1931, pp. 8–25) explained that some variation is normal and expected, based on the numerous sources of variation that typically affect a process outcome. Other variation is unexpected – this variation is driven by a change that affects a process outcome. The job of the process manager is to quickly discover the root cause of this process change. Without knowledge about variation, a manager can mistakenly consider any change in an outcome as actionable.

A good example of what happens when variation is ignored concerns percentile or quartile rankings. Some talent management systems routinely reward (or punish) employees based on the quartile category within which their rated performance falls. Similarly, the U.S. government's healthcare system Medicare is required by law to penalize general care hospitals whose infection rates fall in the highest 25th percentile of patient safety issues. The intent of these policies is to motivate good performance and to identify entities that should be improved or eliminated. The problem is that 25% of any group will fall into the lowest 25th percentile, regardless of their performance. It would be more appropriate to apply an absolute standard when determining the acceptability of a process outcome, where the standard is based on the needs of customers and where variation is accounted for when determining a course of action.

Theory of knowledge

Everyday decisions involve a form of prediction based on science, intuition, or past experiences. We continue to travel the same route to work based on a prediction of how long it will take, the situations we may encounter, and the places where special attention is necessary. If a fundamental change happens, we adjust (e.g., by changing the route). In this way, we continue to refine the theory based on new knowledge. Information (or data) is not helpful unless it can form a basis for prediction. Deming pointed out that many statistical textbooks failed to stress the importance of maintaining the order each number in a data set was collected, because not maintaining the order compromises an analyst's ability to make predictions.

Theory of knowledge also concerns the value associated with a set of data that represent a process outcome. Consider the straight-forward task of counting the number of mistakes while proofreading a manuscript. It is unlikely that two proofreaders would generate the same outcomes from a common manuscript. For example, they may differ in how they account for acceptable words that have better alternatives. They may differ when classifying an unnecessary space character, which a customer would be unlikely to notice. To incorporate these data into a process thinking framework, a formal operational definition needs to be created so that consistency is maintained across proofreaders. Data need to be collected systematically with analysis procedures that maintain its time series orientation.

Psychology

In the system of profound knowledge, psychology refers to the interaction of people and the organization. Psychology includes how a manager should view a worker's contribution and how humans are motivated to behave as a result of the organization's incentive structure. In a healthy organization, workers' contributions depend on their unique talents. Some workers excel in technical skills, some have strong communication skills, and others learn quickly or bring positive energy to their workplace. It is impossible to devise a ranking system that will accurately order their contributions. A good leader will recognize the strengths and weaknesses of each worker. They would create ways for strong worker traits to be spread across the workplace, while providing guidance to workers who need improvement.

Ranking systems and employee review processes usually include schemes that use process outcomes as the basis for incentivizing workers to perform better. These schemes have the unintended consequences, such as discouraging knowledge sharing and encouraging mistake hiding. A perverse incentive exists whereby many workers seek to optimize their ranking regardless of its effects on customers. Consider a small firm that sells software applications to dentists for patient relationship management. Recent data showed that a percentage of new business resulted from cold calls to customers by sales staff, although the sales tracking system was not able to attribute a new customer to a specific staff member. Management incentivized sales staff to make as many cold calls as possible in an effort to increase sales, assuming that the percentage of successful calls would continue. Unfortunately, many sales staff concentrated on making more calls, rather than making effective calls. Sales staff did not take pride in their work because the firm treated them like a call-generating machine rather than a customer–nurturing human.

Illustrative example

Consider how the system of profound knowledge would be applied in the following setting. A business intelligence department consists of analysts who perform quantitative studies for other departments within a firm. Some analytics possess strong IT skills whereby they integrate disparate information so that others can use the data effectively. Other analysts excel at mathematical manipulations that some analysts find impossible. Some analysts can create innovative and informative visualizations of analysis outcomes. Other analysts have superior writing skills to generate clear yet concise reports. Finally, some analysts make excellent oral presentations that inform audiences in entertaining ways.

Appreciation for the system should cause leadership to contemplate ways to best motivate the entire group of analysts for the benefit of customers. They should recognize that no easily collected set of metrics can effectively measure the unique contributions of each analyst. They should understand that creating performance incentives based on one or more visible outcomes, like the number of reports completed per month, will likely only optimize parts of the system while potentially adversely affecting the whole.

Knowledge about variation should cause leadership to be cognizant of the numerous sources of variation that affect what is accomplished in the department. They should avoid creating dashboards that simply compare outcomes to targets such as the number of reports completed per month. Although the number of reports appears to be a valid measure of the group's productivity, setting up an incentive plan based on a target number of reports can lead to dysfunction. It is likely to result in an end-of-month rush to complete reports or holding back report until the next month if the target is already met. Analysts who are forced to concentrate on these metrics will be less effective by rushing report completion or sending customers reports later than planned.

Theory of knowledge should cause leadership to create predictions that can be used as a basis for identifying problems and finding areas needing improvement. They should start by gaining knowledge about customers – how do they judge the quality of the business intelligence department reports? Leadership should create suitable metrics that address the needs of customers, and then use quality analysis tools to quantify the variation in outcomes. They should use the data to better understand decision factors that correlate with better outcomes. They should apply this knowledge to future decision making, including hiring, training, and the purchase of updated hardware and software technologies.

Finally, psychology should cause leadership to be aware of how its workers interact with the management system. They should strive to motivate the group of analysts so that everyone takes pride in their work. Because different analysts possess different skills, the leader may want to organize informal group meetings where analysts inform each other about the reasons for their success. No two workers are alike; they have complementary skills and they can all learn from one another to do their jobs more effectively.

References

Deming, W.E. (1986). *Out of the Crisis*. Cambridge, MA: MIT Center for Advanced Engineering Study.

Deming, W.E. (1993). *The New Economics for Industry, Government, Education, 2/e*. Cambridge, MA: MIT Center for Advanced Engineering Study.

Maleyeff, J. (2021). *Service Science: The Analysis and Improvement of Business Processes*. New York: Routledge.

Shewhart, W.A. (1931). *Economic Control of Quality of Manufactured Product*. New York: Van Nostrand.

3 Service customer needs analysis

Introduction

At the core of a quality service management system resides the customer. The cliché "voice of the customer" should be made practical and operational by determining how customers judge performance of the service they receive. These judgments are based on a multidimensional set of service customer needs. Performance dimensions provide the basis for creating performance metrics that evaluate quality in objective ways, and they are needed to develop satisfaction surveys that quantify customers' perceptions of quality.

This chapter begins by introducing a framework for defining performance that encompasses both the service provider and customer perspective, and the factors that influence them. It describes a procedure by which performance dimensions are determined by introducing the critical incident method, which translates customer feedback to a relevant and unbiased list of performance dimensions. A comprehensive example is provided showing how the critical incident method is implemented using an affinity approach that is applied in a virtual team setting.

Performance

Quality is assured by providing customers with services that satisfy their needs. Although the phrase "exceed customer expectations" is used in business publications, its vagueness and lack of specificity can be less than helpful. A better approach would start with developing a thorough understanding of how service customers evaluate quality. The approach should be robust because some customer needs are implicit. Therefore, even subtle drivers that impact customer satisfaction will need to be uncovered.

The needs of a service customer are multidimensional because they are based on many cognitive and emotional responses to the services received. Needs can be inconsistent across customers, and these needs will almost certainly evolve over time. Applying a sound approach requires a formal system that takes a deep dive into customers' experiences. The system should

DOI: 10.4324/9781003199014-3

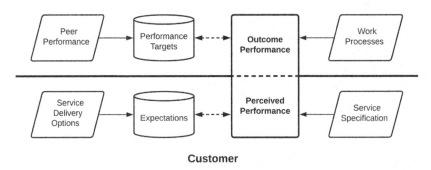

Figure 3.1 Service performance framework.

reevaluate customer needs periodically or as indicated by an analysis of quality-related data.

The integration of many factors should be considered when addressing performance, as shown by the service performance framework illustrated in Figure 3.1. The primary focus of this construct is the performance of the service process. Two viewpoints are shown: (1) outcome performance as viewed by the service provider; and (2) perceived performance as viewed by the customer. Each of these viewpoints is affected by other factors that work together to determine the ultimate satisfaction of customers.

The service provider viewpoint is influenced by performance targets that are set by the process manager or their firm. These targets are usually influenced by peer performance levels either informally or formally (formal systems for incorporating peer performance are discussed in a later chapter). For example, the performance target for customer hold time at a mobile telephone call center may be 10 minutes or less. The quality of process outcomes is determined by the system within which process operates, including technology, training, procedures, and other factors that affect the creation of process output.

The customer viewpoint is influenced by their expectations, which are derived from either prior experience with the process or prior experience with similar services. Process managers should be aware that these expectations can be affected by customers' experiences with similar processes rather than similar firms. For example, a mobile telephone call center customer may consider a 10-minute wait to be unacceptable because they have experienced much shorter waits at their bank's call center. Perceived performance is also affected by promises made by the service provider (i.e., service specifications). Failure to meet these promises can have a detrimental effect on satisfaction, even when performance would have been judged differently had the promise not been made.

How customers judge performance

It is useful to think of a firm's quality system as consisting of a complete, robust, and timely set of data that quantify how well each process is performing. To be complete, it should include both internal measures of performance as well as external measures of customer satisfaction. To be robust, it should include the entirely of how customers define quality. Finally, to be timely, it must continuously monitor data to provide management and service providers with information needed to make prompt decisions.

If a friend is asked: Do you recommend this restaurant? Their short answer would be yes or no; this information will not be entirely helpful unless it is accompanied by an explanation of why the friend likes or dislikes the restaurant. Ideally, your friend would respond yes, then comment further: yes, because the food was good or yes, because the service was friendly. Alternatively, your friend may respond no, then comment further: no, because the restroom was not clean or no, because the service was slow. The importance of their explanation illustrates why a quality system needs to specifically address the multidimensional and nuanced ways that customers judge quality. Without this level of detail, a process manager would be compromised in their ability to consistently understand how well the needs of customers are met, and where improvements should be focused.

Customer needs as well as their expectations change over time. In the early days of the Internet, Internet cafés were common places for customers to purchase refreshments while browsing the Internet. It was common for these businesses to suffer poor reputations because their service providers, although friendly, fast, and knowledgeable about drinks, were ignorant of technology. This example represents a revolutionary change in this service, but more subtle evolutionary changes are also common. Over time, for example, we have come to expect more information to be communicated to us regarding package delivery, appointment schedules, and city services.

Performance dimensions

The term dimensions will be used in this book to denote the categories or criteria that customers use to evaluate a service. A customer's evaluation will include elements that are explicit, implicit, cognitive, and emotional. Other terms that have been used to denote similar concepts include drivers, discriminators, and differentiators. The list of performance dimensions should be customized for each service process and the list should evolve over time. There may be multiple lists of dimensions for different classes of customers, although a process manager should avoid creating a complex system of performance dimensions.

Information required to create the list of performance dimensions should be derived from customers. Consider a bank that interacted with their customers and afterward created a set of six promises. These promises constitute a list of dimensions corresponding to their customer's needs. The list here includes the six promises and a term used to describe the performance dimension (in parentheses):

1   We will make it easy to do business with us (convenience).
2   We will take ownership of your request (completeness).
3   We will treat you as a respected and honored guest (courtesy).
4   We will be knowledgeable regarding your request (knowledge).
5   We will give you solutions to improve your financial life (accuracy).
6   We will safeguard your financial information (privacy).

An unlimited number of possibilities exist for performance dimensions. Although it is useful to summarize each dimension as one term, each dimension should be accompanied by a precise definition. Example dimensions include the following lengthy list: accuracy, usefulness, completeness, responsiveness, timeliness, availability, convenience, competency, integrity, courtesy, friendliness, clarity, simplicity, conciseness, privacy, safety, confidentiality, trustworthiness, honesty, flexibility, cleanliness, and/or appearance. This list should be considered as examples rather than exhaustive.

Some terms should be avoided because they represent multiple dimensions. The best example is quality. Quality is not appropriate for a dimension because it is itself multidimensional. Other multidimensional terms that should be avoided include reliability and consistency. Although business-related metrics, such as server utilization, price variances, and shipment quantities, may be important to the process manager, they play no role in assessing quality for customers. Cost is rarely a dimension of performance because is usually a fixed or negotiated price rather than a measure of process output.

Performance dimension identification

Customers provide the information that determines the list of performance dimensions. A wide range of potential dimensions exists across processes, and the list of dimensions can be broad even for customers of a single process. A total of about 5–7 performance dimension categories will exist for most service process customers, although the list should be customized to the process and its customers. It is acceptable to include some dimensions that not every customer deems critical, but it is not necessary to include dimensions that apply only to a small set of customers. If customers consist of a few clearly defined classifications, a unique list of performance dimensions can exist for each customer class.

The list of performance dimensions should be customized even when services appear similar. Consider the case of a material testing laboratory. For routine testing, key dimensions may include accuracy, speed, and usefulness. However, for specialized testing, key dimensions may include accuracy, speed, and usefulness, plus convenience and communication. The reason for the two additional dimensions is that the specialized service requires close coordination due to the existence of unique sets of testing requirements.

The best set of dimensions includes categories that are mutually independent. For example, the speed of tax preparation and the accuracy of the tax documents are mutually independent because performance for one dimension (e.g., speed) does not tell us about the performance for a second dimension (e.g., accuracy). Pairs of dimensions that would not be mutually independent are: (1) courtesy and friendliness; (2) confidentiality and privacy; and (3) knowledge and competency. The list of dimensions should constitute those that are most important to the short- and long-term success of the firm. There is no need for the performance management system to give precedence (i.e., weighting) to some dimensions over others; in fact this practice may bias analyses. There is also no need to add an overall dimension because the group of dimensions will constitute overall performance evaluation.

Cancer screening process

Consider a process that administers a screening test for cancer, which is provided to individuals within a targeted age group. Screening tests are relatively inexpensive but not always accurate (i.e., they are not as good as other more invasive tests that would be impractical as an asymptomatic routine test). The test may be part of an annual physical, recommended by a primary care physician (PCP), or motivated by a patient's concern. The patient makes their own appointment for the screening test. Results are communicated to the patient and/or the PCP. Follow-up on positive results often may take the form of a surgical biopsy, scheduled by the patient a few weeks later. In the United States, the American Cancer Society provides information on cancer screening online (cancer.org) or via a call center (800-227-2345).

The following dimensions are likely to be important for customers of this process:

1 *Accuracy* (e.g., the screening test should minimize the occurrence of false-negative or false-positive results).
2 *Convenience* (e.g., screening and biopsy appointments should be easy to make or change; test results should be easy to obtain).
3 *Timeliness* (e.g., the screening test should be administered near the appointment time; screening test results should be available promptly; biopsy appointments should be available; biopsy results should be reported promptly).
4 *Clarity* (e.g., risks associated with the screening test should be understood; screening test results and biopsy results should be easily understood).
5 *Privacy* (e.g., no personal information should be disclosed to unauthorized people or groups).
6 *Kindness* (e.g., service providers should recognize the fear associated with cancer and act accordingly when interacting with patients).

Critical incident approach

Customer engagement plays the primary role when deriving the set of performance dimensions for customers of a service process. Numerous customers will need to be engaged so that the information provided is representative of the entire group of customers. A checklist survey that asks customers to choose important dimensions is not a good approach to determine performance dimensions, because the list will include dimensions that the service provider (not the customer) deems important. If surveys are used to create performance dimensions, they need to be open-ended with little or no preconceived categories defining quality. A question such as, "Tell us about your experiences with [our service]" would be appropriate. Written surveys may be more appropriate for internal customers because they are more likely to complete the survey in a comprehensive manner.

Customer focus groups can also be employed to generate the information needed to identify performance dimensions for external customers. Focus groups should be approached with caution, however, because personality differences among focus group members can cause dysfunction. For example, more introverted people may react in a subdued manner due to perceived social pressures. Others in the group may strive to assist in the development of a group consensus, which can lead to inaccuracies when the group leaders are incorrectly accessing the task at hand.

In-depth interviews may be the best method for engaging external or internal customers when determining performance dimension. They mitigate the challenges associated with focus groups, especially because introverted customers feel more comfortable talking one-on-one with a firm's representative. Because the interviewer and customer can interact during the interview, the interviewer can explore customer experiences in greater depth using a more probing dialog. Bias needs to be avoided when choosing interview subjects.

The procedure used to engage each customer should not consist of asking them to list their set of performance dimensions. Although this approach may work for well-informed (perhaps internal) customers, it is generally not a task for which customers are well suited. For example, customers may be confused by the task at hand. They may assume that the service provider is asking for their opinion regarding quality of the service, and they may not focus on providing entirely their dimension list, or they may suggest process improvements to the interviewer.

The recommended approach is referred to as the critical incident method. Statements from customers are sought that concern their experiences. No measure of quality should be sought, only the criteria a customer uses to evacuate quality. The critical incident method is best accomplished using a one-on-one interview, although an open-ended survey can be effective. When employing the method, analysts are often surprised to hear similar statement repeated after only a few customers are interviewed.

Consider a banking customer. The interviewer could ask the customer to start by describing their experiences. If, for example, the customer immediately starts talking about the teller interaction, the service provider may ask them to take a step back and describe their experiences traveling to the bank, parking, finding the location for their service, and other details. Along the way, the interviewer would ask for examples of their experiences (good and bad) at each stage. These sessions should be recorded so that details unnoticed during the interview can be uncovered later.

For a banking customer, the interviewer may record statement such as, "I waited too long before I was helped," "I trust the bank with protecting my identity," "The lines were too long," "I waited in line for a very long time," "I went into the bank and the teller responded immediately to me," "I could not easily find the address of the bank," "I received immediate service for my transaction," "A teller announced my account number in a fairly loud voice," "I could not get the teller's attention even though I was the only one in line." These critical incidents are recorded and later grouped together using an affinity approach.

Affinity diagramming

Affinity diagramming (sometimes called affinity exercise) is effective at determining performance dimensions from a list of critical incidents. The approach described here is also called the K-J method, named after its inventor Jiro Kawakita. It requires a team of 4–10 members and incorporates a structured step-by-step approach. It often proceeds manually using sticky notes, but it can be facilitated by software that duplicates the manual procedure. In fact, electronic applications allow teams in dispersed locations to work together simultaneously.

The affinity approach to determine performance dimensions based on a list of critical incidents is implemented as follows:

1   All comments (i.e., critical incidents) are collected from customers. They are derived from surveys, focus groups, one-on-one interviews, or other sources. Irrelevant comments are removed at this stage.
2   Each comment is summarized on one or more sticky notes (or their electronic equivalent). Only one potential dimension is listed per note and superfluous words are eliminated for brevity. "Fast installation" and "quick email response" are examples of sticky note content.
3   Team members simultaneously move sticky notes into similar categories. They follow no predetermined organizational scheme. This step takes 10–30 minutes depending on the number of notes, with an informal target of 5–8 categories.
4   Each category of incidents is carefully defined and a one-word summary term is assigned to each category. These categories constitute the performance dimensions for customers of the service process.

Step 3 is where affinities are created. The most important rule during this step states that no talking, sighing, or laughing is allowed. This rule is designed to eliminate pressure being imposed by some team members over others. It is expected that there will be disagreements as the team moves from details to categories; these disagreements are evidenced by the movement of some sticky notes multiple times as the definition of each category is crystalized. In fact, categories are expected to evolve as step 3 proceeds.

EH&S reporting case study

Consider a service process that generates environmental, health, and safety (EH&S) reports within a large firm, using a process offered by the sustainability department. Reports are generated on a routine basis each month. The report development process starts by collecting a standard set of performance metrics from each of 15 geographically dispersed divisions. The process creates a series of statistical and visual comparisons that compare divisional performance with prior values and performance targets. Updates on corporate-wide improvement projects are provided and unusually trends are highlighted.

Customers of the report development process reside at corporate headquarters and at each division. Divisional managers use the EH&S reports to highlight areas that deserve attention. Their analysts use information contained in the reports to perform ad hoc analyses, such as tracking progress on ongoing divisional-level improvement projects. Corporate managers deliver a subset of the reports to government regulators. Often, corporate managers are required to explain deficiencies, note progress, and answer other questions posed by government regulators.

The report is generally delivered during the second week of each subsequent month (about 10 days after the month ends). Customers at corporate headquarters and the divisions contact the sustainability department frequently with questions regarding the reports, usually by email. The department endeavors to answer every email question within 48 hours. They meet this standard over 95% of the time.

The new sustainability manager wishes to thoroughly analyze customer experiences, including the identification of relevant performance dimensions. The EH&S reporting process is an internal service, and most customers have been employed by the firm for many years. Hence, the manager is confident that open-ended written surveys would be an effective mechanism for documenting critical incidents. The surveys ask each customer to write about their experiences with the reporting process.

The open-ended surveys were distributed to 37 users of the reports who resided at corporate headquarters and the divisions. A total of 26 individuals responded to the survey. To identify the performance dimensions, a team of six was created, which included three workers in the sustainability department, a manager from operations (with experience in facilitating LSS project teams, who will be the team leader), a customer from one of the divisions, and an analyst from the human resource department. The four steps the team followed to create the list of customer performance dimensions proceeded as follows.

Step 1: Comment collection

The following comments (listed verbatim) were made by customers who returned their survey. The comments from two customers were removed because they were not relevant; they were: (1) This is my first month in this position and have not received any of the reports at this time; and (2) I am retiring soon and overall my experience with the reporting process has been average. The relevant comments from the remaining 24 survey participants are listed here:

1   The reports are often late.
2   They get back to me quickly when I have questions.
3   The reports accurately reflect our safety efforts.
4   The reports are easy to read.
5   My assistant uses the numbers to create reports for me.
6   The reports arrive to my inbox as scheduled.
7   I find that the reports are not very useful.
8   Reports have no errors and always arrive on time.
9   James returns my calls promptly but he is not always helpful.
10 I can't understand the reports.
11 My questions are answered in a few days and the answers are helpful.
12 It would be nice if the reports highlighted our safety improvement projects.
13 The reports are easy to read.
14 My analyst spends a lot of time creating specialized reports for me.
15 I wish the reports were ready on the first of each month to give me more time to take action.
16 The reports are very comprehensive but have little relevance for my new role.
17 The reports never have errors but they are on time.
18 Harriet is one of the smartest workers in your department.
19 My manager cannot understand the EH&S reports very well.
20 The reports are usually on time and easy to understand.
21 They are quick to answer questions.
22 Sometimes mistakes are made in the reports.
23 I don't understand a lot of the technical words.
24 Henry created specialized reports for my division.

Step 2: Comment summaries

Before affinities can be created, a precise list of critical incidents needs to be derived from the comments and then placed onto physical or electronic sticky notes. This step requires translating comments based on two modifications. First, superfluous (i.e., useless) words are removed to facilitate the analysis of relevant information only. For example, comment #18 (Harriet is one of the smartest workers in your department) is posted as "smart workers." Comment #6 (The reports arrive to my inbox as scheduled) is posted as "arrive on schedule." Second, comments that include incidents that clearly span multiple dimensions are separated into two or more critical incidents. For example, comment #8 (Reports have no errors and always arrive on time) is separated into two incidents – "on–time" and "error–free" – and posted on two separate sticky notes. Similarly, comment #20 (The reports are usually on time and easy to understand) is separated into two incidents: "on–time" and "understandable." At the end of this step, a total of 29 critical incidents (i.e., sticky notes) were identified.

Step 3: Affinity creation

The project team's core task was to collaborate for creation of affinities based on the 29 critical incidents. Because project team members did not work at the same location, an online collaboration tool was employed. The tool was used during a teleconferencing meeting so that the exercise would involve all project team members working simultaneously. The teleconferencing application allowed one team member to share their screen so that every team member was keenly aware of the analysis details. A collaborative soft-ware application that creates electronic sticky notes while sharing access to the document was employed. In this way, sticky notes were moved simultan-eously, in much the same way as would be done using physical sticky notes on a white board or wall. The team leader reinforced the rule that no talking whatsoever was allowed during this effort. During this step, some sticky notes were moved many times while the team subconsciously created appropriate affinities. After 22 minutes, team members stopped moving sticky notes and this step was complete. A total of six groupings resulted from the affinity cre-ation exercise; they are shown in Figure 3.2.

Step 4: Performance dimension labelling

The final step consisted of summarizing the dimensions as names and definitions. The task of defining each dimension is made easy because each group's sticky notes includes examples of each dimensions and therefore constitutes a form of definition. The final set of performance dimensions and definitions are listed as follows:

1   *Clarity*: All of a report's calculations, visualizations, and textual informa-tion (and answers to questions about the reports) should be well under-stood by personnel with knowledge of EH&S practice.

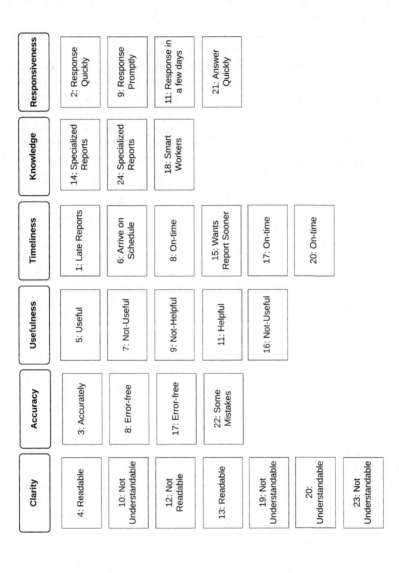

Figure 3.2 Affinity diagram.

2   *Accuracy*: The report's content should not contain erroneous or misleading information, and its text should be presented objectively without exaggerating successes or hiding problems.

3   *Usefulness*: Reports should provide relevant information that meets the technical needs of the various corporate and divisional customers, so that they make informed decisions and provide relevant information to other stakeholders.

4   *Timeliness*: Reports should be completed and made available to users in a timely manner.

5   *Knowledge*: Personnel involved in the reporting process should apply considerable expertise to create analyses and visualizations that maximize the value of input data, and they should be skilled at performing ad hoc analyses for corporate or divisional customers.

6   *Responsiveness*: Personnel involved in the reporting process should respond quickly to questions posed by corporate and divisional users, as well as other stakeholders.

4 Service quality performance metric development

Introduction

The identification of customer performance dimensions sets the stage for the creation of performance measurement system. This system will collect data corresponding both the firm's perception of performance and customers' perception of performance. It starts with the determination of performance metrics (also called performance or quality indicators) and the setting of targets for those metrics. Collection of performance data needs to be done in an unbiased and precise manner. Therefore, it is useful to think of all quality-related data collection as the implementation of an inspection system. The rules governing any inspection need to be adhered to when collecting performance data.

This chapter describes the need for an operational definition that defines each performance metric. It includes rules for ensuring if inspections are unbiased and precise. It introduces the main types of performance data used in quality management and provides examples of performance metric development. The focus is on the types of intangible process outcomes. Examples are presented that illustrate how the inspection rules, metric creation, and data collection are implemented for a diverse set of processes. A comprehensive case study is also presented that highlights the nuances that deserve consideration.

Operational definitions

A quality system seeks to create profound knowledge by integrating performance data and statistical analysis tools, while motivating behavior that ensures customer needs are met now and in the future. The development of this system starts with an understanding of customer needs, culminating with a set of 5–7 performance dimensions. The collection of performance data corresponding to each dimension begins with clearly defined operational definitions. A metric (i.e., a formally defined performance measure) can be based on measurements, observations, or judgments.

The operational definition of a performance metric is required for generating useful data. These definitions are sometimes derived from regulatory

DOI: 10.4324/9781003199014-4

requirements, such as those imposed by government mandates. For example, the U.S. Food and Drug Administration (FDA) provides standards for any food consumed by humans, animal feed, medicines, medical devices, cosmetics, and vaccines (www.fda.gov). Similarly, some operational definitions are based on standards created by professional organizations, such as the American National Standards Institute (www.ansi.org).

The existence of an operational definition is a necessary, though not sufficient, condition for effective collection of performance data. For example, the FDA defines standards for the holes (called eyes) in Swiss cheese as follows: "The cheese shall be properly set and shall possess well-developed round or slightly oval-shaped eyes which are relatively uniform in size and distribution. The majority of the eyes shall be 3/8 to 13/16 inch in diameter." Although this standard sets an effective stage for data collection, it requires a more clearly defined operational definition for implementation at a firm (e.g., to define a slight oval shape).

Some standards are defined by third-party organizations that other firms use as the basis for comparing their process performance with peer organizations. For example, the Benchmark Portal (www.benchmarkportal.com) compares customer contact centers by industry. Their operational definition for abandon rate is:

> The percentage of calls that get connected to the ACD [automatic call distributor] but get disconnected by the caller before reaching an agent, or before completing a process within the IVR [interactive voice response]. The abandon rate is the percentage of calls that are abandoned compared to calls received.

The clarity of this definition serves as a lesson for any data collection for purposes of quality service management.

Operational definitions for inspection of intangible outcomes can be challenging when the performance dimension concerns a form of empathy. A checklist is often used as the basis for the operational definition. For example, courtesy is subjective and can be situational dependent. Its definition could vary depending on the technical background of the customer or the status of the provider-customer relationship. Performance metrics for empathy dimensions are addressed later in this chapter.

Inspection processes

It is useful to consider the collection of a performance metric as an inspection. An inspection is itself a business process. It has suppliers (i.e., the service that generated the outcome), inputs (i.e., the tangible or intangible characteristic being evaluated), a process (i.e., activities such as setup, measuring, analyzing, and recording), outputs (i.e., the result of the inspection), and a customer. The main customer of an inspection is the quality system, where performance data are analyzed for decision-making purposes.

The rules enforced in manufacturing settings also apply to service outcome inspections. Consider the following examples of inspections in various settings: (1) in a hospital, data collection for urgent care readmissions, hospital acquired infections, or cesarean birth deliveries; (2) in a bank, data collection for the duration from application to decision, the loan processor's decision, or the loan default rate; and (3) in any firm, data collection for employee retention, the number of accidents, or customer complaints.

All inspections should be unbiased. This means that, on average, the data recorded is equal to the true characteristic being evaluated. An unbiased inspection for a tangible item is assured through measurement system calibrations. Calibration systems are well established in manufacturing but rarely apply to services, so they are not addressed here. Ensuring unbiased inspections for service processes is generally accomplished through clear operational definitions and training of the individuals that collect performance data.

Inspections should also be precise. This means that inspection results should be repeatable (i.e., each inspector consistently applies the same standard) and reproducible (i.e., the same standard is applied across all inspectors). A formal gauge repeatability and reproducibility (R&R) analysis is performed when tangible items are inspectional. For services, the ability of an inspection system to be precise can be evaluated by auditing the inspection system. For example, call centers routinely record customer interactions and hospitals review cause of death codes based on an audit of patient records.

Inspection processes for metrics that are judgment-based are especially prone to misclassification. Two types of misclassifications are possible. The first type occurs when a process outcome that truly conforms to its operational definition is classified as nonconforming (e.g., a service provider is coded as unfriendly when the interaction was consistent with the firm's operational definition for friendliness). The second type of error occurs when a process outcome that truly does not conform to its operational definition is classified as conforming (e.g., a service provider is coded as friendly when the interaction was inconsistent with the firm's operational definition for friendliness). Firms should realize the existence of these errors and the importance of limiting their occurrence.

Data types

The output of an inspection process is input to the quality analysis system, which performs statistical analyses that drive decision making. There are five types of performance data about which a quality analyst should be aware. They are as follows:

1   *Measurement*: Measurement data are outcomes that fall on a continuous scale. Their collection almost always requires a device, often called a gauge. The most common service process outcome that generates

measurement data is time, which is determined using a stopwatch, clock, or calendar. The consideration of time as measurement data applies even when the data are recorded in whole numbers, such as the number of days to process an invoice or length of stay in a hospital.

2   *Proportion Attribute*: Attribute data exists when the inspector is concerned about a specific characteristic associated with the outcome. There are two types of attribute data. The first type, proportion data, occurs when an outcome is classified in one of two possible categories. Examples include approve-deny, pass-fail, or satisfied-unsatisfied. Proportion data are the most common data type in services and healthcare. They are called proportion data because they are presented as a proportion of time that the targeted category occurs, such as loan approval percentages or fraction of customers who are satisfied. Inspection results are most commonly reported on a common scale (e.g., percentage or fraction) in order to facilitate apples-to-apples comparisons.

3   *Count Attribute*: The second type of attribute data is referred to as count data, where the characteristic of interest can occur more than once for each outcome. Examples include mistakes on an invoice, unscheduled downtime events, or patient falls. Count data are also common in services and healthcare, although not as common as proportion data. Count data should also be reported on a common scale such as number of errors per 1,000 lines of computer code. One caveat should be noted. Some analysts mistake proportion data for count data such as when they count the number of transactions needed to obtain an acceptable outcome (e.g., the number of X-rays needed for a patient's image to be acceptable). This is a mistake because transactions are not outcomes; the feature of interest should be the focus of the data collection.

4   *Nominal Categorical*: Categorical data exists when the inspector classifies each outcome as falling into one of three or more categories (note that proportion data exists when two categories exist). There are two types of categorical data. The first type, nominal data, occurs when no natural ordering exists among the categorical choices. Examples include the type of mistake made during a transaction, the department in which an accident occurred, and the reason for an urgent care facility visit.

5   *Ordinal Categorical*: The second type of categorical data is called ordinal data. Here, a natural ordering exists among the set of categorical choices. The most common example of ordinal data in quality management is associated with customer satisfaction survey data. Customers may be asked to rate their level of satisfaction with a service provider as: very unsatisfied, moderately unsatisfied, neutral, moderately satisfied, or very satisfied. It is unfortunate that analysts sometimes analyze ordinal data by assigning a numerical value to each categorical choice and then analyzing the data as if they were measurements. This practice should not be followed because the numerical values do not represent a true representation of the sensory judgment of the customer.

It is possible for the same outcome to accurately be defined as more than one data type. The most common example occurs when a set of measurement data or categorical data are placed into two categories, which creates a set of proportion data. For example, the proportion of callers who remain on hold for 10 minutes at a customer contact center is derived from a measurement of time. Although proportion data are less valuable than measurement data (because measurement data inherently contains more information), this approach makes sense if a common set of analysis procedures is implemented.

Another popular conversion exists when nominal or ordinal data are converted to a proportion. This approach is popular for customer satisfaction survey results that are converted from ordinal data to proportion data. For example, the analysis may focus on the proportion of customers who choose either moderately satisfied or very satisfied as their response to a survey question. This conversion facilitates a more intuitive analysis approach and eliminates the faulty approach that analyzes the ordinal categories as measurements.

Performance metric development

Each performance metric measures the process's ability to meet customer needs corresponding to one performance dimension. Together, the set of performance metrics covers the entire set of performance dimensions. Although many well-known metrics exist, a process manager should ensure that operational definitions are in place and that these definitions are consistent across the organization. Their application should be practical so that data collection is not burdensome. The myriad of metrics across a firm may number in the hundreds or thousands. The most important metrics are called KPIs.

After the metric's operational definition is created, the process manager needs to ensure that data collection is done in an unbiased and precise manner. An inspection can be analyzed if there is some question regarding its validity. This analysis would start by having the manager (or another process expert) inspect a standard set of customer transactions (e.g., on video or documents). The group of inspectors to be tested would each inspect the same transactions multiple times. Bias would occur if some inspectors evaluated transactions differently from the experts in a consistent manner. Repeatability imprecision occurs when an inspector judges the same transaction differently when shown repeatedly. Reproducibility imprecision occurs when an inspector judges the same transaction differently from other inspectors.

Most metrics can be expressed in a positive frame (called larger-is-better) or a negative frame (called smaller-is-better). When a choice exists, it is usually more convenient to express the metric in the negative frame. For example, the number of mistakes during transactions is often a metric for accuracy. Using this approach with proportion data keeps the numerical results near zero which makes analyses more intuitive and consistent. Some metrics have performance targets (called nominal-is-best), such as cesarean section births in a hospital, although this type is uncommon for service processes.

Metric definitions

The easiest performance metrics to create are those that correspond to common performance dimensions such as accuracy, timeliness, responsiveness, and availability. Common metrics for accuracy include mistakes or returning customers (e.g., because the solution they were provided was unsuccessful). Metrics for timeliness or responsiveness are usually facilitated by technology that measures waiting or transaction time. Examples include time to respond to an email or hold time at a call center. Metrics for the availability dimension require the ability to know when a customer seeks access to the service, but a service provider is unavailable.

Creating a performance metric for some dimensions can be somewhat more difficult, including the dimensions knowledge, competency, clarity, completeness, and usefulness. Some of these outcomes can be measured directly, such as periodically giving a short quiz about government regulations to auditors. Other outcomes can be ascertained based on results expected to occur depending on the outcome. For example, the measurement of a report's clarity can be ascertained by counting the number of questions posed by report readers. Finally, some metrics require a surrogate. For example, competency of a service provider can be estimated by counting the number of nonstandard solutions provided to customers.

The most difficult performance metrics to create are those that concern empathy-related dimensions, such as the dimensions courtesy, friendliness, and kindness. These metrics are usually based on audits of customer transactions that are live, videotaped, or documented. An effective approach to minimize bias and imprecision starts with a list of undesirable elements of the transaction. An example of 15 elements (including an "other" element) that can be used as the basis for a courtesy metric for a call center telephone agent is shown in Table 4.1. The metric would consist of counting the number of nonconforming elements.

The "other" element exists so that the auditor can list any violations of their courtesy definition not shown on the standard list (the number of these violations can be more than one). The list of violations should be reviewed periodically in case the element list needs revision (e.g., when the "other" category contains many violations). The use of a list of elements (rather than a pass-fail audit) allows for both detailed tabulation (i.e., the data are count, not proportions) and can aid in process improvement by identifying specific areas of concern.

Caveats

A performance metric should not be based on a feature or characteristic of the business process. For example, the number of hours that a store is opened is

Table 4.1 Call center courtesy audit

Element of courtesy

Greeting:
    Did not project enthusiasm
    Did not confirm caller name pronunciation
    Did not acknowledge caller's stress
    Did not listen patiently to explanation

Conversation:
    Did not address caller with respect
    Did not listen carefully to caller
    Did not project positive attitude
    Did not use friendly words and phrases
    Did not use simple terms
    Did not engage during quiet times
    Did not speak at appropriate pace

Completion:
    Did not complete call patiently
    Did not verify that solution is understood
    Did not ask patiently for other questions
    Did not project enthusiasm

Other: [Auditor to list]

not a performance metric for the dimension availability. A store that is opened 24/7 has the potential for superior availability performance, but the metric should focus on customers' ability to access the service. Similarly, the number of certified professional service providers (in education, legal, or healthcare services) is not a performance metric. The process manager needs to measure competency or knowledge based on actual service delivery performance.

A performance metric should rarely result from customer input, especially when the customer's input is influenced by their expectations. For example, one should not implement a timeliness performance metric based on the number of customer complaints regarding their waiting time (because this metric does not measure time), or by asking a customer to estimate their waiting time (because this estimate is unreliable and implies that the service provider is inept). Situations where a performance metric derived from customers can be effective are those that are based on cognitive facts rather than emotional reactions. For example, the clarity of a report can be measured according to the number of questions asked by customers after the report is issued. The key distinction is that this metric is not influenced by the level of customer satisfaction.

Examples

A series of examples are provided here to illustrate the creation of a performance metric.

Call center

The customers of a contact center are callers who have problems with installing, operating, or maintaining products sold by a toy company, as well as callers with billing-related problems. The following list of performance metrics would make sense for the call center (the corresponding performance dimension and the type of inspection data are listed for each metric). The list is not complete because the actual metrics would be more comprehensive than the short list given here.

1   *Accuracy*: Number of same issue callbacks per 1,000 callers (count data).
2   *Timeliness*: Average caller hold time (measurement data).
3   *Clarity*: Average talk duration by call category (measurement data).
4   *Convenience*: Number of calls received per week while call center is unavailable (count data).
5   *Courtesy*: Results of listen-in audits expressed as nonconforming elements per audit (count data).

X-ray laboratory

An X-ray laboratory serves patients who make appointments as directed by their PCP and others who arrive randomly from an urgent care facility located in the same building. Patients have a variety of needs associated with potential bone fractures, muscle injuries, organ diseases, motor vehicle accidents, etc. The following list of performance metrics would make sense for the X-ray laboratory (the corresponding performance dimension and the type of inspection data are listed for each metric). The list is not complete because the actual metrics would be more comprehensive than the short list provided here.

1   *Accuracy*: Percentage of images that are discrepant (proportion data).
2   *Timeliness*: Percentage of patients who wait more than 15 minutes (proportion data).
3   *Competency*: Average time to take the image by type (measurement data).
4   *Courtesy*: Results of audits expressed as nonconforming elements per audit (count data).
5   *Usefulness*: Percentage of images that do not help determine patient diagnosis (proportion data).

Internal IT programming

A large firm includes an IT department that serves customers within the firm. The most frequent services provided are troubleshooting hardware and software problems, updating users' operating systems and software, and making modifications to software applications. The following list of performance metrics would make sense for the IT department concerning their software updating process (the corresponding performance dimension and the type of inspection data are listed for each metric). The list is not complete because the actual metrics would be more comprehensive than the short list here.

1 *Accuracy*: Percentage of projects for which mistakes are found within one month of delivery (proportion data).
2 *Timeliness*: Percentage of projects that do not meet the lead time quoted to customers (proportion data).
3 *Competency*: Percentage of projects for which external assistance is needed (proportion data).
4 *Completeness*: Percentage of projects that require modifications (proportion data).
5 *Flexibility*: Percentage of projects whose specifications are changed due to limitations in current skills or technology (proportion data).

Tour guide

A company offers a standard list of tours in and around Shanghai to locations such as Suzhou and Hangzhou, as well as within Shanghai City. Customers are driven in 8–12 seat vans that include a driver and guide. Each tour includes standard stops, but tour guides usually offer some flexibility in the length of stay at each stop. The following list of performance metrics would make sense for the tour company (the corresponding performance dimension and the type of inspection data are listed for each metric). The list is not complete because the actual metrics would be more comprehensive than the short list given here.

1 *Knowledge*: Number of special requests for each tour guide per 100 trips (count data).
2 *Timeliness*: Percentage of customers who are picked up late by at least 15 minutes (proportion data).
3 *Convenience*: Percentage of customers not found in the agreed-upon location (proportion data).
4 *Safety*: Number of customer injuries per 100 tours (count data).
5 *Flexibility*: Percentage of customer groups picked up at the location they reside (proportion data).
6 *Cleanliness*: Number of nonconforming cleanliness elements based on post-trip audits (proportion data).

Target setting

The setting of targets for each performance metric adds perspective to its interpretation. Targets can be based on: (1) comparison with a previous value (often the same time period in the prior year); (2) an internally imposed goal that is consistent with the overall business strategy; or (3) an externally imposed goal based on customer needs, regulatory requirement, or industry standard. If a target is specified for any single metric, then a target should be set for a set of metrics that together account for every performance dimension. Otherwise, process managers may focus on those dimensions that have metrics with targets and ignore other dimensions that are equally important to customers.

W. Edwards Deming cautioned against the setting of targets. He was especially wary of stretch goals, which some managers believe will motivate workers to achieve better performance. Deming stressed that "facts of life" targets can be necessary, such as when defect rates need to be reduced to a specified value for the firm to remain solvent (Deming, 1993, p. 41). He noted that any goal can be achieved by "redefinition of terms, distortion or faking, or running up costs" (Deming, 1993, p. 43). Later in this book, statistical approaches for comparing process performance to suitable targets in ways that do not promote these actions will be described.

The use of targets can interfere with the intent of process thinking, especially when rewards (or punishments) are given when targets are (or are not) met. Even well-intended targets can pose difficulties within a process thinking framework. For example, consider the following scenario. A government agency successfully applies a process thinking approach to the analysis of zoning change approval lead times and, as a result, the percentage of time a 30-day target is met increases from 77% to 100%. It may seem natural to change the target (e.g., from 30 days to 15 days) to encourage even more improvement. The process manager contemplating this change should consider: (1) the factual reason for changing the metric (e.g., is the 30-day lead time too long for some customers?); and (2) the potential effect on worker morale depending on how the change is communicated. This example highlights the need for removing any assignment of blame from the analysis of performance data.

Case study

An earlier chapter introduced a process that administers cancer screening tests. Six performance dimensions were identified at that time. In this section, performance metrics are presented for each performance dimension, including the type of performance data and a discussion of inspection system concerns.

> *Accuracy* can be measured by the percentage of false-positive results (i.e., positive results whose surgical biopsy proves that cancer is not present). These outcomes are proportion data. We can be assured that this metric is unbiased because the biopsies are typically not biased by the result of the screening test. If biopsies are done by different processes (e.g., based on the patient's preference, insurance, or location), accuracy data should be compared across biopsy processes to assure precision.
>
> *Convenience* can be measured based on the percentage of appointments missed by patients (proportion data) and/or the mix of ways in which appointments are made (nominal data). The first metric

needs to be defined precisely to reduce bias (i.e., would a person arriving late constitute a missed appointment?). The process manager should take action to assure that all inspectors use the same definition, across all locations. The second metric is naturally unbiased and precise.

Timeliness can be measured by the time spent in the cancer screening facility (measurement data) and/or the difference between the scheduled time and the start time of the patient's test (measurement data). The duration from test administration to result availability can also be collected (measurement data). In all of these cases, the data can be transformed to proportion data based on how often the measured time exceeds a target. Bias and imprecision would be avoided by carefully specifying the operational definition of the metric (e.g., should the time spent in the facility start with the patient arrival or the scheduled appointment time?) and taking action to ensure that the definition is followed across locations.

Clarity can be measured by the number of questions asked per 100 patients (count data). A standard data collection scheme needs to be established that accounts for various ways a question is asked (e.g., by telephone, email, web site question submission, in-person, etc.). The category of question should also be tracked, such as billing, scheduling, screening tests, or biopsy results (nominal data). These metrics will be unbiased and precise as long as the entire set of inspectors follows the standard reporting procedure.

Privacy can be measured by the number of violations of privacy regulations per month (count data). Because these violations are not always associated with appointments, it may be difficult to specify volume effectively, although the number of violations will likely be small. A precise operational definition is very important. In fact, it would be wise to collect data on both violations and near misses or close calls. For example, if a patient's record is left in a public waiting area, this event would be reported as a violation even though no release of private information occurred.

Kindness can be measured using an audit, similar to the procedure described in Table 4.1 for courtesy (count data). The results can be expressed as a rate of nonconforming elements per 100 patients who have a screening test. Inspection errors can be anticipated, although their occurrence can be minimized by effective inspector training and adherence to the standard inspection process and operational definition.

Reference

Deming, W.E. (1993). *The New Economics for Industry, Government, Education, 2/e.* Cambridge, MA: MIT Center for Advanced Engineering Study.

5 Customer satisfaction survey development

Introduction

The evaluation of quality requires the creation of performance metrics that are each associated with an important customer performance dimension. These metrics provide an internal appraisal of quality. They should be supplemented with measures of customer satisfaction, which is typically accomplished using a customer satisfaction survey. Because a process manager cannot require customers to complete a satisfaction survey, it should be designed and delivered in ways that motivate participation. Satisfaction surveys also need to satisfy rules of inspections regarding an unbiased list of questions and response choices that ensure precision.

This chapter provides a guide to the creation and implementation of a customer satisfaction survey. It discusses the role played by the survey in a quality management system, while describing ways to motivate participation across customers. The importance of creating unambiguous and unbiased questions is stressed, along with the creation of response choices for each question to maximize precision of the survey data. The design of a customer satisfaction survey should be overseen by the process or quality manager because each question should correspond to a critical customer performance dimension.

Purpose of a customer satisfaction survey

Customer satisfaction surveys play an important role in quality management because customers are the ultimate judge of quality. Like performance metrics, each satisfaction survey question should correspond to exactly one performance dimension, and each performance dimension should be measured by at least one survey question. This structure ensures that each dimension is evaluated by both internally derived performance metrics and externally derived satisfaction surveys (including those completed by internal customers). Customer survey results will not always be consistent with performance metric data. For example, a firm may define a responsiveness metric as the percentage of customer emails responded to in less than 72 hours. But customers may wish to hear responses in a timelier manner.

DOI: 10.4324/9781003199014-5

In this case, performance can meet internal targets while customers express dissatisfaction.

The design of a customer satisfaction survey would appear to be a simple matter of listing a variety of questions and asking customer to choose among a common set of responses. In fact, many software applications are available for survey development. However, surveys are often poorly designed, ineffectively administered, or inappropriately analyzed. For example, a medical center's in-patient customer satisfaction survey consists of 4 pages that includes 13 entries of personal information, 107 questions, and 14 requests for written comments. This survey may not result in a sufficient sample size to allow for effective analysis due to its excessive length that discourages participation.

Customer satisfaction survey development should not be delegated to functional entities that have experience with other types of surveys. This practice leads to ineffective surveys because often the developers do not appreciate the nuances associated with satisfaction surveys. They are usually ignorant of inspection rules that ensure unbiased and precise data. Perhaps the most popular consequence can be found in surveys that appear to serve multiple purposes, such as marketing and satisfaction. Because these two survey types (marketing and satisfaction) play completely different roles, they should not be confused or combined. Marketing surveys are used to determine what products, services, or features would be marketable, and the characteristics of current customers. Satisfaction surveys are used to gauge the level of satisfaction with the current product and/or service offerings.

Combining marketing and satisfaction surveys in a quality system is problematic for several reasons. First, it makes the survey longer thereby decreasing participation levels (and the sample size of data). Second, it will demotivate participation because marketing questions are often considered intrusive by customers (e.g., when the survey asks about their annual income). Third, the time spent by customers who complete the survey will not provide both the quality manager and the marketing manager with the in-depth information they both seek.

Process or quality managers should not be wary of developing their own customer satisfaction survey. These surveys are easy to create once the basic requirements for effectiveness are understood. The overall survey design and list of questions are the easiest tasks. The only significant challenge is the setting up of response choices (i.e., potential answers to each question) that satisfy the rules of any inspection – that the resulting data be unbiased and precise. Customer satisfaction survey development combines art (to motivate participation) and science (to create useful data). Their development requires skills that a process manager is likely to possess.

Motivating participation

A customer satisfaction survey will motivate participation when it is short, attractive, or fun. Each survey should be tested to determine the time required for completion. The appropriate completion time depends on the nature of the process and its customers. Internals customers can be expected to spend more time completing a satisfaction survey because the service is important to them as well as the firm. Engaged external customers (e.g., in a business-to-business relationship) will likely devote moderate time for survey completion. More typical external customers will devote only a short time for survey completion. Suggested target completion times of 10–15 minutes (for internal customer), 5–10 minutes (for engaged external customers), and 1–5 minutes (for other external customers) may be appropriate. The survey developer should remember that any survey perceived as taking too long will compromise its effectiveness as a decision tool.

Motivating participation by making the survey easy or fun to complete can be accomplished in several ways. Customers will first notice its overall appearance. They will be intimidated by small fonts and significant textual content. Higher ratios of "white space" (places on the survey that do not include text) create a less-intimidating appearance. The questions and response choices for each question should be easy to understand. In fact, the use of icons or other visual clues can both make the survey easier to understand and fun to complete. Developers should avoid listing response choices that are inconsistent with customers' emotions for the question at hand.

Survey question list

A satisfaction survey should include one or more questions for each customer performance dimension. Each question should be concise and unambiguous. Examples of poor questions are: (1) Was your interaction with the cashier good? (i.e., the term good is ambiguous and can apply to several performance dimensions); (2) Did the call center representative answer your question accurately in a short time? (i.e., two dimensions are addressed – speed and accuracy); and (3) Were you satisfied with the technician's personality? (i.e., the term personality is ambiguous and should be replaced by a more clearly defined term such as friendliness or kindness).

The easiest approach to stating each question is direct – simply ask about the customer's level of satisfaction with the specific issue at hand. Although they are referred to as questions, a statement can also be incorporated. A question that concerns friendliness of a bank teller could be written as: Rate the friendliness of the bank teller who served you. A question that concerns the accuracy of information provided could be written as: Rate your level of satisfaction with the accuracy of the information we provide. A question that concerns clarity of a statistical report could be written as: Please describe your level of understanding when reading our statistical reports.

Questions that do not directly address the customer's level of satisfaction should not be written, such as: How long did you wait for the service provider? Similarly, a question should not ask: Did the technician arrive on time? In both cases, the survey question does not measure the level of customer satisfaction relative to the dimension timeliness. In fact, internal performance metrics should exist to measure the customer's waiting time and whether or not the technician arrived on time. A process manager should also not rely on customers to provide this information because it is not timely and often inaccurate.

Inspection bias is affected by the question's phrasing. The question should not lead the respondent in a positive or negative direction. Behavioral economists use the phrase halo effect because respondents are prone to please the questioner. Some biased questions include the following: Do you agree that the service provider was knowledgeable? It is better to ask: Rate your satisfaction with the service provider's knowledge.

The listing of an overall satisfaction question should proceed with caution, although this question could serve to validate the list of dimensions. For example, if all questions show high satisfaction levels except overall satisfaction, then perhaps a performance dimension has not been identified or addressed in the survey. The listing of an overall satisfaction question risks overt focus on this question at the expense of a more comprehensive analysis of satisfaction. The process manager would lose the ability to better understand root causes of customers' dissatisfaction and may miss the opportunity to solve problems before they become especially problematic.

Survey response choices

A set of potential responses needs to be provided for each survey question; they will be referred to as response choices. The precision of response data constitutes the main criterion when creating the response choices for each question. Although a common set of response choices for all questions can foster understanding and make the survey faster to complete, customized response choices are usually more precise. For any set of response choices under consideration, the survey designer should minimize the chance that two customers with the same opinion would choose different responses.

Precision is controlled both by the number of response choices and the words or symbols used to describe each choice. Examples of choices that may not be precise are: (1) very dissatisfied – dissatisfied – somewhat dissatisfied – indifferent – somewhat satisfied – satisfied – very satisfied; and (2) exceptional – excellent – very good – good – fair – poor – very poor. In the latter case, precision depends on customers clearly distinguishing between very good and good, very good and excellent, exceptional and excellent, and very poor and poor. It is likely that two customers with the same opinion will choose different options.

A good approach for determining a set of response choices is to consider the terms customers would normally use to describe their level of satisfaction. For example, someone evaluating the cleanliness of a hotel room might use terms like spotless, not bad, not too good, or filthy. It would be unlikely for two customers with the same opinion to choose different responses from this list. Choices found on many surveys (e.g., the term somewhat satisfied) are much different from terms used during normal conversation, which can lead to imprecision. The benefit of a customized response choice approach needs to be weighed against the potential for additional survey completion time.

The combining of absolute choices (e.g., good or poor) with relative choices (e.g., average or typical) should also be avoided when determining response choices. Consider the following choices when asking a customer about their rating of service provider friendliness: poor, fair, average, good, or excellent. This set of choices assumes that the average service provider's friendliness is somewhere between fair and good. A respondent may be confused if, for example, they find most service providers to be friendly (i.e., should I choose average or good?).

Number of response choices

Researchers have argued about the optimal number of response choices for a satisfaction survey. There is no one size fits all solution for this decision. In fact, the fallacy of one size fits all also applies to the entirety of questions on the same survey. A survey designer needs to choose: (1) the number of response choices; (2) the format of the response choices; (3) the guidance provided to customers about each response choice's meaning; and (4) the inclusion (or not) of a middle category among the response choices.

The best number of choices is proportional to the amount of nuisance customers place on their satisfaction level. If you asked a friend to rate a film, they may respond by stating: I loved it, I liked it, it was okay, I didn't like it, or I hated it. It is unlikely, but possible, that their opinion will fall between two choices. However, hearing their choice would provide a precise satisfaction level for the film. Some surveys do a poor job duplicating this common sense approach. For example, a written satisfaction survey may include: Rate your level of satisfaction with the film and list response choices as: very satisfied, somewhat satisfied, neutral, somewhat dissatisfied, or very dissatisfied. This list of response choices does not correspond to how one typically speaks about a film, and the term neutral is difficult for many individuals to comprehend.

The range of emotion one feels about a service dimension varies by dimension, and therefore providing the same number of choices for every question is not necessary. A good approach is to consider the intensity of the customer need relative to the targeted performance dimension. For some dimensions (i.e., information security) customers may be equally concerned about any breach of security. In these cases, a simple yes–no choice may be offered to this question: Are you confident that your privacy will be maintained by our service providers?

For most performance dimensions, 4–7 response choices make sense. When 5 or 7 choices are provided, customers will perceive the middle choice as precise between satisfied and dissatisfied. At times, this emotion is hard to convey; in these cases, 4 or 6 response choices can be used whereby each customer is forced to "choose a side" of the satisfaction scale. With 4 or 6 choices, the center two choices typically convey minor dissatisfaction and minor satisfaction, and therefore the middle value is unnecessary. Because emotions operate on a continuum, a mathematician may claim that the chance of someone with emotions "exactly" at the center of the scale is effectively zero. The decision to use 6 (versus 4) or 7 (versus 5) choices depends on the range of emotions experienced by the customer and the ability of the survey to precisely convey emotions within this range.

The format used to convey response choices also impacts survey effectiveness. There are good reasons to use icons instead of text when, for example, customers differ in their spoken language. The use of icons can also motivate participation by making the survey appear fun to complete. Icons can reduce the survey's completion time, which will enable more details to be uncovered in a short timeframe. They are particularly appropriate when technology is used to deliver surveys because they require less room than text on an online application. Examples of icons that convey levels of satisfaction include faces (☹, ☺, and ☺) or thumbs up or down (👍 👍, 👍, 👎, and 👎 👎).

Fallacy of numerical equivalents

Numerical values for response choices are often created by survey designers who will be evaluating the results using methods associated with measurement data. The use of these numerical scales is discouraged. They are usually implemented in one of two ways. The first approach consists of indicating a numerical equivalent for each qualitative description, such as Very Good (5), Good (4), Fair (3), Poor (2), and Very Poor (1). This approach incorrectly assumes that the qualitative emotions experienced by a customer fall on a linear scale. It assumes that the emotional distance between very good and good is equivalent to the emotional distance between good and fair. A survey designer has no reasonable basis for making this assumption.

The second approach typically used to incorporate a numerical scale occurs when a set of numbers (e.g., 1 through 10) are shown as the response choices. Often the endpoints are anchored and described as the range of potential emotions, such as completely dissatisfied (1) and completely satisfied (10) with no qualitative descriptions associated with intermediate values. This approach leads to significant response imprecision. Two customers with the same level of satisfaction will likely choose different numbers, especially if they fall away from the anchored endpoints.

Some analysts convert qualitative response choices to numerical values, even when it may not have been the survey designer's intention. This approach, that typically calculates the average score for each question, is also problematic. Consider a question with the following response choices (with the assumed numerical values noted): Very Good (5), Good (4), Fair (3), Poor (2), and Very Poor (1). If 54 customers complete a survey question and the average score is 3.54, it would be impossible for a process manager to envision an equivalent qualitative emotion. They may be forced to compare this score to a previous score, say 3.83 based on 62 customers. In these cases, a process manager tends to compare the numerical averages while being ignorant of or unable to quantify expected variations. Changes that appear substantial on a numerical scale (e.g., 3.83–3.54) may represent statistically insignificant or unimportant differences in the average emotions of customers.

When deciding on the number of response choices, it is useful to think ahead of the survey's analysis and its use in decision making. The survey designer should determine the level of detail that would be most appropriate. For example, many process managers would be well-informed if they knew that, for the timeliness dimension: (1) 82% of their customers were satisfied; (2) 34% of customers were thrilled; and (3) 11% of their customers were unsatisfied. This information implies that there may be some problems with a subset of the service providers or with customers having specialized needs. The process manager would be advised to begin RCA by studying the performance metric(s) associated with timeliness.

Survey administration

Satisfaction surveys should convey competency and be presented to customers in a convenient manner. It should include a level of formality consistent with the firm's relationship with its customers, ranging from professional to whimsical. The survey should always start with a brief introduction, including its purpose. It should also include instructions describing how it should be completed and submitted. Finally, it should ensure customers that their privacy will be maintained. The introduction section should be kept brief, because it consumes the already limited completion time, and it provides no useful satisfaction data.

A process manager should use the concepts detailed above to create the list of questions and response choices for each question. Although already mentioned, the following rules are worth repeating for satisfaction survey designers:

1   Include at least one question for each performance dimension.
2   Use an open-ended textual format for smaller customer groups because small sample quantitative analyses are not reliable.
3   Avoid the inclusion of questions not associated with customer satisfaction, such as marketing-related questions.
4   Make each question concise and unambiguous.
5   Create response choices that are consistent with how a customer would describe their emotions.
6   Motivate participation by making the survey fun and easy to complete.
7   Keep surveys as short as possible using a suitable target completion time that depends on the customer audience.

The survey should be presented to customers in a visually appealing way that is easy for them to complete. Increasingly, technology is used to facilitate survey administration, but it should be used only when almost all customers would comply. For example, in brick-and-mortar establishments like retail stores, government agencies, airports, or public libraries, surveys can be shown on a touch screen whereby customers passing the screen can pause to answer survey questions. In cases where customers cannot be expected to spend sufficient time to complete the entire survey, a random subset of questions (even one question) can be shown on an electronic touch screen. The intent should be to maximize the number of questions answered rather than the number of customers who complete an entire survey.

Examples

Two examples are provided here that illustrate survey design and deployment. The first example is targeted at internal customers of an environmental health and safety reporting process, and the second example concerns external customers of a cancer screening process.

EH&S reporting process

An earlier chapter introduced a service that generates EH&S reports within a large firm, using a service process offered by the sustainability department. Reports are generated on a routine basis each month, with customers located at corporate headquarters and 15 geographically dispersed divisions. Reports show statistical and visual comparisons that compare divisional performance with prior values and performance targets. Other details were provided earlier.

The critical incident method was used to obtain customer information about their experiences with the process, and an affinity approach yielded six performance dimensions. They were accuracy, timeliness, usefulness, clarity, responsiveness, and knowledge. A customer satisfaction survey was created as shown in Figure 5.1, designed for internal customers of the EH&S reporting process. The six performance dimensions are explicit, representing one question each (using bold text within each of the six questions). The questions are kept somewhat general to encourage comments or elaboration from survey participants. This transparent approach is effective at getting internal customers to feel involved in quality improvement. More open-ended content is also consistent with the expected small sample size, which will preclude extensive quantitative analysis in favor of a more qualitative analysis approach.

Internal customers may offer suggestions for improvement even when they respond favorably to some aspect of the service they receive. Including the rating scale is critical in this regard. Without each customer's pairing of ranking and comments, context would be lost when evaluating the nature of the open-ended comments. The format of the response choices is customized for each question, with more choices where more nuance is expected in a customer's emotional response. There is little rationale for using especially simple terms or icons, because the group of survey participants will be found within the firm and language skills will be consistent across customers.

Environmental Health & Safety Reporting
Customer Satisfaction Survey

The sustainability department seeks to provide services to our internal customers that consistently meet your evolving needs. This survey concerns our monthly EH&S reports. Your candid feedback will help us understand where we can make improvements. We especially value your comments. **Thank you for your time!**

Part 1: Please rate your satisfaction with the **accuracy** of our monthly reports.

☐ Reports are flawless   ☐ Reports sometimes contain errors   ☐ Reports often contain errors

Comments: _____

_____

_____

Part 2: Please rate your satisfaction with the **timeliness** of our monthly report distribution.

☐ Always arrives on time   ☐ Usually arrives on time   ☐ Sometimes arrives on time   ☐ Never arrives on time

Comments: _____

_____

_____

Part 3: Please rate your satisfaction with the how **useful** our monthly reports are for your work.

☐ I can't live without them   ☐ They are pretty useful   ☐ They have limited use   ☐ They are useless

Comments: _____

_____

_____

Part 4: Please rate your satisfaction with **clarity** of the information (text, tables, graphs) contained in our monthly reports.

☐ Crystal clear   ☐ A few confusing parts   ☐ Numerous confusing parts   ☐ Everything hard to understand

Comments: _____

_____

_____

Part 5: Please rate your satisfaction with the speed of our **responsiveness** to your questions and other inquiries.

☐ Quick as lightning   ☐ Plenty fast   ☐ Could be faster   ☐ Slow as molasses

Comments: _____

_____

_____

Part 6: Please rate your satisfaction with the specialized **knowledge** the EH&S reporting team brings to the reporting process.

☐ They are experts   ☐ They are pretty knowledgeable   ☐ They know barely enough

Comments: _____

_____

_____

Figure 5.1 EH&S reporting process customer satisfaction survey.

Cancer screening system

An earlier chapter introduced a process that administers a cancer screening test. Screening tests are relatively inexpensive and, although they are not perfect indicators of cancer, they serve as an effective early warning for most

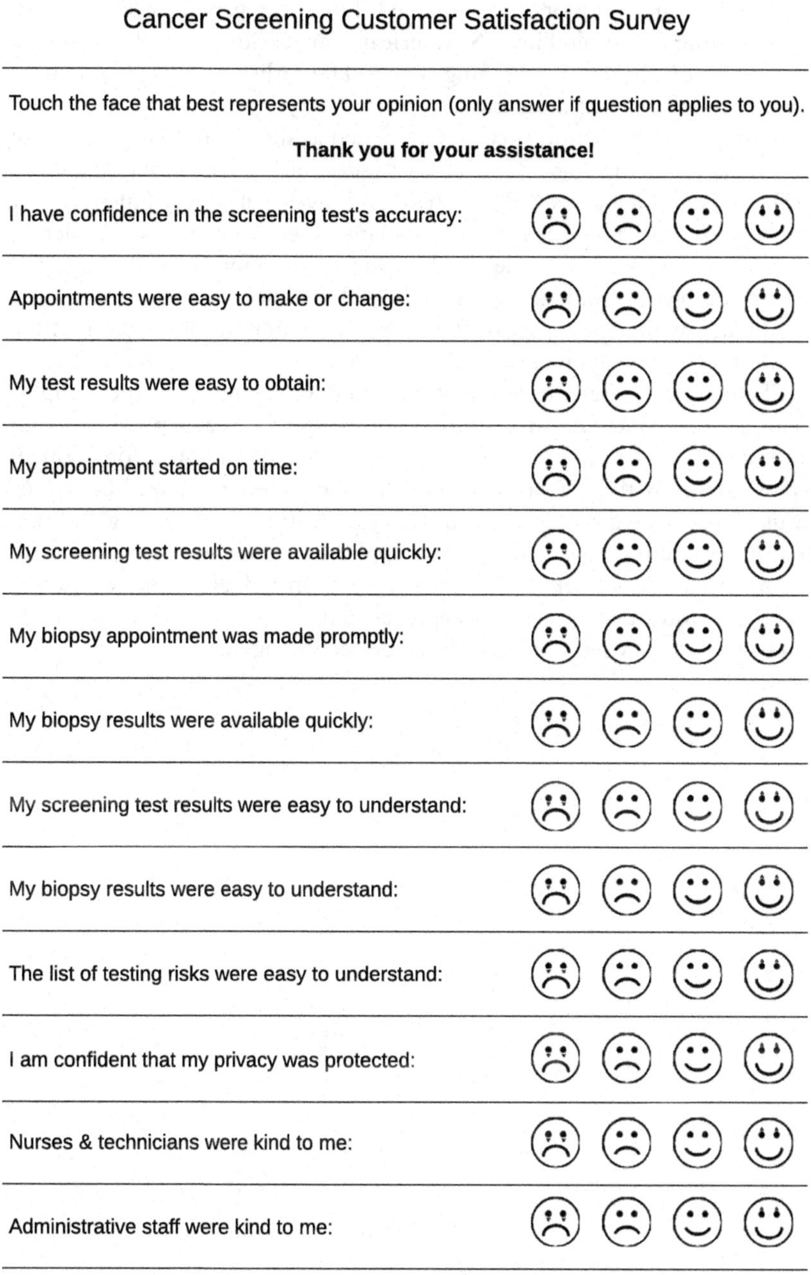

Cancer Screening Customer Satisfaction Survey

Touch the face that best represents your opinion (only answer if question applies to you).

Thank you for your assistance!

I have confidence in the screening test's accuracy:	☹ ☹ ☺ ☺
Appointments were easy to make or change:	☹ ☹ ☺ ☺
My test results were easy to obtain:	☹ ☹ ☺ ☺
My appointment started on time:	☹ ☹ ☺ ☺
My screening test results were available quickly:	☹ ☹ ☺ ☺
My biopsy appointment was made promptly:	☹ ☹ ☺ ☺
My biopsy results were available quickly:	☹ ☹ ☺ ☺
My screening test results were easy to understand:	☹ ☹ ☺ ☺
My biopsy results were easy to understand:	☹ ☹ ☺ ☺
The list of testing risks were easy to understand:	☹ ☹ ☺ ☺
I am confident that my privacy was protected:	☹ ☹ ☺ ☺
Nurses & technicians were kind to me:	☹ ☹ ☺ ☺
Administrative staff were kind to me:	☹ ☹ ☺ ☺

Figure 5.2 Cancer screening customer satisfaction survey.

people. Patients make their own appointment and usually get the results from their PCP. A surgical biopsy is scheduled should the patient receive a positive screening test result. The U.S. American Cancer Society is a key resource for patients of any cancer screening system. The earlier analysis identified six customer performance dimensions.

A customer satisfaction survey was created as shown in Figure 5.2. What are evaluated in the survey are *accuracy* (question 1), *convenience* (questions 2–5), *timeliness* (questions 6–7), *clarity* (questions 8–10), *privacy* (question 11), and *kindness* (questions 12–13). Icons are large to enhance survey completion on a touch screen display. Ideally, the touch screen format will encourage survey completion, and the facial icons will enhance customer motivation by adding a whimsical aspect to the survey (although in the medical setting humor may not be appropriate).

The objective when developing this survey was to minimize the complex terms for the nontechnical customers and to use icons as replacements for more description response choices. This practice also allowed for a longer list of questions that can be answered in about 3–5 minutes. The survey would be delivered using a touch screen monitor in the testing location or using a computer or smart phone application. Not including space for comments is not problematic because the anticipated large sample size will allow for a quantitative analysis approach (and it would be impractical to allow comments when using touch screen technology).

6 Basic tools for service quality analysis

Introduction

Quality analysts make use of several quantitative and qualitative tools in their quest to implement a process thinking approach. The tools employed by a quality analyst must be intuitive and useful so that the process manager and other stakeholders appreciate their meaning. When several tools are available, less complex alternatives should take precedent. Each tool serves a specific purpose, and some tools apply only to certain data types. A quality analyst needs to appreciate each tool's caveats and limitations. They should not be applied haphazardly, but in reaction to the issue being addressed, the nature of the process, and the type of data available to the analyst.

In this chapter, many of the standard qualitative tools for quality management are described. It starts with the presentation of rules for information collection to ensure that useful data are collected. Eight useful quality tools are described with examples. A common business process involving job hiring in a human resource department is used as the basis for all examples. The examples highlight how the tools are integrated for process analysis and improvement projects. The chapter ends with a set of application guidelines based on a checklist of concerns.

Information and data collection

Information and data are used in quality management to understand a process under study. Information usually starts with a description using a SIPOC framework, including the activities that transform inputs to outputs. During initial stages of a project, the best approach is referred to as "go and see" whereby the project team visits the process and learns first-hand about its activities, customers, and problems. This approach contrasts with an approach that uses documented information about the process. This information may lack relevance because it often represents the process as it should operate instead of how it actually operates.

The numerical or categorical data used by a quality analyst consists of values that quantify its inputs and outputs, or potentially influence the quality of process output. These variables will likely include performance

DOI: 10.4324/9781003199014-6

metrics and customer satisfaction survey results. Before any analysis begins, the following questions should all be answered affirmatively:

Does the analysis have a clear objective? Without a definitive objective, time will be wasted because the scope of information may be too broad, irrelevant data may be collected, or important information may be ignored.

Is the data collection (i.e., inspection) process unbiased and precise? Data should be collected using an unambiguous procedure that is well documented with all data collectors trained effectively to remove bias and ensure precision.

Does the data collection account for all relevant factors? Timing is critical for identifying root causes during process analysis; therefore, all data should include a time stamp showing the time each variable was created rather than when they were entered into a database.

Are all extraneous factors controlled or recorded? The factors that may affect process outcomes need to be held constant or their values recorded if they are not precisely controlled.

Will supplemental notes be recorded? Because root cause identification is always important, data collectors need to record any unusual or unexpected circumstances they encounter while collecting data.

Care should be taken to avoid using only the data that are conveniently available. A quality analyst will be tended to make use of data already collected for productivity assessment or when data readily available from technologies that support service delivery. For example, websites can automatically record visits, bounce rate (visitors entering site and leaving quickly), click-through rate (percentage of visits that choose link), returning visitors, pages per session, and time spent on each page. Communication technology can record time of call, hold time, call duration, and caller location, among others. Analysts should account for every customer performance dimension in the data they consider for use.

Analysis approaches

George E.P. Box (1919–2013), a renowned industrial statistician, once stated, "Every process generates information that can be used to improve it." This chapter concerns qualitative approaches that can be used to thoroughly understand a process under study. The approaches avoid assigning blame to individuals by seeking root causes of a process's success and failure. Their main purposes are to describe process activities and factors that affect its performance, identify process activities that do not add value for customers, and find the root causes for problems that arise. They focus on the analysis of relationships (i.e., correlations) among process variables and process outcomes.

A key component of quality improvement is RCA, which refers to any effort to diagnose the source of a problem. RCA looks beyond symptoms to find causes, much like a physician tries to find the causes of a patient's pain. RCA concentrates on correlations between variables and outcomes, with the analyst determining how certain variables (inputs from suppliers, external factors, operating conditions, etc.) impact outcomes. A method known as stratification is associated with correlation analysis. Stratification seeks to determine if the relationship between two variables is affected by a third variable. Ignoring stratification affects can lead to missed opportunities to leverage knowledge of critical relationships that affect process quality.

Qualitative quality analysis tools

The qualitative tools of quality management are easy to implement, although they need to be implemented properly. They are most effective when applied in concert to diagnose and solve a problem. The essential quality tools described in this chapter are useful because they provide a mechanism to use common approaches, common software, and common terminology to solve problems that all stakeholders can understand and play a role in applying.

Kaoru Ishikawa may have been the first quality leader to propose many popular quality analysis methods in his landmark book *Guide to Quality Control* (Ishikawa, 1982). Many practitioners still refer to Ishikawa's Seven Basic Tools of Quality for collecting and analyzing data and information. Like Ishikawa's seven tools, the methods presented in this chapter are effective because of their usefulness and simplicity. They are applied in most process or quality improvement programs. The tools are summarized here and detailed later in this chapter (a few of the tools have been discussed earlier in the book and will not be repeated here).

1   SIPOC is used to describe the business process for purposes associated with a process analysis or improvement effort (for more details see Chapter 2, pp. 000).
2   Process flowcharts are displays of the process activities, so that an analysis can be performed based on a common understanding of the process flow.
3   Fishbone diagrams are hierarchical displays of all known potential causes of a problem, which combine the knowledge of all project team members; they are also called cause-and-effect or Ishikawa diagrams.
4   Check sheets are used to collect data and visualize relationships in real time to enhance data collection, while serving as a visual means to highlight patterns that may support an analysis.

5   Pareto charts are displays of the number or impact of a variety of problems or other issues, so that priorities can be set for addressing the most impactful concerns.
6   Affinity exercises are used to organize disparate information by relationship, class, type, or group (for more details see Chapter 3, pp. 000).
7   Scatter plots are displays of numerical data that evaluate the relationship between two or more variables (usually controllable inputs and a process outcome) so that cause and effect can be confirmed or refuted.
8   Contingency tables are displays of categorical data that evaluate the relationship between two or more variables (usually controllable inputs and a process outcome) so that cause and effect can be confirmed or refuted.

Examples are provided for a business process to illustrate how the methods are integrated to solve problems. The business process will concern activities in a human resource department, which mainly serves internal customers. The illustrations given here will focus on an employee hiring process. The process starts with receiving a job description from the customer (an internal department within the firm), continues with candidate identification, followed by two rounds of interviews (one done remotely and the other in person). The process ends with the initiation of salary negotiations.

Process flowchart

A service process flowchart displays the activities that take place during service delivery. It includes activities that actually take place rather than the activities that should take place or the activities that are designed to take place. The more generic use of the term flowchart contrasts with the term process map, which is well-suited for manufacturing process analysis. Process maps contain more detailed information relevant to production systems, such as inventory locations, changeover times, and cycle times. A service process flowchart requires more flexibility in its design and rarely incorporates numerical information to quantify intangible activity characteristics. In addition, it would be difficult to document service activity durations in simple terms because they are subject to random variations.

A process flowchart is especially helpful in highlighting places where delays, mistakes, and other inefficiencies add unnecessary time to process completion or interfere with the process's ability to deliver customers a high-quality service. These activities are called non-value-added, or wasteful, and ideally they should be removed from the service process. Examples of activities that do not add value for customers include: (1) time spent by the service provider looking for information; (2) time spent by the customer waiting for service to begin; (3) delays due to the late arrival of information from another department; or (4) time spent by the service provider correcting a mistake.

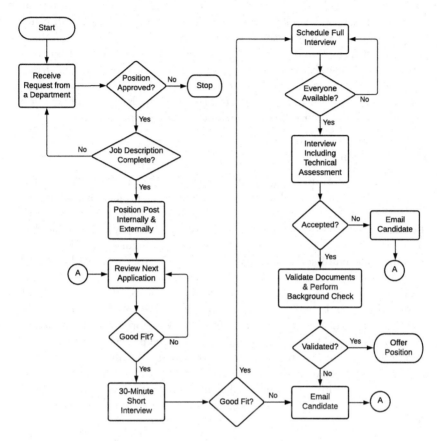

Figure 6.1 Process map for job recruiting process.

Figure 6.1 is a flowchart for the human resource hiring process. Service process flowcharts use fewer standard shapes in favor of customized designs that are consistent with the goals of the analysis and the nature of the process. Some flowcharts are organized chronologically, while others include swim lanes that show the role played by various stakeholders (i.e., departments). It is recommended that a few standard shapes be used to facilitate some level of consistency. They include: (1) an oval for start and end indicators; (2) a rectangle for process activities; (3) an arrow to denote flow; (4) a diamond for decision branching; and (5) a circle to show where the flow shifts from one location to another location.

The evaluation of the human resource hiring process flowchart would identify the following activities as wasteful: (1) when job descriptions are not approved; (2) when job descriptions are incomplete; (3) when applications are reviewed for candidates who are rejected; (4) when an applicant is rejected after the 30-minute call; (5) time spent arranging the on-site interview; (6) when an applicant is rejected after the on-site visit; (7) when an applicant is rejected based on a fraudulent resume; and (8) when an applicant is rejected based on a background check. Each of these activities can cause the process to take longer than it would under ideal or perfect conditions.

A project team would endeavor to remove the wasteful activities in convenient and cost-effective ways. They may find some "low hanging fruit" (easy-to-remove activities), or they may need more data to support their analysis. Many of the information and data analysis methods they would employ are detailed in the section that follows and in subsequent chapters.

Fishbone diagram

A fishbone diagram uses a hierarchical design to list all known and potential causes of a problem. It combines the knowledge of all project team members (and others), each of whom has limited ability to fully understand all of the potential causes of a problem. The fishbone diagram will be updated as more learning takes place. Biased opinions or the assignments of blame are minimized or eliminated by displaying problem causes in a public setting using a common format.

A fishbone diagram is organized with the problem (effect) at the head of the display and the known potential causes presented by category. It resembles the bone structure of a fish. The main categories can be labelled in a way that is related to the process and helpful to the project team. Common main categories are customers, service providers, machines, systems, and external factors, although the main categories may be adjusted as the details are added. Sometimes a branch called management is shown, which can include the social, physical, and organizational environment within which the process operates.

The fishbone diagram can help find root causes that are well known to some workers but not to others (e.g., newly hired employees). It differs from a process flowchart because: (1) it is not organized according to the flow of the process; (2) it does not list all activities that take place; and (3) it focuses on problem solving only, usually a current concern of the project team. A fishbone diagram is shown in Figure 6.2, which represents reasons why a candidate is rejected during the human resource job hiring process. Although some rejections are expected, they are considered a problem because they waste time and therefore their occurrence should be minimized.

The fishbone diagram shows that several causes of rejection are found in the requesting department (i.e., the customer of the process). The request department may cause a rejection because some interviews were scheduled after the best candidate was identified, a key technical skill was described poorly on the job description, or a key manager was busy and needed to skip the 30-minute interview thereby delaying the hiring decision. Other causes (one per main branch) include a poorly trained human resource management employee, an applicant who is untruthful, issues with job placement agencies, an incorrect cover letter, and the position placed on hold by upper management.

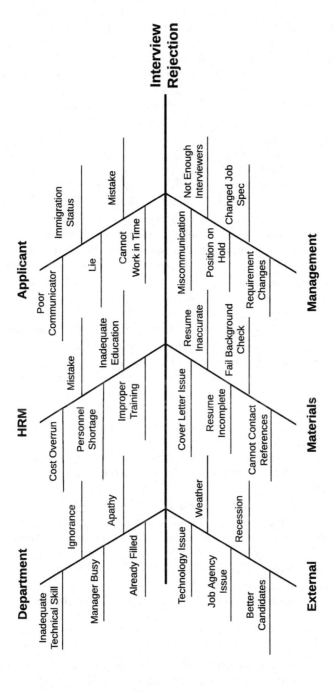

Figure 6.2 Fishbone diagram of interview rejection causes.

Check sheet

A check sheet combines data collection and data visualization using a multi-dimensional approach that facilitates stratification analyses. The method was developed by Ishikawa when computers were not widely used, and visualizations were created manually. They are valuable because today we automate data collection but struggle to display the data in meaningful ways. Many project teams lack the specialized expertise necessary to create visualization using software applications. Although many standard visualizations are available using well-known software applications (e.g., Excel), they often lack the effectiveness necessary to highlight nuances in the data.

Every check sheet is customized based on the process analyzed and the problem being solved. Check sheets are designed to be completed in real time, and they are especially effective for studying impactful problems that do not occur frequently. As such, they are often used to tabulate data concerning mistakes or errors. Examples of effective check sheet applications in various firms include tabulating (1) hospital-acquired infections; (2) workplace accidents; (3) errors on consumer request forms; or (4) customer complaints.

The use of a check sheet is illustrated in Figure 6.3, which shows the reasons for rejecting candidates during the human resource hiring process. This check sheet can be analyzed on a continuous basis because it collects real time data in visually effective ways across multiple dimensions. It shows data across four dimensions: hiring department, job level, interview type (short or long), and reason for rejection. It lists the predominant reason for rejection across hiring departments along each row, and the combination job level and long or short interview along each column. A code is used to denote each reason for rejection, using a set of letters: fraudulent resume (R), failed background check (B), technical skill deficiency (T), inadequate writing ability (W), insufficient communication ability (C), poor cultural fit (F), salary/benefits conflict (S), and other (O).

The following observations can be made at this point in the data collection: (1) the most request reasons for rejection concern codes T and R; (2) rejection code R dominates the rejections for R&D department; (3) rejection code T dominates the rejections for IT department; (4) rejections in the operations and supply chain (O&SC) department most frequently occur after the long interview; (5) rejections in the human resource management department most frequently occur after the short interview; and (6) most rejections for other reasons are shown for the S&M department (perhaps there is a mistake or a new cause has arisen). A project team would be wise to explore the implications for these tendencies and take appropriate action.

Pareto chart

A Pareto chart is used to display issues affecting process performance and their impact, so that appropriate action can be taken. It is based on the theories of Vilfredo Pareto (1848–1923) who discovered that 80% the Italy's

Jul 1 - Aug 15	Job Level / Short or Long Interview											
	Executive		Manager		Technical		Clerical		Operational		Other	
Hiring Dept.	Short	Long	Short	Long	Short	Long	Short	Long	Short	Long	Short	Long
Operations & Supply Chain (O&SC)	R	STC		RCR	R	TOS		WT		CWRT	B	RRWB
Sales & Marketing (S&M)	FO	OOO	R	OOB	CRRO		RWO	OO	OO		ROCORT	FFOO
Accounting & Finance (A&F)	SB	RT	CC	TTT	F	TT		BTT	F	TT	CTT	FTB
Information Technology (IT)	CCC	SW		TBTRTTRB	CCT	TTTT	CCRCR	RTTSSW	TR	TTWTT	BBTT	ROC
Human Resource Management (HRM)	SF	W	CO	C	TTT				SSW		RWC	
Research & Development (R&D)	OCWCC	BFTTB	RRR	WBBTW	CTOT	TSRTST	RRR	FFTTF	RRWRRR	RTRTBRT	RRRBRR	RRRTST
Other	F	FCFF			CC			B	CRR	FTT		TT

Figure 6.3 Check sheet for reasons for interview rejection (July 1 through September 15).

wealth belonged to about 20% of the population. Subsequently, this 80–20 rule became known as the Pareto principle. Although the 80–20 percentages can vary, often a minority of possible causes are responsible for the majority process impacts. Ishikawa may have been the first to suggest the use of Pareto charts for quality analysis and improvement.

A Pareto chart reduces subjectivity or the influence of "loud voices" in favor of an objective fact-based approach. Typically, the chart is used to display impacts of problems such as mistakes, complaints, or defects. For quality improvement, it forces attention on issues that disproportionately impact the quality of process outcomes. One caveat should be noted. A Pareto chart should not be used as a control mechanism. It can be influenced by random variations. Frequently updating and analyzing a Pareto chart can lead to confusion or priority shifting. It is best used infrequently, with large data sets.

The structure of a typical Pareto chart consists of categories (horizontal axis), the impact of each category sorted from the highest to the lowest impact (left vertical axis), and the cumulative impact of causes using a concave curve (right vertical axis). An example illustrating the structure of a Pareto chart is shown in Figure 6.4. This chart displays the reasons for rejecting applicants over a three-month period in the human resource hiring process. The impact for this example is the number of rejected applicants, using the same codes used in Figure 6.3.

The Pareto chart is useful because it prevents a project team from solving problems that have minor impacts on customers or the firm. The chart shown in Figure 6.4 proves that reasons T and R (technical skill deficiency and fraudulent resume) represent over 70% of the rejections. That is, two of the eight reasons (i.e., 25% of the reasons) constitute over 70% of rejections. A project team should explore the root causes of rejections for reasons T and R and take action to reduce their likelihood. It is not important that the

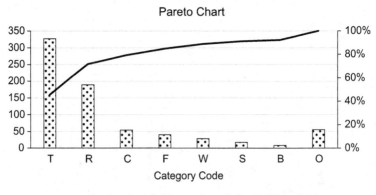

Figure 6.4 Pareto chart for interview rejection reasons (third quarter).

80–20 rule be followed precisely – the key is to have a project team focus its attention on the most impactful issues affecting performance.

Scatter plot

Scatter plots are well-known visualizations for comparing two data sets, although they can be modified to include stratification with three or more variables. They are used in quality analysis to determine the relationship among process variables and a process outcome. For example, a painting process for a metal filing cabinet may be studied to determine the relationship between the application temperature and the quality of paint adhesion. Simple scatter plot development requires paired data (often called X and Y). Each data pair is plotted as a point and the visual trend explaining the relationship between X and Y constitutes the analysis focus.

Many analysts do not appreciate the three aspects of scatter plot analysis. First, there is often no relationship among the variables. An analyst must be wary of overreacting to a presumed trend when, in fact, no relationship exists. Second, not every relationship can or should be described by a mathematical formula. Many analysts mistakenly assume that every relationship is described by a linear equation. Third, an analyst should be aware that stratification effects can be hidden in a scatter plot. These effects may be caused by a third variable that affects the relationship between the two variables under study.

Consider Figure 6.5 that shows the relationship between a candidate's age (X) and the number of days required to make a hiring or rejection decision (Y). This analysis may be motivated by a hypothesis that setting up interviews for younger applicants is faster than their older counterparts due to their technical savvy. The scatter plot shows the applicant's age (horizontal axis) and the time to decision (vertical axis). For example, there was a 23-year-old

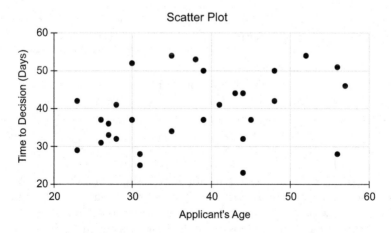

Figure 6.5 Scatter plot of applicant's age versus time to decision.

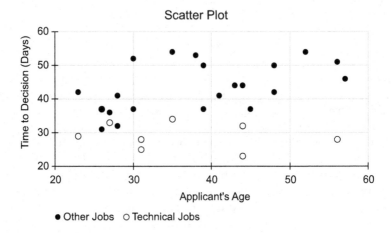

Figure 6.6 Scatter plot with stratification.

applicant whose time to decision was 29 days (the point at the bottom left of the display).

According to this scatter plot, no relationship is evident, because there are no obvious differences in time to decision as applicants' age changes. Therefore, an analyst would rightfully conclude that the applicant's age does not affect the time to decision. Let's assume that a third variable, job type, is suspected as having an effect on this relationship. As a result, a stratified scatter plot is developed, where unfilled dots are used to denote technical jobs and filled dots are used to denote other jobs, as shown in Figure 6.6.

Time to decision appears to increase as age increases for "other" jobs, but not for technical jobs. There may be a small negative relationship between age and days to decision for technical jobs, but the sample size is small and more data would be needed to verify this relationship. In addition, the time to decision tends to be lower for technical jobs over all applicant ages. These insights can help a project team find ways to reduce time to decision for older candidates who apply for nontechnical positions.

A final caution regarding the use of scatter plots concerns the routine insertion of a trend line. This practice will cause a viewer to focus on the line rather than the points (because people tend to use simple heuristics when they are able). A viewer may misinterpret a scatter plot by: (1) claiming that a small upward or downward trend exists when in fact no relationship exists (because random variation will cause the trend line to deviate from perfectly horizontal); (2) not noticing a quadratic relationship when the linear trend line is horizontal; or (3) not noticing an important but nuanced relationship (e.g., when few points exist in one region of the plot). The only time that a linear trend line is appropriate is when the analyst first confirms that a relationship exists and then determines that the relationship appears linear.

Table 6.1 Contingency table of degree and annual merit category

	Bottom 25%	Next 25%	Next 25%	Upper 25%	Total
No degree	2	8	4	7	21
	(10%)	(38%)	(19%)	(33%)	
Undergraduate degree	17	12	21	23	73
	(23%)	(16%)	(29%)	(32%)	
Master's degree	27	26	22	15	90
	(30%)	(29%)	(24%)	(17%)	
Doctorate degree	6	4	2	2	14
	(43%)	(29%)	(14%)	(14%)	
Total professionals	52	50	49	47	198
	(26%)	(25%)	(25%)	(24%)	

Contingency table

A contingency table (also called a cross-tabulation or pivot table) displays the relationship between two categorical variables. Like scatter plots, the analyst is interested in the relationship between a process variable and a process outcome. A table is employed because a scatter plot cannot be used to display categorical data. Contingency tables should be employed with caution, however, because they are difficult to interpret without an associated statistical routine to determine if the differences shown in the table are statistically significant. This difficulty is encountered even by experienced analysts.

Consider Table 6.1, which displays a contingency table for the human resource job hiring process, with rows showing educational background of the R&D department's professional employees (engineers, scientists, and technicians). Columns show where each employee was categorized in the latest set of annual performance merit reviews. For example, 23 employees with an undergraduate degree were rated in the top 25% in the annual merit review, which represents 32% of all employees who entered the firm with that degree. The purpose of the contingency table is to study the relationship between incoming background and job performance.

Although graphical displays are easier to analyze, development of a contingency table can be helpful, intuitive, and easy to understand. Here, it appears that employees with lower levels of degrees have performed better in annual merit reviews than those with a master's or doctorate degree. It is worth repeating that these results should be supported by a statistical analysis, especially when sample sizes are small or when sample sizes vary in each row or column of the table.

Application guidelines

An analysis tool or graphical display should support a transparent and constructive discussion of a problem or issue affecting a business process.

A quality analyst should appreciate that every analysis tool has a specific purpose, and each tool has its limitation. These tools should not be applied arbitrarily or haphazardly. They should be applied in a sequence based on the results from prior analyses. An analysis should affirm the following questions before implementing a qualitative quality analysis tool:

1   *Is it accurate?* When software applications are used to develop visualization, the developer should always check for accuracy prior to release for public consumption. An accuracy check should include the title, axes labels, and legend labels.
2   *Is it intuitive?* A viewer should be able to grasp the display's meaning with little or no associated explanation. Clear descriptive titles and axis labels are a must. Comprehensive but complex displays should be avoided in favor of multiple intuitive visualizations.
3   *Is it objective?* An analyst should not imply either explicitly or implicitly that they seek to influence viewers' impression of a display. Although there may be disagreement among viewers regarding root causes, the effects shown on the display should be unbiased.
4   *Is it helpful?* A display needs to support the making of decisions and, as such, developing a display without a clear reason should be avoided. For example, it is usually unhelpful to create multiple visualizations of the same data set unless there is a clear reason.

Reference

Ishikawa, K. (1982). *Guide to Quality Control.* Tokyo: Asian Productivity Organization.

7   Statistical tools for service quality analysis

Introduction

Statistics plays an important role in quality management because of the random variations present in process outcome data. Statistical methods are analogous to fog lights on a car that enable a driver to see objects that would otherwise be hidden from view. They constitute the quantitative toolbox of every quality analyst who applies a process thinking approach to the analysis of process performance and customer satisfaction data. Statistics in quality management are somewhat dissimilar from more traditional statistical applications. They require specialized training to maximize their effectiveness and prevent misapplications; an analyst needs to be especially concerned with process variation over time.

This chapter complements the basic qualitative tools covered earlier in the book by providing a description of fundamental statistical methods. It introduces the run chart to evaluate the process variation over time and the histogram to evaluate the pattern of process variation. To supplement these graphical approaches, numerical summaries are used to quantify the variation of a process outcome. Combining calculations with information about the pattern of variation enables an analyst to predict an expected range of process outcomes, which is helpful for determining when action is warranted. It also enables the analyst to compare performance with standards or other comparison process outcomes while accounting for variation.

Statistical framework

The statistical analysis of process outcome data (e.g., performance metrics or satisfaction survey results) involves the creation and interpretation of visualizations and numerical calculations. Each analysis method has a specialized purpose and a set of interpretation rules. A quality analyst's primary challenge concerns the firm's decision makers, who may not understand statistics. In fact, even accurate displays can be confusing or misleading, correct calculations can be misunderstood, and interpretation can be inconsistent. The analyst needs to be mindful of these potentials by ensuring that each statistical application is objective, clear, and intuitive. An organization

DOI: 10.4324/9781003199014-7

can prevent misapplications by enforcing the consistent use of a few statistical methods that are applied in consistent ways.

Applying statistical methods within a process thinking framework is unlike many traditional statistical applications. The most important difference is that process-oriented statistical methods focus on understanding the behavior of a dynamic process, rather than the characteristics of a static population. Consider the concept of drawing a sample from a population, which is a mainstay of classical statistics. The analysis of process data must always account for potential process changes during the data collections period, and therefore the classical population-sample concept is invalid. Process-oriented statistics also plays a more active role in decision making because it uses recent outcome data for, in effect, prediction of future outcomes. The methods employed by a quality analyst use visualizations that directly support root cause investigation. They also help the decision maker prevent overreacting to process variations.

Consider a publishing firm that uses copyeditors to review manuscripts, where data are collected over a three-month period. For each manuscript reviewed, the total number of words and the number of corrections is recorded. An analyst using a classical approach may begin by calculating the average correction rate. Although this calculation may be correct, it is useless if the process was undergoing changes during the months of data collection. The average calculation is valid only if the copyediting process was unchanged over time. This process may undergo changes during the data collection period caused by temporary employees, changes in training courses, fatigue caused by excessive overtime, employee turnover, or major changes in the types of manuscripts reviewed.

According to W. Edwards Deming. "statistical techniques taught in books, however interesting, are inappropriate because they provide no basis for prediction and because they bury the information contained in the order of production" (Deming, 1986, p. 132). A construct that describes the process thinking approach to data analysis is shown in Figure 7.1. Note that compared to traditional statistics teaching, the terms process (instead of population) and data (instead of sample) are used. In the copyediting example, the analysis would be the same if data from all manuscripts or data from some of the manuscripts were analyzed. In both cases, the aim of the analysis should be to derive an accurate understanding of the process under study.

Analysis approaches

A process thinking analysis approach is designed to accomplish three tasks simultaneously: (1) create a visualization of process outcomes; (2) determine if action needs to be taken; and (3) assist in root cause identification. The methods are process-focused because they are cognizant of the myriad of factors that may affect process performance. The following list of questions is usually among those that are addressed:

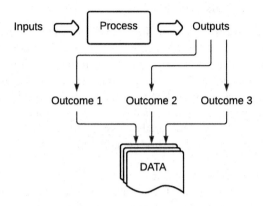

Figure 7.1 Framework for process-oriented quality analysis.

1   Has the process changed?
2   If the process changed, what is the nature of the change?
3   If the process did not change, what is the range of outcomes expected in the future?
4   What is the likelihood that the process meets customers' needs?
5   How does the quality of the process compare with benchmark processes?

Key definitions

The following definitions are used throughout this chapter. They also form the basis of the quantitative methods covered later in the book. They are:

1   *Stability*: Denotes a process that is unchanged over time. A stable process will generate outcomes that follow a consistent pattern of variation during the data collection period. The magnitude of variation is not relevant to this definition – a stable process may operate with low or high levels of variation.
2   *Central tendency*: The central value of outcomes from a stable process. It is usually quantified by the average, although in some cases the median is used to measure central tendency.
3   *Dispersion*: The amount of variation exhibited by outcomes from a stable process. It is usually quantified by the standard deviation, although in some cases the range is used to measure dispersion.
4   *Distribution*: The pattern (or shape) of outcome variation for a stable process. The most common distribution is the normal (bell-shaped) distribution, although the shape of many process distributions is right- skewed.
5   *Probability*: The likelihood that an event of interest occurs. In quality management, the event is associated with a process outcome and we often wish to estimate the likelihood that an outcome will meet customer needs.

Quantitative quality analysis tools

Quantitative quality analysis tools need to be understood by all process managers as well as by others who make process-related decisions. The methods described here are relatively simple, but they need to be implemented properly using a consistent and structured approach. Haphazard use of a statistical method can lead to misapplications. The statistical tools detailed in this chapter are summarized here. An analyst needs to be aware that some statistical tools apply only to a subset of the potential data types, and that each tool serves a specific purpose. The statistical methods detailed in this chapter are:

1   *Run charts:* A display of process outcomes over time to determine if its statistical characteristics have changed. They are sometimes called time series plots. They apply to both measurement and attribute data.
2   *Histograms:* A display of the pattern of process variation for a set of measured outcomes between the minimum and maximum value of the data set. They apply only to measurement data derived from a stable process.
3   *Average:* A calculation that estimates the central tendency of outcomes from a stable process. It applies to both measurement and attribute data.
4   *Standard deviation:* A calculation that estimates the dispersion of outcomes from a stable process. It is calculated either from data (in the case of measurement data) or a theoretical formula (in the case of attribute data).
5   *Prediction range:* An estimate of low and high outcome values from a stable process. It is accompanied by a percentage of outcomes expected to fall within the range (usually 95% or 99.7%). It applies to both measurement and attribute data.
6   *Confidence interval:* A range of values expected to contain a process parameter (e.g., the average of a measurement outcome or the likelihood of a proportion outcome). It is accompanied by the degree of certainty (usually 95%). Its length is inversely proportional to the same size of the data set. It applies to both measurement and attribute data.

Run chart

A run chart serves one purpose – to determine if a process is stable based on the analysis of variation over time for a process outcome. A process can be stable with respect to one process outcome (e.g., accuracy of information provided to a customer) but unstable relative to a second process outcome (e.g., customer waiting time). The run chart provides information concerning the nature of instability so that its root causes can be readily identified. Although no process will remain perfectly stable over time, we call a process stable when the outcome is not noticeably affected by the process changes that occur.

Consider data collected from a firm that sends invoices to customers for services completed. The time (number of days) it took to process an invoice

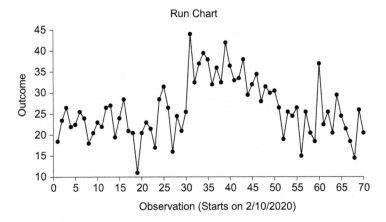

Figure 7.2 Run chart for days to process an invoice.

was recorded for a 70-day period (one invoice was audited per weekday). The first day of data collection was on February 10, 2020. The last day of data collection was May 15, 2020. The run chart is shown in Figure 7.2 (this run chart was created using a template found on the book's companion web site). The goal is to focus on the trend of outcome variation over time rather than its magnitude. Hence, all run charts will highlight process variation by zooming in on the vertical axis while ignoring targets values associated with the outcome.

A stable process will generate a run chart with points that randomly fall above and below an unchanged average, with the magnitude of the variation similar as the points move from left to right. A most basic interpretation of a run chart is based on a so-called squint your eyes test. That is, if a quick glance at the run charts shows no obvious instability, then the process is probably stable. A more comprehensive test would require the development of a control chart, which will be covered in a later chapter.

The run chart in Figure 7.2 does not appear stable because of the significant increase in the outcome starting from day 31 (March 23). Let's assume that an RCA discovered that this day corresponded to the first day of work from home (WFH) at this firm (because of the COVID-19 pandemic). There appears to be an initial period of higher-than-expected days to process an invoice. Afterward, there appears to be a downward trend, which would correspond to improved process performance (i.e., reduction in days required to process an invoice). By day number 50, the process appears to return to the level experienced before the WFH policy was implemented.

Because the performance data from days 31–50 will not reoccur (assuming that the firm's WFH procedures have been standardized) these data should be removed because the intent is to predict future process performance. The revised run chart is shown in Figure 7.3 (note that the vertical axis scale was

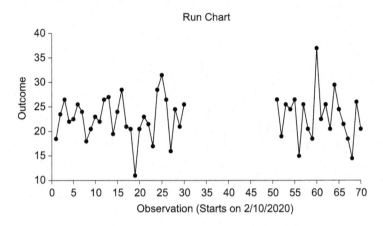

Figure 7.3 Revised run chart for days to process an invoice.

changed to zoom in on the variation). The gap (where data were removed) remains, although it is not relevant to the run chart's interpretation. This revised run chart appears stable. The two potential outliers (days 19 and 60) are best evaluated during the graphical analysis of distribution, which is effective at detecting the presence of extremely unusual outcomes.

Histogram

A histogram serves one purpose – to display measurement data from a stable process in order to determine the distribution of a process outcome. The histogram is valid only for measurement data. It can be helpful in identifying outliers (isolated unusual points), although control charts will be more effective for this task. A histogram is constructed by first dividing the range of all outcomes into bins, also called cells or classes, which evenly subdivide the entire range of the data. The number of observations, called the frequency, is counted for every bin. A bar chart with connected bars is constructed with the height of each bar representing the frequency of its bin.

The interpretation of a histogram focuses on the comparison of the bin frequencies (i.e., its shape) to various standard distributions. The most common distribution is the normal distribution, which is characterized by a bell shape (or bell curve). Normal distributions occur naturally when a process outcome is affected by many sources of variation, with none of the sources being especially dominant. Most non-normal processes are right-skewed, meaning that the bars extend farther to the right of the peak bar than to the left of the peak bar. Right-skewed distributions are common for durations of service activities, where some customers require significantly more time than a typical customer and most customers experience relative short service durations.

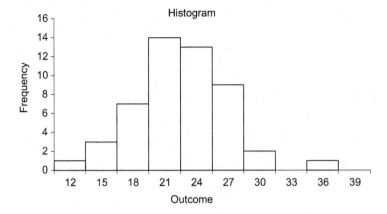

Figure 7.4 Histogram of days to process an invoice.

The histogram should display only data from a stable process because it does not contain information about the data's time orientation. An analyst has no choice but to assume that the distribution shown on the histogram is how the process can be expected to operate in the future. It would be useless, for example, to create a histogram for the unstable process data shown in Figure 7.2. This process underwent changes which would be ignored if a histogram were created using all 70 data points. As an aside, some novice analysts mistakenly assume that: (1) an unstable process will never resemble a bell curve (not true); or (2) a skewed distribution is symptomatic of an unstable process (also not true).

The histogram for the days to process an invoice is shown in Figure 7.4, using data shown in the stable run chart (Figure 7.3). This display was created using a template found on the book's companion web site. The histogram's bins each cover a range of 3 days (e.g., the first bin, which contains one data point, falls between 10.5 days and 13.5 days).

The histogram for days to process an invoice includes one extreme value shown on the right side. This value, approximately 36 days to process an invoice, is identified as day 60 (April 24, 2020) based on the stable run chart (Figure 7.3). Outliers can be natural for the process (e.g., a relatively rare event that can be expected to occur in the future), or they can be caused by an extraordinary event the process manager hopes does not reoccur (e.g., a mistake in data collection). In the latter case, they provide a good learning opportunity, and their root cause should always be investigated. For this data set, we will assume that an investigation is undertaken, and a cause is found. A new employee started on this date (a Friday) and the human resource department failed to notify the accounts payable department of this event.

If we assume that a change is made to the human resource processes to ensure that all departments are notified about new employee start dates, then the day 60 outcome may be removed and the histogram redone

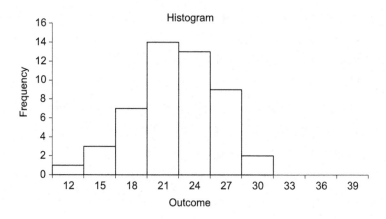

Figure 7.5 Revised histogram of days to process an invoice.

(Figure 7.5). This histogram appears as a discernable pattern similar to a bell shape. Therefore, we can assume the process operates according to the normal distribution. Readers will note that data value from day 19, which appeared to be a potential outlier on the run chart, was not shown to be an extremely unusual value on the histogram. This observation illustrates that the histogram identifies outliers better than the run chart. In almost all cases, no outcome should be declared an outlier unless the histogram shows a gap (a bin with no values) between the main part of the histogram and the extreme point.

The sample size used to develop a histogram has a tremendous influence on how closely it represents the actual process distribution. When the sample size includes 100 or more outcomes, the histogram will generally be a close representation of the process distribution. With smaller sample sizes, the histogram pattern may not accurately represent the process distribution due to random variation effects. In fact, a histogram is not recommended when the sample size is less than 40. The number of bins also affects interpretation. The number of bins shown on a histogram should increase as the sample size increases. It is generally recommended that the number of bins be approximately equal to the square root of the sample size (e.g., about 10 classes for 100 outcomes, about 6 or 7 classes for 40 outcomes). This rule would exclude potential outliers.

When the sample size is less than 100, it is recommended that normality is assumed if: (1) most of the data are contained in the center of the histogram; and (2) a tapering off (tail) appears on both sides of the center of the histogram. For the example presented, the sample size is 49 after removal of the unstable process data and outlier. The process can be assumed normal because both of the above conditions hold. If the sample size were greater than 100, normality would be confirmed only when the histogram closely resembled a bell-curve pattern.

Numerical summaries

A statistic is a numerical summary calculated from a set of data. The main statistics used in quality management are the average and standard deviation. Statistics are not affected by the bias associated with interpretation of visualization, but they need to be understood in context. Because they are routinely calculated using statistical software, care must be taken to avoid simplistic or misleading interpretations. For example, any numerical summary of data from an unstable process is meaningless. Some statistics are meaningless even for stable data sets, such as the calculation of a standard deviation for attribute data.

The simplest and most common statistic is the average (also called the mean). Statisticians refer to the average of a set of data as the sample average to distinguish it from the process mean. The process mean can never be calculated because the process will continue operating into the future – it can only be estimated based on the sample average. For clarity, we will consistently use the term average if it is based on a sample of data and mean if it refers to the process. The notation used to denote the sample average includes a bar above a letter that denotes the outcome. For measurement data, values are denoted by the letter x and therefore the sample average is denoted by $\bar{x}$ (pronounced x-bar). The use of the notation $\bar{x}$ is so commonplace that many quality analysts routinely refer to the sample average as x-bar.

The calculation for the sample average of measurement data is well known and shown in Equation 7.1. The data are labelled according to the order of production as $x_1, x_2, ..., x_n$. In Excel, the function "average" will display the average of data contained in specified cells (empty cells are ignored). The value n denotes the sample size; the Excel function "count" will display the sample size for a range of specified cells.

$$\bar{x} = \frac{x_1 + x_2 + \cdots + x_n}{n} \qquad\qquad 7.1$$

For proportion and count data, each process outcome includes a numerator (the number of occurrences) and a denominator (called the subgroup size). For weekly data on loan activity, the numerator and denominator might be the number of loans approved and the number of loan applications, respectively. The sample average for proportion and count data is calculated as the total of the numerators divided by the total of the denominators. In Excel, the function "sum" will display the total of data contained in specified cells (empty cells are ignored).

The best statistical calculation for calculating dispersion for a set of measurement data is the sample standard deviation, denoted by s (Equation 7.2). This calculation is only valid for measurement data. The sample standard deviation is an estimate of the process standard deviation. The square of the standard deviation is called the variance. In Excel, the function "stdev" will display the standard deviation of data contained in specified cells (empty cells are ignored).

$$s = \sqrt{\frac{\left(x_1 - \bar{x}\right)^2 + \left(x_2 - \bar{x}\right)^2 + \cdots + \left(x_n - \bar{x}\right)^2}{n-1}}$$

7.2

The standard deviation can be interpreted as the average amount by which individual outcomes vary around the process mean. As seen in its equation, a deviation (difference between the outcome and $\bar{x}$) is calculated for each outcome and squared (to make each deviation a positive value). The total of the squared deviations is then averaged by dividing by $n-1$, to obtain an estimate of the average squared deviation. The square root of the average squared deviation, s, is the standard deviation. Dividing by $n-1$, rather than n, is a theoretical adjustment necessary to remove the bias caused by using $\bar{x}$ in the calculation as an estimate of the process mean.

Consider the stable data set shown in Figures 7.3 and 7.5 that represents days to process an invoice. Recall that unstable process data and one outlier were removed. The following statistics were calculated: $\bar{x} = 22.54$ days. $s = 4.14$ days, and $n = 49$ days. Although the sample average and sample standard deviation are precise calculations, their interpretation should be focused on the process that generated the data. An analyst should always be cognizant that they are estimates of process parameters. The best description would be as follows: On the basis of a set of 49 outcomes, the process is stable and normal, and the days to process an invoice is estimated to average 22.54 days and operate with an estimated standard deviation of 4.14 days. These statistical calculations are included in a template found on the book's companion web site.

Prediction range and confidence interval

Understanding how to cope with random variations constitutes a quality analyst's main challenge. All analyses to support decision makers, and all associated recommendations, should directly address the impact of randomness. This section details calculations for creating a prediction range (to determine an expected range of future process outcomes) and a confidence interval (to create a margin of uncertainty associated with the estimate of a process parameter). Although prediction ranges and confidence intervals will be implemented throughout this book, their introduction here will focus on their application to measurement data. Calculations of prediction ranges and confidence intervals are included in a template found on the book's companion web site.

Recall the invoice processing system where the process was stable, the mean time to complete an invoice was estimated to be 22.54 days with an estimated standard deviation of 4.14 days. Two scenarios are presented to illustrate the need for prediction ranges and confidence intervals:

1   Let's assume that the most recent invoice was processed in 31 days, which exceeds the average by over 8 days. A process manager would like to know if the 31-day outcome is consistent with the expected performance of this process. If it is not, then action should be taken to identify the root cause of this extraordinary outcome. The calculation of a prediction range will help the manager determine if action should be taken.

2   Let's assume that corporate headquarters did a benchmark analysis and concluded that the target mean processing time should be 20 days or shorter. The process manager would like to know if the current 22.54-day average is consistent with this standard. That is, would a process whose mean is 20 days generate a sample average of 22.54 days based on a data set with 49 outcomes? The calculation of a confidence interval will answer this question and determine if a process improvement effort is warranted.

A prediction range includes a lower and upper value that almost all future outcomes will fall within as long as the process remains stable. A typical prediction range is usually defined as a range containing 99.7% of future outcomes and is calculated by Equation 7.3 (where X denotes the process outcome). When the 3 in the equation is replaced with 2, the prediction range covers 95% of future outcomes. This prediction range formula is valid only for measurement data from a stable process that follows a normal distribution (Chapter 8 will provide prediction ranges for attribute data). The prediction range for the invoicing process (using the sample average and standard deviation listed above) shows that the days to process an invoice would fall within a range of 10.1 days and 35.0 days 99.7% of the time. Days to process an invoice will fall outside this range only 0.3% of the time, a rate of 3 invoices per 1,000.

$$\bar{x} - 3s \leq X \leq \bar{x} + 3s \qquad\qquad 7.3$$

Recall the first of the two scenarios described above, where the most recent invoice was processed in 31 days. According to this prediction range, the process manager should take no action because the 31-day outcome is within this process's prediction range of 10.1 days and 35.0 days. That is, although it exceeds the current estimated average by over 8 days, we cannot rule out that the current outcome exceeds the average due only to random variation.

Unlike a prediction range that quantifies an expectation of future outcomes, a confidence interval quantifies a margin of uncertainty associated with the estimate of a process petameters (usually the mean). The percentage assigned is the likelihood that the interval contains the process parameter, rather than a percentage of time an event will occur. The precise definition is as follows: "A 95% confidence interval for the process mean is a range of values within which we will find the true process mean with 95%

confidence." It is rare in quality management to create confidence intervals using percentages that differ from 95%.

When data are measurements and the process is stable and normal, the confidence interval for the process mean can always be determined. It can also be determined for measurement data when the sample size exceeds 30, without the requirement of normality. The 95% confidence interval equation is shown as Equation 7.4, where the Greek letter μ denotes the process mean (recall that $\bar{x}$ is the sample average of the data set and n is the sample size of the data set). For the invoicing process, we are 95% confident that the process mean is between 21.4 days and 23.7 days.

$$\bar{x} - \frac{2s}{\sqrt{n}} \leq \mu \leq \bar{x} + \frac{2s}{\sqrt{n}} \qquad\qquad 7.4$$

Recall the second of the two scenarios described above, where headquarters set a target mean of 20 days or less to process an invoice. The process manager should take notice because the 95% confidence interval for the process mean (21.4–23.7 days) does not include the 20-day target. That is, we have statistical proof that process performance does not meet the 20-day requirement. The process manager may want to initiate a process improvement project with the aim of reducing the mean time to process an invoice. They should be aware that a fundamental change to a stable process requires the consideration of all factors affecting performance, not just the actions of service providers.

Statistical analysis process flow

The precise sequence of procedures documented in this chapter should be followed within a process thinking quality system. The analysis should focus on understanding the process that generated a data set, while accounting for variation. Every statistical method needs to conform with its basic assumptions in order to avoid misapplications. All conclusions should be focused on what the data has taught the analyst about the process. The analyst should reinforce the idea that the analysis is devoted to predicting how the process would be expected to operate in the days and weeks ahead.

The flowchart shown in Figure 7.6 presents a process flow for the statistical analysis of measurement data. Readers will note that: (1) the run chart initiates the analysis and the analysis will stop there if no ability to remove data to establish stability exists; (2) a histogram is developed only for a stable process; (3) a prediction range can be calculated only for a stable and normal process; and (4) a confidence interval can be calculated only if the process is stable and normal, or if it is stable and the sample size is 30 or more. The remainder of this section summarizes guidelines for implementing these statistical analysis tools.

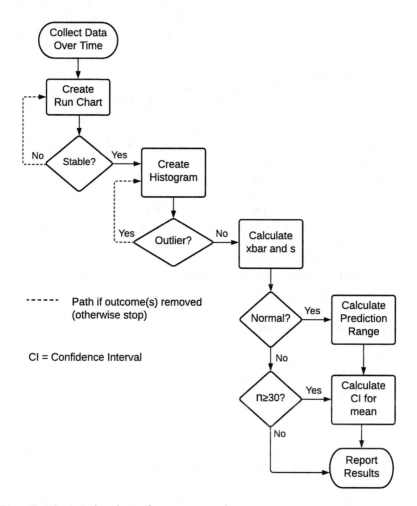

Figure 7.6 Statistical analysis of measurement data.

Rules for run charts

The following rules apply to the creation and interpretation of a run chart.
A run chart should:

1 Be used only to confirm the stability of a process.
2 Display only one set of process data.
3 Be shown as points connected by straight lines, so that both the individual data and its pattern over time can best be evaluated.
4 Be scaled independently by zooming in on the variation of the process data.

5   Be revised (and rescaled) when instability is identified, a root cause if found, and that cause will not affect future process outcomes.
6   Not include a trend line because this annotation can mislead a viewer.

Rules for histograms

The following rules apply to the creation and interpretation of a histogram. A histogram should:

1   Be used only to determine the distribution of a stable process that generates measurement data.
2   Be created only for a stable process.
3   Not be created when the sample size is less than 40.
4   Show only one set of process data per display.
5   Include a number of bars approximately equal to the square root of the same size.
6   Retain an outlier if no root cause is found.
7   Not include a superimposed bell curve because this annotation can mislead a viewer.

Rules for statistical calculations

The following rules apply to the calculation and interpretation of numerical summaries. They should:

1   Be calculated only using data from a stable process.
2   Include only a standard deviation calculation if the data are measurements.
3   Include a prediction range if the process is stable and normal.
4   Include a confidence interval for the process mean if the process is stable and normal, or if the process is stable and the sample size is at least 30.

Reference

Deming, W.E. (1986). *Out of the Crisis*. Cambridge, MA: MIT Center for Advanced Engineering Study.

8 Theoretical foundations for statistical quality analysis

Introduction

The quality of a business process cannot be managed effectively without using statistical methods to analyze the variation of process outcomes. Every statistical method includes a theoretical construct at its core, called a probability model. These models predict the amount of variation that can be expected under assumed conditions. They enable the quality analyst to distinguish between events that require attention and outcome variation that is random. Although probability models can be complex, their scope is made narrowed and their use is made convenient by focusing on service process quality.

This chapter starts by describing a probability model in the context of the process thinking approach to quality management. Models are explained as a simplified structure that mimics a more complex phenomenon. Three probability models are described in detail, with numerous examples provided as illustration. They are the binomial model for proportion data, the Poisson model for count data, and the normal model for measurement data. Coverage also includes procedures for using these models to analyze other forms of process outcome data, including categorical data and customer satisfaction survey results.

Probability models

Decision making under uncertainty is a field of study that uses probability laws to enable a decision maker to contend with variation. Its application to quality management is required because of the random variation present in process outcome data. Probability laws are used to implement the "theory of knowledge" in Deming's system of profound knowledge. Their use is fundamental to process thinking and avoids pitfalls associated with approaches that do not account for variation. A quality analyst need not be an expert in probability theory. They should, however, possess a fundamental understanding of probability concepts especially the assumptions that underlie the statistical methods they apply.

DOI: 10.4324/9781003199014-8

Humans make decisions every day that involve uncertainty, either explicitly (when playing a game of chance) or implicitly (when deciding when to leave for work). These decisions require us to make a prediction. For example, we may evaluate a potential decision by predicting the chance of winning a game or the likelihood of arriving late for work. The use of probability models is essential in quality management because decision making needs to be formalized to ensure accuracy, enforce consistency, and enhance understanding. Although many practitioners are intimidated by probability calculations, all software applications embed them automatically. Therefore, the quality analyst just needs to understand their underlying conceptual foundations.

A probability model (also called a probability distribution) is a mathematical formula that calculates the likelihood that an event will occur. The use of a probability model ensures that decision makers are not fooled by the randomness of outcomes. They are especially effective at guarding against tampering, which occurs when action is taken because of random variation rather than real events (Deming, 1993, pp. 190–204). Tampering often affects an organization's culture when every negative change in performance outcome data elicits a reaction by the manager, often to blame the service providers, even though the process has not changed.

A probability model is used to evaluate process stability by identifying outcomes that are inconsistent with the variation expected for the process under study. They are also used to predict the likelihood that customer needs are met. And they are used to compare this likelihood to desired targets, while accounting for random variation. Finally, they are used to determine if interventions meant to improve quality were successful. The probability models described in this chapter are implemented using a template that is included in the book's companion web site.

Like all mathematical or prediction models, a probability model is accurate only when conditions required for its use are met. Fortunately, for cases where data are proportions or counts, a few key probability models apply to almost all service processes. These typical models, the binomial and the Poisson, apply to proportion and count data, respectively. When data are measured, the normal model often applies to outcome data. Almost every set of service process outcome data can be analyzed using one of these models.

Binomial model for proportion data

The binomial model applies to process outcomes that are classified as proportion data. Conditions governing its use are known as Bernoulli trials, named after the mathematician Jacob Bernoulli (1655–1705). The binomial model applies when

1   Outcomes are classified in one of two categories, most often a successful outcome and an unsuccessful outcome. This condition can also apply when data are measurements or categorical, as long as two categories

are created to classify each outcome. For example, a customer can be classified as satisfied if they choose 5, 6, or 7 on a 7-point satisfaction scale.

2　Outcomes are independent from one to the next, meaning that the outcome itself does not affect the process. This condition almost always applies in a service process; an unusual exception occurs when an unsuccessful outcome places stress on a service provider that affects their service of future customers.

3　The probability that an outcome is equal to the category of interest does not change over time. This condition applies when the process is stable. Hence, the binomial model is often used to determine an expectation for stable process outcomes, which is then used to detect instability.

When the binomial model is applied, the category of interest is called a success (the alternative category is called a failure). The classic and simplest application of the binomial model would be calculating probabilities associated with a coin flip (e.g., where heads is considered a success). The conditions of Bernoulli trials are met (two categories – heads or tails, independence from flip to flip, and a stable 50% probability for heads). The binomial model is by far the most useful for modeling service process outcomes. It can be used in conjunction with analyses involving outcomes such as on-time service, missed due dates, customer returns, loan defaults, and proposal acceptances.

The binomial model calculates the probability that x successes would result from n Bernoulli trials, where the probability of a successful outcome is p. The number of trials is usually called the sample size or the subgroup size. Its mathematical equation is not shown but it is available in any probability or statistics textbook. A function exists in Excel for calculating binomial probabilities, called *binomdist*$(x, n, p, false)$. The *false* parameter specifies that probabilities are not accumulated starting from $x = 0$. If *true* were specified, the probabilities would be accumulated. For example, if $n = 8$ and $p = 0.2$, the function *binomdist*$(3, 8, 0.2, false)$ would be equal to 0.1468, and would represent the probability that the outcome is equal to 3. The function *binomdist*$(3, 8, 0.2, true)$ would be equal to 0.9437, and would represent the probability that the outcome is 0, 1, 2, or 3.

Binomial example

Consider the following example. A consumer product firm's customer relationship manager wishes to anticipate the number of product returns, where the historical average return rate is 7.5% and 100 products are sold during a one-month period. Probabilities corresponding to each potential outcome (i.e., number of returns) can be calculated using an Excel function binomdist, with $n = 100$ and $p = 0.075$. Figure 8.1 shows each potential outcome (horizontal axis) and the probabilities associated with each outcome (vertical axis). For example, the probability that 10% of products are returns

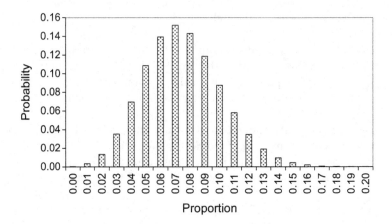

Figure 8.1 Binomial probabilities (*n* = 100, *p* = 0.075).

(i.e., 10 product returns) is equal to 0.0874, which was derived using the function *binomdist* (10,100,0.075, *false*). The calculations were implemented and the display was created using a template found in the book's companion web site.

Its ability to predict likelihoods corresponding to all possible process outcomes makes the binomial model extremely useful in quality management. Its use is also made convenient because a prediction range can be readily determined based on the outcome's mean, standard deviation, and distribution (i.e., shape). The distribution of binomial probabilities will follow a normal bell-shaped pattern when $np \geq 5$ and $n(1-p) \geq 5$. The formula for calculating the process mean (denoted by μ) is straightforward: $\mu = p$. The process standard deviation (denoted by σ) is calculated using Equation 8.1.

$$\sigma = \sqrt{\frac{p(1-p)}{n}}$$ 8.1

Returning to the product returns example, we can calculate the mean proportion of expected returns ($\mu = 0.075$) and the standard deviation of this proportion ($\sigma = 0.0263$). We also know that the pattern will be bell-shaped (i.e., approximately normal) because $np = 7.5 \geq 5$ and $n(1-p) = 92.5 \geq 5$. The prediction range associated with 99.7% of future outcomes can now be calculated using the "3-Sigma" formula ($\mu \pm 3\sigma$) detailed in a previous chapter.

The prediction range for the percentage of returns indicates that outcomes would be expected to fall between 0.000 and 0.154 (0%–15.4% products returned) in 99.7% of months with 100 products sold, as long as the process remains stable. The bell-shape assumption and this production range can be verified visually based on Figure 8.1. Knowing this range enables the customer relationship manager to avoid reaction to changes in return rates that are due only to random variation. If a month of returns (assuming 100 products sold) falls outside this range, then the manager should assume that the process has changed and seek to identify root causes.

Sample size effects

An important phenomenon associated with proportion outcomes is the impact of sample size on prediction ranges. The 99.7% prediction range for the product return percentage (0%–15.4% for $n = 100$) would change to 2.5%–12.5% for $n = 250$ and to 4.0%–11.0% for $n = 500$. The difference in the prediction range lengths is due to the standard deviation of proportions formula (Equation 8.1), which shows that the standard deviation is inversely proportional to the sample size. No analyst, however skilled, can determine the appropriate reaction to a proportion outcome without knowledge of the sample size that generated the outcome.

The normal distribution can be used to create prediction ranges for proportion outcomes, as long as the sample size (n) is sufficient to satisfy the requirements that $np \geq 5$ and $n(1-p) \geq 5$. When the sample size is insufficient, the prediction range cannot be determined because the shape of the probabilities will be skewed. An example is shown in Figure 8.2, where a customer relationship manager wishes to determine the range of product returns in one week with only 25 products sold. The inadequacy of the sample size is easily overcome by accumulating more data prior to making a decision based on a prediction range (i.e., outcome data can be analyzed monthly instead of weekly).

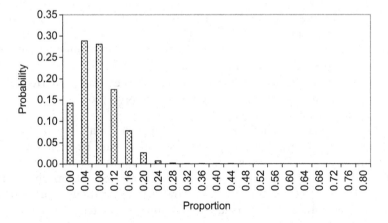

Figure 8.2 Binomial probabilities ($n = 25$).

Proportion outcomes

Although service processes appear to be very different from one another, their underlying conceptual underpinnings are remarkably similar. These similarities allow for the handling of all proportion data in similar ways regardless of the firm, process type, or outcome definition. Examples of outcomes that will follow a binomial model include the following (each outcome would be preceded by "the proportion of"):

- *Bank*: Loan approvals, job interview hires, customer ATM usage.
- *Hotel*: On-time check-in, rooms needed special cleaning, customers who check out early.
- *Health care*: Discrepant x-rays, hospital readmissions, false-positive rate screening test.
- *Help desk*: Same reason callbacks, workers absent, customers who wait.
- *Government*: License approvals, families with pets, unemployed job seekers.
- *Convenience store*: Customers who buy lottery tickets, product returns, expired food items.
- *Airline*: On-time flights, passenger no shows, passengers who check baggage.
- *Education*: Admitted applicants, accepted admission offer, graduation within five years.
- *Factory*: Parts delivered on-time, parts failing inspection, workers who leave before one year.
- *Insurance*: Customer renewals, on-time payments, policies cancelled.

Poisson model for count data

The Poisson model, named after the mathematician Siméon Denis Poisson (1781–1840), applies to process outcomes that are count data. The conditions governing its use are referred to as a Poisson process, which is similar conceptually to Bernoulli trials. A Poisson process generates data whereby each outcome takes on an integer value (0, 1, 2, etc.) with no finite maximum value. The process stability condition means that the mean rate associated with the outcome remains constant over time. This mean rate is referred to as a mean unit count. There are two versions of a Poisson process about which a quality analyst should be aware.

The first version of a Poisson process occurs when outcomes occur at a constant rate over time, but there are no definitive trials. Examples include the number of falls during the patient's stay in a hospital, or the number of outages at a power plant over a one-week period. The second version occurs when outcomes occur at a constant rate over space, but do not correspond to definitive trials. Examples include the number of scratches on a part, or the number of mistakes made on a loan application.

The Poisson model calculates the probability that x occurrences would result from a Poisson process where the mean unit count is denoted by u (the Arabic letter not the Greek letter μ) and the sample size is n. The equation is not shown but is readily available in a textbook on probability or statistics. A function exists in Excel for calculating Poisson probabilities, called $poisson(x, \lambda, false)$, where $\lambda = nu$ (which represents the mean count for the entire sample). The *false* parameter specifies that probabilities are not accumulated starting from $x = 0$. If *true* were specified, the probabilities would be accumulated. For example, if $n = 50$ and $u = 0.2$, the function $poisson(3,10, false)$ would be equal to 0.0076, and would represent the probability that the outcome is equal to 3. The function $poisson(3,10, true)$ would be equal to 0.0103, and would represent the probability that the outcome is 0, 1, 2, or 3.

Poisson example

Consider the following example. An IT manager wishes to anticipate the number of network outages over a six-month period, where the historical rate is 1.25 outages per month with no seasonal trends. The Poisson process assumptions apply because the potential outcome values are 0, 1, 2, etc., with no finite maximum. Probabilities corresponding to each potential outcome can be calculated using the template provided in the book's companion web site. With $n = 6$ (months) and $u = 1.25$, the mean count over six months is $\lambda = nu = 7.5$. Figure 8.3 shows the probabilities associated with each potential outcome (i.e., rate of outages per month). For example, the probability of exactly 9 outages (i.e., 1.5 outages per month) is 0.1144 derived using the following function $poisson(9, 7.5, false)$.

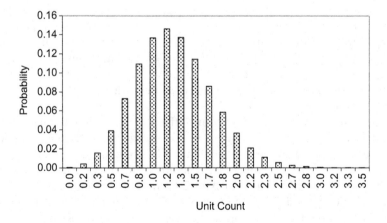

Figure 8.3 Poisson probabilities ($n = 6$, $u = 1.25$).

Some analysts can be confused when interpreting Poisson outcomes. For example, the occurrence of 9 outages over six months corresponds to a rate of 1.5 outages per month, which is the outcome of interest. The historical outage rate of 1.25 per month would translate to an average rate of 7.5 outages in six months. Outcomes such as 0.50 outages per month or 2.00 outages per month would not be considered usual, based on the Poisson probabilities.

The Poisson model is useful to a process manager because, like the binomial, the outcome's prediction range is easy to determine. Poisson probabilities will follow a bell-shaped pattern when $\lambda = nu \geq 5$. The formula for calculating the mean unit count (denoted by μ) is straightforward: $\mu = u$. The standard deviation of the unit count (denoted by σ) is calculated using Equation 8.2.

$$\sigma = \sqrt{\frac{u}{n}} \qquad\qquad 8.2$$

The prediction range for 99.7% of future outages would be expected to fall between 0.00 and 2.62 outages per month (i.e., 0–15.7 outages over six months). This range was calculated using the mean unit count ($\mu = 1.25$) and the standard deviation of the unit count ($\sigma = 0.456$). The prediction can be verified visually from Figure 8.3 (but note that the prediction range precludes the need to calculate all outcome probabilities). The width of the prediction range would likely be surprising to an IT manager because they should take action only when the number of outages in six months is 16 or more.

Sample size effects

Practitioners can be confused by the sample size for some count outcomes. In some cases, there can be more than one correct option. For example, the outages prediction could have been calculated using $n = 1$ (one six-month period of operation) and $u = 7.5$ (a mean rate of 7.5 outages per six months). In this case, the 99.7% prediction range would be 0–15.6 outages per six-month period. These values are equivalent to the earlier prediction range of 0.00–2.62 outages per month.

The sample size for count outcomes affects their prediction ranges. For example, if the IT manager wishes to analyze outage data collected over one year, the 99.7% prediction range would be 3.4–26.6 outages per year, which is equivalent to 0.28–2.22 outages per month. This range is narrower than the previous prediction range of 0.00–2.62 outages per month when the data collection period was six months. The placement of n in the denominator of the standard deviation formula (Equation 8.2) reinforces this concept. It is apparent mathematically and intuitively that the level of variation in a unit count decreases for larger sample sizes or longer time periods.

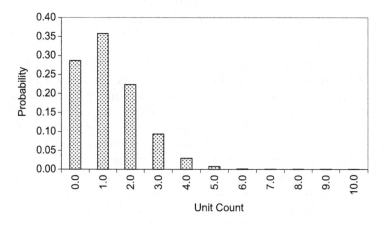

Figure 8.4 Poisson probabilities ($n = 1, u = 1.25$).

The normal distribution can always be used to create prediction ranges for proportion outcomes, as long as the sample size (n) is sufficient to satisfy the requirement that $nu \geq 5$. When the sample size is insufficient, the prediction range cannot be determined because the shape of the probabilities will be right-skewed. An example is shown in Figure 8.4, where the IT manager wishes to determine the range of outcomes in one month. Although they cannot create a prediction range for a one-month period, the IT manager can allow more time to transpire before utilizing a prediction range.

Count outcomes

Like the binomial model, the conceptual underpinnings are remarkably similar for the analysis of count data regardless of the process type or the firm within which the process exists. An analyst need not be specialized in an industry or discipline to apply the Poisson model to a broad range of processes. Examples of outcomes that will follow a Poisson model include the following (each outcome would be preceded by "the number of"):

- *Bank*: Fraudulent transactions per month, transactions per customer.
- *Hotel*: Incoming calls per room, emergency events per week, service requests per room.
- *Health care*: Codes per ICU bed, patient falls per month.
- *Help desk*: Complaints per customer, inquiries per call.
- *Government*: Traffic accidents per day, hurricanes per year.
- *Convenience store*: Lottery tickets bought per customer, stolen items per day.
- *Airline*: Delays per day, incidents per flight.

- *Education*: Edits per manuscript, questions per student per week.
- *Factory*: Scratches per part, worker injuries per month.
- *Insurance*: Claims per auto policy, clicks per web site link.

One caveat regarding count data and the use of the Poisson model requires mention. Data for an outcome that is conceptually a proportion is sometimes mistakenly considered to be a count. The most frequent example is the counting of the sample size required to generate a targeted number of successful outcomes. Examples include the number of images required to get a clear X-ray, the number of locations checked before the correct part is found in a warehouse, or the number of surveys sent until 50 customers agree to complete the survey. These outcomes should be evaluated as proportion data (e.g., if three X-rays are required to obtain a good image, the data should consist of three proportion outcomes: bad, bad, and good).

Normal model probability calculations

Unlike the binomial or Poisson, there is no theoretical model that consistently applies for outcomes classified as measurement data. When outcomes are measured, data must always be collected and analyzed to determine the outcome's probability distribution. A previous chapter of the book described the process that should be followed when analyzing measurement data using a run chart and histogram, including the calculation of the sample average ($\bar{x}$) and sample standard deviation (s). In this section, we assume that the process generating the measurement data is stable and that outcomes follow a normal distribution. This coverage would also apply to proportion or count outcomes whose distributions are bell-shaped.

An important feature of the normal distribution is that its shape is completely determined by the process mean (its center, called μ) and the process standard deviation (its width, called σ). Greek letters are used to distinguish these parameters from their estimates (i.e., $\bar{x}$ is an estimate of μ and s is an estimate of σ). As shown in Figure 8.5, σ characterizes the bell curve's width as measured from μ to the curve's point of inflection (where it changes from sloping down to sloping up). For the example shown ($\mu = 50$, $\sigma = 10$), points of inflection occur at the values 40 and 60.

The normal mathematical equation is very complex, and therefore analysts make use of special functions found in any statistical software. The Excel function for calculating normal probabilities is $normdist(x, \mu, \sigma, true)$, which calculates the probability that the outcome will be less than x (i.e., the area under the curve that is less than x). The false parameter is never used for practical application of the normal model (it is used to draw the normal curve). A template found on the book's companion web site includes a display of the normal distribution, 95% and 99.7% prediction ranges, and various probability calculations.

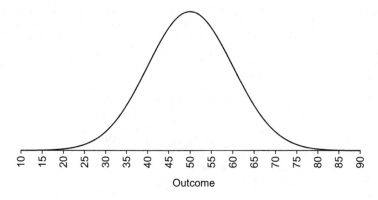

Figure 8.5 Normal distribution ($u = 50, \sigma = 10$).

Normal example

Consider the following example. A process for completing requests for passport renewal generates a set of data consisting of the number of days required to complete a renewal. The run chart (not shown) confirms that the process is stable, and a histogram (not shown) confirmed that the process is normal. The estimated process mean ($\bar{x}$) is 50 days and the estimated process standard deviation (s) is 10 days. The normal model for this outcome (number of days to complete a renewal) would be consistent with Figure 8.5. The probability that a passport renewal will be processed in more than 60 days is 0.159, because $normdist(60,50,10,true) = 0.841$. This means that the probability that completion time is less than 60 days is 0.841, and therefore the probability is 0.159 and that it will take longer than 60 days.

Comprehensive guide

Figure 8.6 provides a guide for probability modeling for statistical quality analysis. The guide applies to stable process outcomes (i.e., after a run chart or control chart has confirms stability). If the process is not stable, a root cause needs to be identified and the process modified, and this guide would not be used. Analyzing an unstable process with a probability model is not appropriate because an unstable process does not operate with a consistent set of process parameters.

Applying the normal model for proportion data and count data from a stable process can always be accomplished when the sample size meets minimum requirement based on the normality rules shown in the guide. For measurement data, a histogram should be used to confirm normality of the stable process. For non-normal measurement data, nominal data, and ordinal data, the guide suggests that each outcome be converted to a proportion.

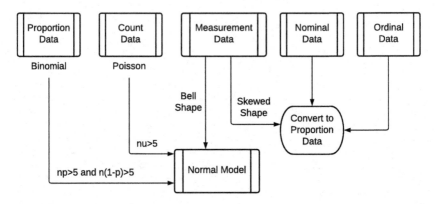

Figure 8.6 Guide to probability model determination (process stability is assumed).

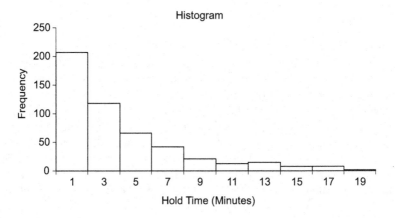

Figure 8.7 Hold time histogram (*n* = 500).

Conversion of measurements to proportions

The following example illustrates how a measured outcome is converted to a proportion, which the guide recommends in the case of a skewed (i.e., non-normal) process. Consider a call center that records the hold (i.e., waiting) time for each caller. A large data set of 500 calls is analyzed and the run chart shows that the process is stable. The histogram for hold times is shown in Figure 8.7; the process is clearly not normal (especially considering that the histogram's accuracy is high because of the very large sample size of 500 calls).

The measured outcomes can be converted to categories by establishing a hold time limit. This limit need not represent a desired outcome; it only serves the purpose of converting measurements to proportions. If a limit of 10 minutes is implemented, each of the 500 outcomes would be classified as either conforming (i.e., less than 10 minutes) or nonconforming (i.e., greater than 10 minutes). The new outcome of interest is the proportion of hold times longer than 10 minutes. For the set of 500 calls, 46 had hold time greater than 10 minutes. This process is stable (from the run chart of measured outcomes) and the stable mean proportion would be 0.092 (the ratio of 46 and 500). Process outcomes can now be modeled using the binomial model with $p = 0.092$. Although the limit chosen for converting measurements to proportions was arbitrary, it should ensure that normality rules would apply to the resulting proportion data set.

Conversion of categorical data to proportions

Consider the handling of nominal outcomes. Each of these outcomes will fall into a category among the three or more possible categories that have no natural ordering. To convert these outcomes to proportions, one of the categories would be chosen as the category of interest (the other categories would be aggregated). For example, if a hospital records the cause of death, a targeted outcome of interest may be a pandemic-related death. The binomial model would then apply for the proportion of deaths caused by the pandemic.

When process outcome is ordinal, each of the outcomes will fall into a category among the three or more possible categories that have a natural ordering. This situation is handled like nominal data, except that several categories will be combined into two aggregated categories based on the desirable and undesirable categories. A common example of this approach would concern the analysis of a customer satisfaction survey.

Consider a survey question: Rate your level of satisfaction with the cleanliness of our facility, with five response choices: very dissatisfied, somewhat dissatisfied, neither dissatisfied nor satisfied, somewhat satisfied, and satisfied. The following stable results are obtained (with the percentage of customers indicated for each category): very dissatisfied (6.1%), somewhat dissatisfied (12.6%), neither dissatisfied nor satisfied (19.3%), somewhat satisfied (37.6%), and very satisfied (24.4%). In this case, the outcomes can be converted to proportion data by aggregating the highest two categories. As a result, we would estimate that 62.0% of customers are satisfied (37.6% plus 24.4%) and 38.0% are not satisfied. The binomial model can now be applied (with $p = 0.62$) and normality would be assured given a sufficient sample size.

Introduction to a statistical control chart

Statistical control charts are used in quality management to evaluate process stability based on the outcome's expected variation, which is quantified using a probability model. Control charts were invented by Walter Shewhart (Shewhart, 1931), and they remain an essential element of any quality system. Many types of control charts are implemented depending on the type of outcome data being analyzed. Although there are many types of control charts, they share common features. These features are based on the normal distribution and the concepts described in the pages that follow.

Shewhart appreciated that process outcomes vary even when the process remained stable. He referred to the natural variation exhibited by a stable process as resulting from numerous "common causes." These causes each contribute a small amount and they are too numerous to list. When only common cause variation is present, the process is said to be in a state of statistical control (or simply "in control"). Common cause variation is usually represented by normal distribution.

When a process is unstable (or becomes unstable after a period of stability) process variation will appear inconsistent with normal distribution expectations. Shewhart referred to an unstable process as being "out of control." The quality analyst should be able to detect when the process change occurred and the reason for the change. Shewhart referred to the reason for the change as an "assignable cause" of instability. The assignable cause can have either positive impacts or negative impacts on process outcomes. Its identification supports better process understanding and exemplifies the process thinking mindset.

A control chart appears like a run chart except it includes horizontal lines that traverse the chart. These lines are based on the normal distribution, and they form the basis for determining if the process is stable using a set of rules that Shewhart recommended. The Shewhart rules are derived from the normal probabilities listed here and illustrated in Figure 8.8. Specifically:

- About 68% of outcomes will fall within the range $\mu \pm 1\sigma$
- About 95% of outcomes will fall within the range $\mu \pm 2\sigma$
- About 99.7% of outcomes will fall within the range $\mu \pm 3\sigma$
- About 50% of outcomes will fall above μ
- About 50% of outcomes will fall below μ

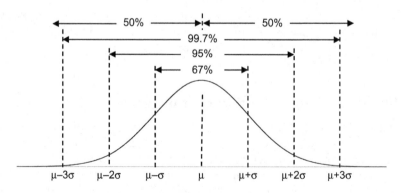

Figure 8.8 Basis for Shewhart rules.

Control charts are designed to detect instability in a timely manner. The set of Shewhart rules, detailed in subsequent chapters, will provide a means for determining if a process is stable. The pattern shown on the control chart aids in the detection of instability soon after the assignable cause becomes impactful. This quick detection ability is important for the identification of the assignable cause.

References

Deming, W.E. (1993). *The New Economics for Industry, Government, Education, 2/e.* Cambridge, MA: MIT Center for Advanced Engineering Study.

Shewhart, W.A. (1931). *Economic Control of Quality of Manufactured Product.* New York: Van Nostrand.

9 Service process stability analysis

Introduction

Control charting is the most important statistical analysis tool in quality management. A control chart is used to implement process thinking by leveraging the graphical features of a run chart and the theoretical framework of probability modeling. It determines if a process is stable, while providing a visualization that uncovers causes of process changes. Most process managers find control charting to be intuitive, and they are extremely effective at identifying process instability. They also prevent overreaction to changes in process outcome data by accounting for the random variation that will exist even when a process is unchanged.

This chapter focuses on attribute control charts for the analysis of proportion or count data. It starts by providing an overarching construct that places control charting in a process thinking SPC system. Proportion (called P) charts and unit count (called U) charts are described. Several examples are provided to illustrate how these control charts are implemented, and how requirements associated with their effective use are validated. Implementation suggestions are also made regarding how to design the proper control charting application, and how to deal with customer satisfaction data or measured outcome data.

Statistical process control

Process stability evaluation is almost always the initial step when statistical analyzing process outcome data, including data derived from performance metrics or customer satisfaction surveys. Figure 9.1 shows a construct, known as SPC, as applied to attribute (i.e., proportion or count) data.

An important term in SPC is subgroup, defined as the number of outcomes collected for each point plotted on a control chart. The subgroup frequency is defined as the period corresponding to each subgroup. For example, control charting in a bank may consist of a subgroup frequency of one month and a subgroup size equal to the number of customers served each month. The sampling frequency is usually chosen for convenience (one day, week,

DOI: 10.4324/9781003199014-9

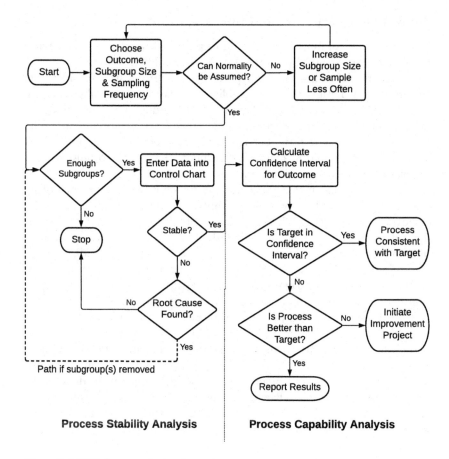

Figure 9.1 SPC framework: Attribute data.

or month). For attribute data, the analyst needs to be cognizant of both the requirement of normality for each subgroup, as well as the need to include a minimum number of subgroups. These requirements are provided later in this chapter.

An analyst needs to be careful when choosing the control chart type, which is solely determined by the outcome data – proportion data for a P chart and count data for a U chart. Once the control chart is created, process stability is evaluated using the set of rules developed by Walter Shewhart. If the process is deemed unstable, a root cause should be sought. If the cause is found and removed, it is possible for the control chart to be reevaluated after deleting subgroups that no longer represent the process. If the process is declared stable, the ability of the process to meet stated goals (e.g., benchmarks, conformance rates, etc.) is then evaluated by a process capability analysis (PCA).

Control chart structure and interpretation

A control chart combines the time series plot shown on a run chart with interpretation rules based on normal probabilities. There are many types of control charts depending on the type of data, subgroup size, and how the data are recorded. All control charts follow the basic structure illustrated in Figure 9.2. The horizontal axis identifies the subgroup (always in the order they are generated by the process) and the vertical axis identifies a normally distributed summary statistic (determined by the subgroup outcomes). The control chart illustrated in Figure 9.2 includes a bell curve to illustrate the role played by the normal distribution.

Each control chart includes a center line, which is the average value of all subgroups. They also show two control limits – the upper control limit (UCL) and lower control limit (LCL). The UCL and LCL are positioned three units of standard deviation above and below the center line; they are commonly called 3-Sigma limits. A control chart may also include intermediate limits delineating the 1-Sigma and 2-Sigma limits above and below the center line. A stable process would be expected to show a pattern that moves from left to right with a pattern that is consistent with normal probabilities.

A set of Shewhart rules (also called Western Electric rules) is applied to check the control chart for instability. They are based on how often points plotted on a control chart would fall into zones that are delineated by the center line, the 3-Sigma control limits, and intermediate 1- and 2-Sigma limits. Although many quality analysts use modified versions of these rules, the original four rules Shewhart used at Western Electric are recommended. An analyst should declare a process to be unstable when any of the following occurs (the control chart shown in Figure 9.2 should be declared stable, because no Shewhart rules are violated).

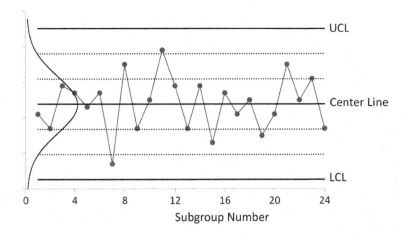

Figure 9.2 Control chart structure.

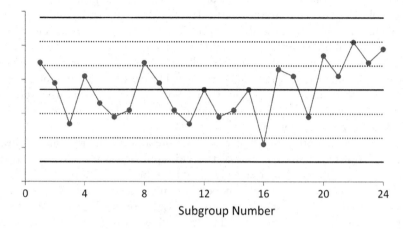

Figure 9.3 Generic control chart (unstable process).

1   One or more points outside of the 3-Sigma limits.
2   Two of three consecutive points outside of 2-Sigma limits (in the same direction).
3   Four of five consecutive points outside of 1-Sigma limits (in the same direction).
4   Eight consecutive points on the same side of the center line.

The process whose outcomes generated the control chart shown in Figure 9.3 should be declared unstable, because at least one Shewhart rule is violated. In this case, four of the last five points fall outside of 1-Sigma limits (in the same direction). This is a violation of Shewhart rule number 3. Shewhart rules operate with a default assumption that the process is stable; they declare a process unstable when statistical proof of instability exists. A quality analyst should endeavor to find a root cause of instability whenever a Shewhart rule is violated.

A control chart needs to include enough subgroups to validate stability. Although there is no generally accepted minimum, 18 subgroups constitute a reasonable minimum for the number of subgroups. When each subgroup frequency is one month, 1½ years of historical data would be required to meet this standard. Showing too many subgroups can be problematic because more opportunities would exist for falsely declaring a stable process to be unstable. Thirty subgroups represent a reasonable maximum, although there is no generally accepted standard in this regard.

Power and false alarms

Shewhart rules create control chart decision criteria that: (1) maximize the control chart's power to recognize an unstable process; and (2) minimize the probability of a false alarm, which occurs when a stable process is declared unstable. Each of the four Shewhart rules contributes to the power of a control chart as well as its false alarm probability. Larger subgroup sizes increase the power of a control chart without impacting its false alarm probability. Therefore, a quality analysis should collect as much outcome data as possible while adhering to practical restrictions. The addition of more subgroups increases the control chart's power but also increases its false alarm probability. Therefore, a quality analysis should maintain the recommended 18–30 subgroup configuration.

It may be tempting for an analyst to ignore a Shewhart rule that is "just barely" violated to avoid a false alarm. This approach is not recommended because the control chart is already giving the benefit of doubt to the stability assumption. Similarly, it may be tempting to seek a root cause when a Shewhart rule is "almost" violated to increase a control chart's power. This approach is also not recommended because it creates an environment where opinions dominate objective rules, and it risks tampering with a stable process. Alternatively, an analyst should not try to increase the power of a control chart by changing the control limits. For example, changing the control limits from 3-Sigma to 2.5-Sigma would significantly increase the false alarm probability.

Sometimes a process outcome occurs too infrequently for control charting because normality rules cannot be validated. For example, a P chart may need subgroups that span multiple months to accumulate the required sample size for normality. For outcomes that have a significant impact on customers or the business, it may be wise to investigate the root cause of every occurrence of the outcome (similar to the approach taken for automobile accidents). For less impactful occurrences, data can be accumulated over two lengthy time periods (e.g., quarterly) and the two data sets compared statistically. A two-sample hypothesis test analysis would be employed.

Proportion (P) control charts

A Proportion (P) chart is used to evaluate the stability of a process that generates proportion data. Random variation for proportion data is described by the binomial model. The size of subgroup i is denoted by n_i and the average subgroup size is denoted by $\bar{n}$. The P chart will plot k proportions, with outcomes labelled as $p_1, p_2, \cdots, p_k$. The average proportion over all subgroups is denoted by $\bar{p}$. A P chart is statistically valid when normality can be assumed for the average sized subgroup, which is confirmed when both $\bar{n}\bar{p} \geq 5$ and $\bar{n}(1-\bar{p}) \geq 5$. The UCL and LCL for subgroup i on a P chart are shown in Equation 9.1.

$$\bar{p} \pm 3\sqrt{\frac{\bar{p}(1-\bar{p})}{n_i}} \qquad 9.1$$

Consider a labelling process at a pharmacy. An analysis of labelling quality consisted of inspecting 200 labels each week over 20 weeks. The number of labels with mistakes were (starting from week 1): 6, 5, 9, 4, 2, 11, 8, 4, 5, 7, 10, 6, 4, 4, 7, 8, 3, 7, 6, and 11. Notes were taken, indicating that a new pharmacist started work on week 7 and that a substitute inspector was used during weeks 4 and 15. The average proportion of labelling mistakes over the data collection period was 0.03175 (a total of 127 mistakes over 4,000 labels inspected). A P chart is valid because between 18 and 30 subgroups exist and normality applies to each subgroup since the product of 200 ($\bar{n}$) and 0.03175 ($\bar{p}$) is equal to 6.35, which exceeds 5, and the product of 200 and 0.96825 ($1 - \bar{p}$) also exceeds 5. The P chart is shown in Figure 9.4. For example, in week 1, 6 mistakes in 200 labels constitute a proportion of 0.03.

There are no Shewhart rule violations on the P chart for labelling mistakes, so the process should be considered stable over the 20-week data collection period. Because the process is stable, there is no need to review the notes (this is important because there should be no room for bias in the chart's interpretation). We can state that the likelihood of a labelling mistake is estimated to be 0.03175, and this likelihood can be expected to continue into the future unless the process changes. For this P chart, the UCL is 0.0689 (from Equation 9.1). The LCL calculation would place it below zero; since a proportion cannot be less than 0, no LCL exists.

When subgroup sizes change from subgroup to subgroup, there is no change in the development and interpretation of the P chart, although the control limits will change as the chart moves from left to right. Consider this example. In a hospital's maternity ward, an important metric is the percentage of births for first-time mothers who undergo a cesarean section procedure. This procedure, called a primary cesarean section (PCS) birth, should be performed when necessary. There is no desire to minimize or maximize the metric, although hospitals tend to be concerned when their PCS metric

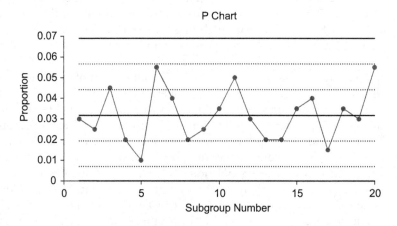

Figure 9.4 P chart for labelling mistakes.

Table 9.1 PCS data

Month	First-time births	PCS births	Notes
1	116	33	
2	86	28	
3	80	23	
4	97	35	
5	103	32	Dr. Yuan hired
6	111	33	
7	93	26	
8	82	29	
9	101	22	Dr. Cooper retired
10	87	20	
11	111	30	
12	100	23	
13	117	15	
14	83	17	Updated checklist for decision on C-sections
15	105	21	
16	114	28	
17	93	21	
18	81	16	
19	112	16	
20	95	26	
21	103	15	
22	111	27	Hired new head nurse, Ms. Dixon
23	91	23	
24	88	14	
25	104	32	
26	89	21	
27	95	25	

compares unfavorably with peer hospitals. This hospital's peers had a proportion of PCS births averaging 20.32%. Table 9.1 shows a set of data collected over the past 27 months, including the number of first-time births and the number of PCS births. Notes taken during data collection are also shown in case they are needed later for root cause identification.

The P chart for PCS births is shown in Figure 9.5. The control limits (including intermediate limits) change from month to month because of the differences in subgroup sizes (i.e., number of births). The vertical axis is scaled so that it starts just below the LCL and ends just above the UCL. The control limits for month 1 (with 116 births) are closer than the control limits for month 2 (with 86 births). This difference is consistent with the calculation of a proportion's standard deviation, which increases as the sample size decreases. The P chart shows a violation of Shewhart rule number 4 – there are 8 consecutive points falling on the same size of the center line (months 1–8). Consulting the notes, it seems clear that Dr. Cooper's retirement may have contributed to the process change (a fact that would be easy to confirm through interviews and additional data collection).

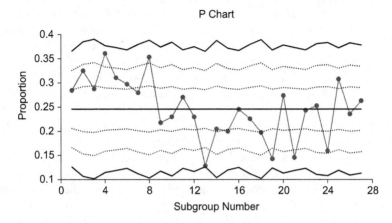

Figure 9.5 P chart for PCS births.

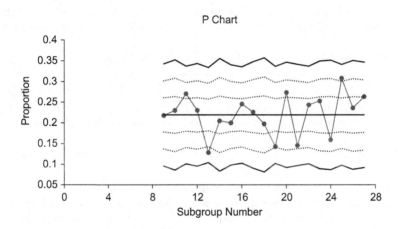

Figure 9.6 P chart for PCS births (revised).

In the case of PCS births, a root cause was found that will not reoccur (assuming Dr. Cooper will not return to the hospital). The control chart should be revised by removing months 1–8 because they no longer represent the process as it currently exists. The analyst should remove data according to the process change rather than remove subgroups at their discretion. The revised P chart (Figure 9.6) includes 19 subgroups and no Shewhart rule violations. Therefore, the process should be declared stable. A template on the book's companion web site created the P charts shown in this chapter. It leaves a blank space where data are removed, so that an analyst will remember this action.

Declaring a process stable has implications important to the communication of results. The center line on the revised P chart is 21.915%, which is the average proportion of PCS births during the last 19 months. This fact is correct, but not informative. Because the purpose of the analysis is to predict future performance, it would be best to state: The likelihood of a PCS birth at this hospital is estimated to be 21.915%. In fact, by declaring the process stable, this likelihood estimate applies to both the past and the future. To help understand the implication of stability, consider months 19 and 20. Although those months had different PCS rates, the likelihood of a PCS birth was the same – 21.915% in both of those months. The difference in the monthly data was due to normal variation. In other words, as stated earlier in the book, the data changed but the process remained the same.

It is important to note that the peer hospital average proportion of PCS births (20.32%) played no role in the analysis of process stability. Of course, the hospital under study would be interested in comparing their PCS birth occurrences with their peer group. A stable process may or may not meet customer needs effectively. It is tempting to compare the estimated likelihood of a PCS birth at this hospital (21.915%) to the peer group rate (20.32%). This is an appropriate comparison, but it needs to be performed using a statistical confidence interval so that the margin of uncertainty associated with the estimated 21.915% is accounted for. This analysis will be described in the next chapter on PCA.

A few final thoughts regarding P charts: Some analysts are annoyed by the changes in control limits when subgroup sizes are unequal. They may consider using the average subgroup size for every subgroup to maintain a constant set of control limits. This practice is not recommended, because it can lead to inaccurate control charts when the subgroup sizes vary considerably.

An alternative control chart, called the NP chart, is also available to quality practitioners. This control chart shows the number of occurrences of the outcome (e.g., the number of labelling mistakes) instead of showing a proportion. NP charts are valid only when the subgroup sizes do not change and, in these cases, they look identical to a P chart. There is no reason to use an NP chart because a P chart is appropriate in every case of proportion data. Consistently using fewer types of control charts also enhances communication across an organization.

Unit count (U) control charts

A U (unit count) chart is used to evaluate the stability of a process that generates count data. It has many features in common with P charts, such as normality verification, number of subgroups validation, and Shewhart interpretation rules. They only differ because random variation for count data is described by the Poisson model. The U chart will plot unit counts, defined as the number of occurrences divided by the subgroup size. For example, if 10 audits are done and a total of 24 nonconforming elements are found, the unit count is 2.4. The k unit counts are denoted by $u_1, u_2, \cdots, u_k$, and the average unit count over all subgroups is denoted by $\bar{u}$. The subgroup size is sufficient for the required normality assumption when $\overline{nu} \geq 5$. The UCL and LCL calculations for subgroup i are shown in Equation 9.2.

$$\overline{u} \pm 3\sqrt{\frac{\overline{u}}{n_i}} \qquad\qquad 9.2$$

Consider an office manager at a consulting company who is monitoring corrections made on proposals written by associates. Each proposal is inspected by a senior staff member, and data are tabulated for the past 28 weeks (Table 9.2). For example, in week 1, five proposals were inspected and a total of two corrections were made. The current goal at the firm is to average one or fewer corrections per proposal.

The U chart is shown in Figure 9.7, where the control limits differ by subgroup due to the subgroup size differences. This U chart was created using a template included on the book's companion web site. An evaluation using

Table 9.2 Proposal inspection data

Week	Proposals	Corrections	Unit count	Notes
1	5	2	0.40	
2	7	5	0.71	
3	6	5	0.83	
4	4	8	2.00	
5	4	9	2.25	
6	7	8	1.14	
7	6	3	0.50	
8	8	8	1.00	
9	7	15	2.14	
10	8	13	1.63	
11	6	7	1.17	
12	5	5	1.00	
13	4	12	3.00	New architect hired, Joe Bigley
14	4	9	2.25	
15	10	25	2.50	
16	10	9	0.90	
17	7	11	1.57	
18	10	9	0.90	
19	5	9	1.80	
20	8	12	1.50	Created template for proposals
21	10	8	0.80	
22	9	11	1.22	
23	8	9	1.13	
24	4	9	2.25	
25	4	7	1.75	
26	10	11	1.10	
27	7	15	2.14	
28	9	9	1.00	Updated client database

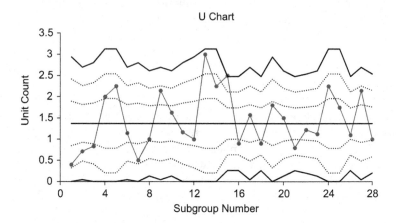

Figure 9.7 U chart for proposal corrections.

Shewhart rules shows that the second rule is violated because subgroups 13 and 15 have outcomes that fall beyond 2-Sigma limits. Hence, the process would be declared unstable. According to the notes taken during data collection, a new architect (Joe Bigley) was hired in week 13. Let's assume that our investigation indicated that Joe was not fully trained until the end of week 15. The inadequate training of the new architect would form the root cause of the instability, and weeks 13, 14, and 15 may be removed assuming that action is taken to ensure more timely proposal preparation training.

The revised U chart is shown in Figure 9.8, where the data for subgroups 13–15 were cleared. Although the gap in the chart (where subgroups 13–15 existed) may appear awkward, this approach reminds a quality analyst (and other viewers of the control chart) that data were removed from the original data set. Some software will create revised control charts with subgroups shown but ignored in the control limit calculations. This practice should be avoided, because it can mislead a reader of the control chart who likely assumes that all data were used to determine control limits. Note that the subgroup causing the Shewhart rule violation (#15) is not where the root cause was found. This is a normal situation when identifying root causes of an unstable process – the rule violation should cause an analyst to study the entire chart pattern as they begin instigation of root cause.

Because the revised U chart has no violations of the four Shewhart rules, the process would be declared stable. The goal of one or fewer corrections per proposal was not considered in the U chart analysis but will be considered during the next stage of the SPC framework.

Some textbooks (and practitioners) also use C (count) charts for count data. These charts show the total count by subgroup, rather than the unit count. They are valid only when the subgroup size is unchanged over time. Because they are limited by the constant subgroup size assumption, and U

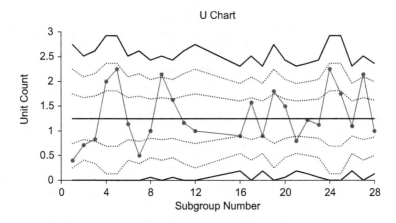

Figure 9.8 U chart for proposal corrections (revised).

charts are always valid, there is no need to implement C charts within an organization.

Rational subgrouping

Rational subgrouping refers to the determination of how process outcome data are collected and aggregated. The ideal control chart configuration would conform to a "one process one chart" rule. Practical requirements make this determination a combination of art and science. The science requires subgroups to conform with normality and minimum number of subgroups requirements. The art requires a control chart that represents the process as precisely as possible. It is rarely advisable to set up one control chart for each service provider because usually the intent is for services to be delivered in a consistent manner. It is advisable, however, to set up a control chart for each major service type. For example, if control charts are used to show time to approve a zoning change in a government office, one chart may be used for commercial applications and another chart for residential applications. In these cases, process outcomes would likely be expected to differ and therefore two processes exist.

A useful interpretation of the normality rules focuses on the average number of expected occurrences of the outcome by subgroup. The requirement of normality for the P chart can be stated as follows: The average number of successes, np, and the average number of failures, $n(1-p)$, need to both be at least 5. For the U chart, the average number of occurrences per subgroup of the occurrences that are counted, nu, needs to be at least 5. Subgroup sizes need to be large enough to satisfy these assumptions, which is also a good approach for assuring that the sample sizes are sufficient for powerful detection of instability.

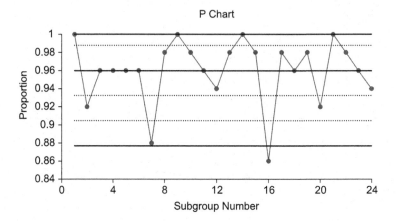

Figure 9.9 P chart with insufficient subgroup size.

When either a P chart or a U chart has insufficient subgroup sizes, a telltale sign is visible on the charts. For U charts, an insufficient subgroup size would result in too many unit counts of 0.0. For P charts, an insufficient subgroup size would result in too many proportions of either 0.00 or 1.00. An example is shown in Figure 9.9, where the subgroup size is 50 and the average proportion of successes is 0.960. The lack of normality would be confirmed because $50(1 - 0.96) = 2$ is less than 5. Although the first Shewhart rule is violated (subgroup 16), the process shown is actually stable and perfectly consistent with the skewness expected in binomial distribution when $n(1 - p) < 5$.

Control charts for measurement data

Measured process outcomes fall on a continuous scale, albeit sometimes rounded for convenience. The most likely measured outcome from a service process concerns time, most often customer waiting times or customer service times. The theoretical foundations of control charting of measurement data are more complex than those for attribute data. Because they mainly apply to manufacturing operations, readers interested in measurement control charts are advised to consult a more general text on quality management or one that focuses on manufacturing.

Two approaches are recommended for the stability analysis using measurement data from a service process. The first approach would utilize a run chart, described earlier in this book. Although its interpretation is more subjective, a run chart can be effective at identifying instability and its root cause. An analyst needs to be careful not to overreact to random variation. The second approach would utilize a P chart after converting the measurement data to proportion data. For example, a mobile phone store that collects data on customer service times can translate the measurements of time to the proportion of customers who took longer than a specified time to be serviced. This specified time need not be an actual standard or target. It should be created so that subgroups average at least five callers with waiting times below or above the specified time.

Customer satisfaction survey analysis

The analysis of process outcomes using SPC also applies to customer satisfaction survey results. Many survey results include outcomes that are ordinal categorical. Although ordinal data have a natural ordering, it is unwise to analyze survey data by assuming they are measurements. These conversions make invalid assumptions about the magnitude of customer emotions across response choices, and their numerical results are difficult to interpret. A statistically valid approach would use a P chart to analyze stability, with one P chart per survey question. For each question, response choices that correspond to either satisfaction or displeasure would be totaled thereby converting the ordinal data to proportions.

Consider a 7-choice list of answers to this survey question: "Indicate your level of agreement with the following – My service provider was friendly." The survey was administered to 200 customers, though not all customers responded. The response choices, assumed measurement equivalent (score), and the number of customer responses by response choice during the last month were as follows:

Score = 1: Completely disagree – 2 customers
Score = 2: Disagree – 3 customers
Score = 3: Somewhat disagree – 4 customers
Score = 4: Neither agree not disagree – 7 customers
Score = 5: Somewhat agree – 16 customers
Score = 6: Agree – 24 customers
Score = 7: Completely agree – 19 customers

The total number of customers completing the survey was 75, and the average score was 5.40. This score appears to place the average customer response between somewhat agree and agree (slightly close to somewhat agree). Often this value is compared to a target value and action is taken if the target is not met or exceeded. Comparison of the average with a target ignores the impact of random variation and is not consistent with process thinking. Some analysts use a statistical hypothesis test or confidence interval assuming normality, but the scaling problem remains.

A more effective approach would be to convert the survey responses into two categories (e.g., satisfied or not) and analyze the survey results using a P chart. For example, all responses in the highest three categories of a 7-point scale could be combined as representing a satisfied customer. We see that 59 of the 75 customers were satisfied with the friendliness of the service provider, a proportion of 0.787 (78.7%). This value would be plotted on a P chart. This approach is statistically valid because proportion data will follow a binomial model. It is also intuitive because a process manager and others in the firm can appreciate the meaning of a satisfaction percentage.

Aggregation of responses across survey questions is not recommended. Although it may appear as effective for simplifying an analysis, all nuances will be lost when evaluating customers' emotional responses to service delivery. For example, satisfaction with respect to multiple dimensions may be confounded by combing questions that span more than one dimension. Similarly, focusing solely on the analysis on an overall satisfaction question should also be avoided. Although tempting, this approach will be ineffective at identifying the satisfaction level for each performance dimension. It will also compromise root cause identification when a process becomes unstable.

Control charts for monitoring performance

The examples presented in this chapter show how control charts are implemented for evaluating a set of outcome data. Any new application of control charting would need to start by using this approach to develop a baseline for future comparisons. For example, the labelling mistakes data in Figure 9.2 showed that the process was stable with a center line of 0.03175 (3.175%). These data were collected on a weekly basis over the previous 20 weeks. Consider the inspections that will take place in future weeks, such as week 21. The outcome of these inspections would need to be added to the P chart.

When adding new data to a control chart, two options are available. The first option is to freeze the center line at the current value, so that future results are judged based on this likelihood. This method assumes that the current center line will form the basis of future evaluations. This approach is unnecessary and can cause confusion because it suggests that the control chart is being used to evaluate outcome acceptability. It also complicates the application of P charts, requiring software applications that are more feature laden.

The recommended option is to recalculate the center line and control limits as new subgroups are added to the control chart. Within this option, two alternative approaches can be implemented. The first approach is to add data that expands the control chart's length by adding new data and maintaining the previous data. The second approach plots a constant number of subgroups by dropping the oldest data when new data are added. This approach is recommended because it maintains a consistent look and feel for the P chart, which enhances communication across the organization. In addition, it focuses the most recent set of process outcomes. Finally, it prevents the necessity of wholesale control chart restructuring so that no more than 30 subgroups are shown.

10 Service process capability analysis

Introduction

Statistical process control (SPC) integrates process stability analysis and process capability analysis (PCA). Stability is analyzed using control charts, and PCA compares the performance of a stable process to a target that will be referred to as a benchmark. The integration of control charts and PCA ensures that only stable processes are compared to a benchmark. Benchmarks are based on performance targets that the process manager creates in their quest to meet customer needs in a competitive manner. They may be internally derived, or they may be based on external comparisons to peer organizations.

This chapter details the procedure employed to perform a comprehensive PCA for a service process, which is also referred to as statistical benchmarking. It details the statistical techniques that account random variation of process outcomes, when the outcomes consist of proportions or counts. Some attention is also devoted to PCA for measured outcomes. The determination of suitable benchmarks is discussed using several illustrative examples. A scenario is described that illustrates the potential for misapplication when a firm utilizes a third-party company to assist with statistical benchmarking.

Benchmarking service process performance

A stable process that meets the needs of customers at a satisfactory performance level is called an acceptable process. Some stable processes are unacceptable because, although they generate outcomes within a predictable range, many of these outcomes do not meet the benchmark target set by the firm. For example, consider a stable loan process with a mean unit count of 3.2 mistakes per application. This mistake rate may be considered unacceptable because other banks process loans at a much lower mean unit count. Some unstable processes may be acceptable some or all of the time. However, an analyst cannot perform an accurate PCA for an unstable process because a predictable range cannot be determined for future outcomes.

DOI: 10.4324/9781003199014-10

Service customers' needs are usually intangible, and they can be difficult to define precisely. They are unlike manufacturing processes that have tangible outcomes with clearly defined design specifications. Service customer needs are multidimensional, and they evolve over time. Internal customer needs can be easier to define because the process manager has better access to customers. The setting of performance targets (i.e., benchmarks) will take different forms across process types. They rarely apply consistently from one process to another.

The comparison of performance data to a benchmark will be referred to as statistical benchmarking. Benchmarks can be established internally based on the needs of the organization. In these cases, care should be taken to set reasonable benchmarks rather than benchmarks that attempt to improve performance by setting a standard that is beyond the current process capability. These stretched goals assume that employees can improve quality simply by working harder; they often cause workers to artificially manipulate data for fear of punishment.

A benchmark can also be externally derived by obtaining performance information from professional organizations that focus on specific industries or process types. Benchmarks for call centers are readily available for companies that pay a fee for access; they are useful for comparing performance of call centers for various industries. Sometimes, groups of organizations hire a third-party firm to compare their performance with the aggregate performance of similar processes. Many hospitals employ this approach, which is a requirement of important accreditation systems. Governments often publicly disclose benchmark information for public sector or tax-supported services, such as the Medicare health system in the United States.

SPC perspective

The SPC construct for attribute outcome data (Figure 10.1) shows the integration of process stability analysis and PCA. It reinforces the requirements that a process must be stable for any analysis of its capability to be accurate and meaningful. And it accounts for random variation throughout. For example, the stable P chart center line estimates the likelihood of an outcome; this estimate should include a margin of uncertainty before it is compared to a benchmark likelihood.

To perform the PCA, uncertainty associated with P and U chart center lines is quantified using a statistical confidence interval. If the benchmark lies within the confidence interval, then the process may or may not perform as well as the benchmark. In these cases, it would be fair to conclude that process performance is consistent with the benchmark (the process manager typically desires this result). If the benchmark falls outside the confidence interval, then the process is proven to be either better than or worse than the benchmark.

If process performance is proven to be worse than the benchmark, an action plan would start by ensuring that the benchmark enforces an

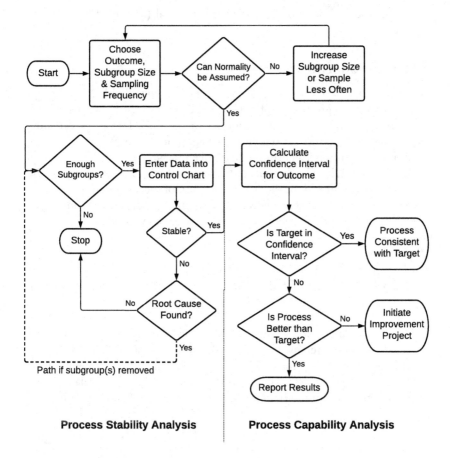

Figure 10.1 SPC framework: Attribute data.

apples-to-apples comparison. If the benchmark is deemed appropriate, the process manager should initiate a quality improvement project. In the meantime, it would be wise to place short-term controls on process output while the quality improvement project is undertaken. If process performance is proven to be better than the benchmark, the process manager may wish to publicize this result.

The PCA procedure assumes that the comparison benchmark is a definitive value that is not subject to random variation. This assumption is valid when the benchmark is derived from a very large sample of outcomes. Although no standard exists, the methodology presented would be appropriate when the comparison benchmark is based on 20 or more similar processes. The definitive value benchmark requirement precludes the necessity to calculate a confidence interval for the benchmark. Such a calculation would be impractical because an external benchmark's provider will usually not provide sample size information. In cases where the benchmark cannot be assumed definitive, a confidence interval (described here) would be utilized.

PCA for proportion outcomes

Consider a pharmacy's labelling process, where a P chart (with 20 subgroups and a constant subgroup size of 200) showed the process to be stable with an estimated labelling mistake likelihood of 0.03175. The PCA can now commence because process stability has been confirmed. With no suitable benchmark, we simply calculate a confidence interval for the true likelihood of a labelling mistake. The formula in Equation 10.1 is used to determine the 95% confidence interval for the true proportion of success based on a sample of size N drawn from a stable process generating proportion outcomes. The value N is the total of all subgroup sizes that were used to display the stable P chart.

$$\overline{p} - 2\sqrt{\frac{\overline{p}(1-\overline{p})}{N}} < p < \overline{p} + 2\sqrt{\frac{\overline{p}(1-\overline{p})}{N}} \qquad 10.1$$

For the labelling process, a total of 4,000 labels were inspection over the 20-week period covered by the P chart. Hence, $N = 4,000$ and $\overline{p} = 0.03175$, and the 95% confidence interval for the true likelihood of a labelling mistake is $0.0262 < p < 0.0373$. This confidence interval can be calculated using a template included in the book's companion web site. The proper description of this confidence interval is: We are 95% sure that the probability of a labelling mistake at this pharmacy is between 2.62% and 3.73%. With no comparison benchmark available, this explanation would conclude the PCA. Alternatively, an analyst can provide perspective by consulting the customer satisfaction survey results for the same performance dimension. If customers are satisfied, then currently performance can be considered acceptable; otherwise, the process should be improved.

To illustrate the SPC approach when a suitable benchmark exists, consider a hospital's maternity ward. An important metric is the percentage of PCS births. There is no desire to minimize or maximize the metric, although a hospital would be concerned if their PCS rate was inconsistent with peer hospitals. The rate for PCS births at peer hospitals averages 20.32%. PCS data covering 27 months were evaluated using a P chart, which showed that the process was unstable. After the root cause of instability was found and removed for the process, the P chart shown in Figure 10.2 was created.

The likelihood of a PCS birth at his hospital is estimated to be 21.91% (i.e., the P chart center line), based on the past 19 months of data that totaled 1,880 first-time births. As shown in the template's output screen (Figure 10.3), we are 95% sure that the true likelihood of a PCS birth at this hospital is between 20.01% and 23.82% (small inconsequential differences

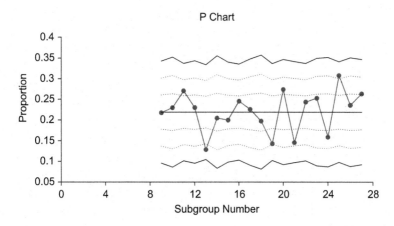

Figure 10.2 P chart for PCS births (revised).

Process Capability Analysis Template (Proportion Data)
(Enter Values in Shaded Areas)

Assumptions: (1) process is stable and (2) outcomes are normally distributed.

Estimate of Proportion "Success"	0.21915	Benchmark Outcome (optional)	0.2032
Sample Size for Estimate	1880	Degree of Confidence	95%
Lower Confidence Interval Limit	0.20007		
Upper Confidence Interval Limit	0.23823	**Performance Consistent with Benchmark**	

Figure 10.3 PCA for PCS births.

may exist between a hand calculation and the template's results due to rounding effects). The benchmark rate of 20.32% is within this confidence interval, that is, performance is consistent with the benchmark. Although it is possible that the true likelihood of a PCS birth at the hospital may be higher or lower than the benchmark likelihood, no action should be taken.

PCA for count outcomes

A PCA for count data is almost identical to a proportion data PCA, except the Poisson distribution is used to calculate the comparison confidence interval instead of the binomial. Consider a consulting firm's office manager who monitors corrections made to proposals written by associates. Data are collected when a proposal is reviewed by a senior staff member prior to its submission to a customer. Correction data were tabulated for the previous 28 weeks and the current target is no more than one correction per proposal.

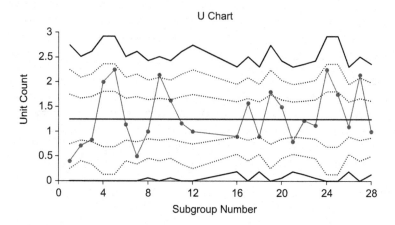

Figure 10.4 U chart for proposal corrections (revised).

A U chart showed the process to be unstable, but after finding and removing a root cause the stable U chart in Figure 10.4 was created. Its center line is 1.247 (i.e., an estimated rate of 1.247 corrections per proposal over 25 weeks).

Because the U chart is stable, we can perform a PCA that evaluates performance relative to the benchmark rate of one or fewer corrections per proposal. Equation 10.2 calculates the 95% confidence interval for the mean unit count based on a sample of size N drawn from a stable process generating count outcomes. The value N is the total of all subgroup sizes that were used to display the stable U chart.

$$\bar{u} - 2\sqrt{\frac{\bar{u}}{N}} < u < \bar{u} + 2\sqrt{\frac{\bar{u}}{N}} \qquad 10.2$$

After removing the unstable subgroups, a total of 174 proposals were inspected. The estimated rate of corrections (i.e., unit count) was 1.247 corrections per proposal. Hence, $N = 174$ and $\bar{u} = 1.247$, and the 95% confidence interval for the true correction rate per proposal is $1.08 < u < 1.41$ (see Figure 10.5). This confidence interval was calculated using a template included in the book's companion web site. The proper description of this interval is as follows: We are 95% sure that the current correction rate is between 1.08 and 1.41 corrections per proposal. The benchmark correction rate of 1.0 falls below this confidence interval, and therefore process performance is proven to be worse than the benchmark. Before initiating quality improvement project to improve performance of the proposal writing process, the process manager should confirm that 1.0 is an appropriate target given the nature of the process under study.

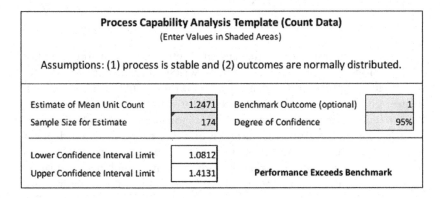

Figure 10.5 PCA for proposal corrections.

Sources of benchmarks

An ideal benchmark would be derived from a large number of peer organizations that operate similar processes with identically defined outcomes. Peer groups should be configured based on factors that affect process outcomes. Usually, size would not be an effective basis for peer grouping unless performance for different sized organization is expected to perform differently. Healthcare peer groups are usually created based on factors such as teaching versus nonteaching hospitals, urban versus rural hospitals, and children versus adult care hospitals. Call center peer groups are usually created by industry type. It is rarely necessary to create peer groups based on customer volumes because the PCA accounts for sample size.

An organization often relies on a third-party firm for identifying comparison benchmarks. These firms collect performance outcomes from a group of similar organizations based on precisely defined standards. The benchmarking firm aggregates performance data and provides each client with a report detailing how well their performance was compared to similar organizations. The benchmarking firm may provide detailed peer group comparisons when the client base is expansive.

For attribute outcomes, the information clients provide to a benchmarking firm will generally be the average outcome and the sample size corresponding to the specified period. Time periods are often delineated by quarter (i.e., three months). The data collected by the benchmarking firm from each of its T clients consist of their average proportions $(\bar{p}_1, \bar{p}_2, \cdots, \bar{p}_T)$ or their average unit counts $(\bar{u}_1, \bar{u}_2, \cdots, \bar{u}_T)$, as well as their sample sizes $(N_1, N_2, \cdots, N_T)$. The only useful statistic the firm can generate is the weighted average for each outcome. The statistic would represent the likelihood of a success or the mean count rate of the group of T clients, as shown (for proportion data) in Equation 10.3 (a similar calculation would exist for count data).

$$\bar{P} = \frac{\bar{p}_1 N_1 + \bar{p}_2 N_2 + \cdots + \bar{p}_T N_T}{N_1 + N_2 + \cdots + N_T}$$ 10.3

Several statistical summaries that appear helpful for benchmarking are not valid for proportion or count data. The unweighted average (the average of each client's proportion) is not an accurate measure of the likelihood within the peer group because it does not account for sample sizes. Measures of dispersion, such as the standard deviation of proportions or counts across the T clients, is not valid because the variation of a proportion or count depends on sample size (i.e., the T outcomes are derived from T separate processes each with a unique sample size). Similarly, percentile rankings or quartile assignments for each client are also useless statistics because of sample size differences.

Comparison of a service process outcome to a benchmark requires an apples-to-apples association, especially regarding their outcome definition. Effective statistical benchmarking also requires that customers' expectations are similar across the comparison processes. Some outcomes (such as hold time per call at a call center) have consistent definitions, although comparing call center needs to account for industry type. For example, the customer hold time expectation for a business-to-business call center would likely differ from the customer expectation for a business-to-consumer call center.

Industries that undergo accreditation or certification by a standards organization often enforce consistency across outcome definitions. These industries include healthcare, education, and many services. But many performance outcomes are not consistently defined across organizations. In these cases, benchmarking should be undertaken with caution. At an IT help desk, a metric that tabulates same issue call backs requires that every IT help desk use the same metric definition, including a timeframe and a clear delineation of a new problem versus an unsolved problem.

Internal performance comparisons

There are times when a process manager wishes to compare two similar processes, usually within the same extended enterprise. In these cases, the conceptual approach shown in the SPC framework (Figure 10.1) is appropriate with a few modifications. These modifications can also be applied to external benchmark comparisons when the sample size generating the benchmark is known. An analyst should start by confirming that the outcome being compared is defined and measured in consistent ways. The statistical analysis begins the approach by evaluating the stability of each process. If one or both processes is not stable, then a root cause should be identified and resolved. In these cases, a comparison cannot be made until stability is assured for both processes. Once stability is confirmed for both processes, each process's likelihood of success or mean count rate can be compared.

Comparing outcomes of two processes with similarly defined outcomes focuses on the gap in their performance. This gap is estimated as the difference between the center lines on the two stable P or U charts. The gap is analyzed statistically using a 95% confidence interval for the difference in the center line values. The relatively complex formula for this confidence interval can be found in a statistics textbook. The book's companion web site includes a template that calculates the 95% confidence interval for the difference in: (1) two proportions; (2) two counts; or (3) two measured outcomes.

The confidence interval for the difference in process performance corresponds to one of the following: $p_1 - p_2, u_1 - u_2, \mu_1 - \mu_2$ (for proportion data, count data, and measurement data, respectively). The confidence interval is valid as long as normality rules are met for both processes. The rules for the normality of attribute data (i.e., based on the binomial and Poisson models) are based on requirements presented earlier. For measurement data, no distributional assumptions are made if the sample sizes of both data sets are 30 or more (otherwise, the processes need to both follow a normal distribution).

Consider the proposal correction process analyzed earlier in this chapter, where the stable U chart is shown in Figure 10.4 (with a total sample size of 174 proposals and a center line of 1.247 corrections per proposal). Let's assume that another department also writes proposals, and an identical inspection procedure has been implemented. That department's U chart is also stable, with a total sample size of 141 proposals and a center line of 1.455 corrections per proposal. Figure 10.6 shows the confidence interval for the difference in the two mean unit counts.

The 95% confidence interval for the difference in the mean unit counts for the two processes extends from −0.472 to 0.056. This means that we are 95% sure that the difference of the process mean unit counts falls within this range. Because this interval includes the value 0.0 (i.e., no difference) we conclude that correction rates are similar. If the confidence interval did not include 0.0, then a difference in the mean unit counts would be statistically

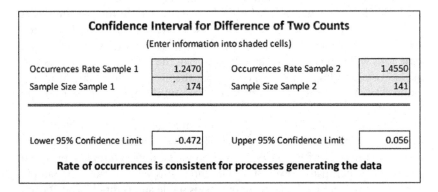

Confidence Interval for Difference of Two Counts

(Enter information into shaded cells)

Occurrences Rate Sample 1	1.2470	Occurrences Rate Sample 2	1.4550
Sample Size Sample 1	174	Sample Size Sample 2	141

Lower 95% Confidence Limit	-0.472	Upper 95% Confidence Limit	0.056

Rate of occurrences is consistent for processes generating the data

Figure 10.6 Confidence interval comparing proposal corrections.

significant. The analysis would conclude that the two processes operated dissimilarly, and approach action would be taken.

PCA for measured outcomes

A PCA in manufacturing settings typically uses measurement data and concludes with an estimated rate at which products conform to design specifications. This procedure is complex and unnecessary for services, where measurement data are uncommon. The best approach would start by converting the measurement data to proportions. A P chart will be utilized to confirm stability and a confidence interval would be used to compare performance to a suitable benchmark. Most cases of measurement data in services concern waiting or service times. In these cases, a threshold time would be created and each customer would be documented as conforming or nonconforming to the threshold time.

When data sets are small, measured outcomes cannot be converted to proportions with adherence to the binomial distribution's normality assumption. In these cases, the measured outcome data can be maintained and the data evaluated as follows. Stability would be confirmed using a run chart. If the run chart clearly shows that the process is unstable, the root cause of instability would be identified and appropriate action taken. A PCA would not be performed until the process is declared stable. If the analyst deems the process to be stable, a histogram would be created to determine the outcome's distribution, and calculations of the sample average and standard deviation would be calculated. Evaluating acceptability of the stable process would be done using a confidence interval for the stable process's mean outcome.

Consider an IT department that modifies computer code for applications used within a small firm. Customers are internal and requests are infrequent. The outcome of interest is the total lead time from creation to closure of a help ticket. Over the past two years, 45 code modification requests were made. The run chart in Figure 10.7 shows the 45 lead times.

The run chart appears stable except for a potential outlier at observation 34, which is best evaluated by a histogram. The histogram, shown as Figure 10.8, is right- skewed and inconsistent with a normally distributed outcome. This skewness is expected because of the nature of the process – some jobs will naturally take much longer than the average and few jobs will take a corresponding amount shorter than the average. The value at observation 34 (239 days) is clearly not an outlier and therefore does not require investigation.

For the 45-outcome data set, the sample average lead time was 86.2 days, and the standard deviation was 45.9 days. The 95% confidence interval for the mean lead time is: $72.5 < \mu < 99.9$ days (calculated using a template provided in the book's companion web site). The interval is valid because the sample size is 30 or more. In summary, the process is stable and right-skewed. We are

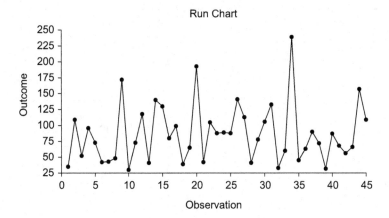

Figure 10.7 Run chart for IT lead time (in days).

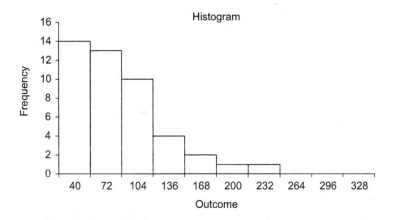

Figure 10.8 Histogram for lead time (in days).

95% sure that the mean lead time is between 72.5 days and 99.9 days. The analysis would stop here if no benchmark comparison for lead time exists.

PCA for customer satisfaction analysis

SPC is easily adapted to the analysis of customer satisfaction. The procedure is best described with an example. Consider the firm that housed the IT department's application modification process analyzed in the previous section. A customer satisfaction survey is sent every month to a sample of internal customers throughout the firm. The survey questions focus on the IT department's ability to service customers across five key dimensions of performance, including timeliness of service. The data in Table 10.1 shows

Table 10.1 Customer satisfaction survey results for timeliness

Month	AD	MD	SD	SA	MA	AA
1	1	2	2	4	11	8
2	0	2	3	4	10	7
3	1	1	2	3	9	14
4	1	3	4	2	10	7
5	0	2	3	3	12	8
6	0	2	4	4	13	9
7	1	4	5	3	12	8
8	0	3	3	2	11	7
9	1	2	4	6	10	6
10	1	1	2	3	9	7
11	0	3	3	4	10	7
12	0	2	3	3	11	7
13	0	2	4	2	9	6
14	1	1	4	6	10	5
15	1	2	3	5	10	6
16	0	3	5	6	12	9
17	1	3	4	5	11	8
18	1	5	6	3	8	6
19	2	3	5	4	9	4
20	1	5	6	3	7	3
21	3	6	5	6	7	4
22	2	3	7	7	6	5
23	2	5	5	6	8	3
24	3	4	4	8	7	2

the customer satisfaction results collected over the past two years where customers responded to the following: I am satisfied with the timeliness of the IT department. They were asked to choose one of the following response choices: absolutely disagree (AD), moderately disagree (MD), slightly disagree (SD), slightly agree (SA), moderately agree (MA), and absolutely agree (AA).

The survey results were converted to proportions by classifying the highest two categories (moderately agree and absolutely agree) as satisfied customers. For example, in month 1, 19 of the 28 customers who completed the survey indicated satisfaction, a proportion of 67.9%. The P chart (Figure 10.9) shows 0.679 as the first month's proportion.

The P chart includes several Shewhart rule violations, including the first 8 points falling above the center line, points 19–23 having 4 of 5 points falling below 1-Sigma of the center line, and points 20–22 having 2 of 3 points falling below 2-Sigma of the center line. An investigation should be undertaken to find the root cause of this instability because it is clear that customers have become increasingly less satisfied over time. The PCA would not continue until the process was stabilized.

It is interesting to consider the P chart customer satisfaction results in light of the earlier analysis that showed the lead times to be stable. This phenomenon is not unusual. It appears that, although the IT department

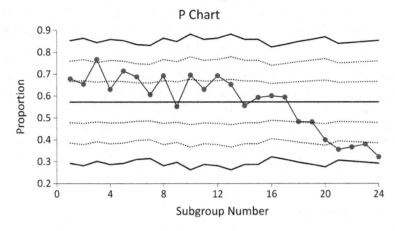

Figure 10.9 P chart for satisfaction with timeliness.

has maintained a consistent level of service, its customers have increasingly higher expectations. These higher expectations are likely due to many factors. They include new employees who work at firms with more responsive IT departments, or the existence of similar support processes within and outside the firm that have improved over time.

Preventing benchmarking mistakes

Mistakes are common when inexperienced or untrained analysts compare performance to a benchmark. This phenomenon is prevalent within service organizations, where fewer standard analysis routines exist compared with manufacturing settings. Some organizations mistakenly compare their quarterly data with a benchmark without accounting for random variations. Other organizations misinterpret information received from third-party benchmarking firms. These mistakes are rooted in the shortage of statistical expertise within many service organizations.

Consider the use of a percentile ranking. Many people know percentiles from their school days because they are often used to communicate standardized test results. A high school student who scores at the 82nd percentile on a standardized test has done better than 82% of the other test takers. Percentile rankings are appropriate because the differences in students' abilities are profound, and scores are not significantly affected by random variation. But percentile ranking comparisons can be problematic when used to compare business process outcomes. The main reason for the misapplication is that we expect all firms to operate similarly. We do not expect, for example, the PCS likelihood to differ across hospitals. In these cases, random variation can cause substantial changes in percentiles from one period to the next, even when a process is unchanged.

Consider a group of 20 identical processes with different sized customer populations, where an outcome takes the form of proportion data. By definition, two of the processes will have outcomes that fall among the top 10th percentile and two of the processes will have outcomes that fall among the bottom 10th percentile. These 4 of the 20 processes operate no differently from the others (because the processes are identical), yet they are highlighted as being either superior or inferior to other processes. A change from period to period in their percentile score may be large even when no differences exist across the processes. Because smaller samples will experience more outcome variation, organizations that serve fewer customers will often see especially large percentile changes that have no meaningful statistical (or business) relevance.

Comprehensive example

Consider a performance analysis for a manufacturer with licensed dealers that sell their kitchen appliances. About one month after each appliance purchase, a link to an online customer satisfaction survey is sent by email to the purchaser. Survey results are tabulated each quarter. For the current quarter, the percentage of customers who are satisfied with the knowledge of the sales staff member for 20 dealers in a region is analyzed. Table 10.2 shows the survey results, sorted by satisfaction percentage.

Table 10.2 Appliance dealer customer satisfaction results

Dealer name	Surveys completed	Number satisfied	Satisfaction percentage
B&G Appliance	9	9	100.0
Victory Appliance	6	6	100.0
Appliance Center	38	35	92.1
AAA Appliances	17	15	88.2
Harvard Appliances	56	48	85.7
5MC Appliances	30	25	83.3
Modern Appliances	53	44	83.0
P&L Appliances	15	12	80.0
DNC Appliances	89	71	79.8
Harris Appliances	94	70	74.5
John's Appliances	79	56	70.9
Appliance Town	63	39	61.9
RUX Appliances	78	45	57.7
Billings Appliances	44	24	54.5
Y&A Appliances	28	15	53.6
Gentry Appliances	34	15	44.1
ABC Appliances	18	7	38.9
Pete's Appliances	5	1	20.0
City Appliances	8	1	12.5
Edison Appliances	4	0	0.0

The overall average satisfaction rate for the 20 dealers was 70.1% (538 of the 768 respondents chose satisfaction for the question concerning sales staff knowledge). Readers are reminded that the table presents a list of proportion data, each with a unique sample size. It should not be surprising that dealers at the top and bottom of the list tend to exhibit smaller sample sizes. This phenomenon could have been predicted based on the behavior of binomially distributed proportion outcomes, because the magnitude of variation increases as the sample size decreases.

This example illustrates the fallacy of sorting a group of proportions, especially when their sample sizes differ. The binomial model and P chart development both stressed that proportions cannot be evaluated without consideration of sample size differences. Ranking appliance dealers based on the proportion of satisfied customers is a useless exercise. Calculating any measure of dispersion, such as standard deviation of the 20 proportions, is also meaningless. Similarly, calculating percentiles or grouping the proportions by quartile is unhelpful. The only meaningful statistic that can be derived from the set of 20 proportions is the weighted average proportion (70.1%). This value provides a suitable benchmark for the likelihood that a customer across this region is satisfied with sales staff's knowledge.

The proper analysis of these performance data would proceed dealer-by-dealer based on the PCA procedure used earlier in this chapter. Ideally, a P chart would be analyzed for each dealer, with unstable processes (i.e., dealers) identified. Those dealers would be asked to find a root cause of their instability, and why it caused an increase or decrease in the satisfaction likelihood. For dealers with a stable process and a sample size large enough to assume normality, a 95% prediction range for that dealer would be calculated with the assumption that the likelihood of a satisfied customer is 0.701 (the aggregate group mean). This prediction range is the expectation of the quarterly satisfaction percentage assuming that the dealer's satisfaction likelihood is equal to the group's mean likelihood. Those dealers with a reported proportion within this interval perform consistently with the group. Others whose reported performance falls outside the prediction range are proven to be either better or worse than the group.

Consider 5MC Appliances, with 30 surveys returned and a satisfaction rate of 83.3%. Assuming stability, the 95% prediction range for the likelihood of a satisfied customer at 5MC extends from 53.3% to 86.8%. Although this range is not a confidence interval, it uses Equation 10.1 with $p = 0.701$ (instead of $\bar{p}$) and $N = 30$. This dealer's customer satisfaction is consistent with the benchmark, because their reported 83.3% proportion lies within the prediction range. On the contrary, consider Modern Appliances with a lower satisfaction rate of 83.0% based on 53 surveys. Assuming stability, this dealer's 95% prediction range extends from 57.5% to 82.6% (note that the length of this range is smaller than the interval for 5MC due to their larger sample size). Modern Appliances can claim that their customer satisfaction is higher than the benchmark, because their reported 83.0% proportion lies above the prediction range.

Table 10.3 PCA for appliance dealer satisfaction

Dealer name	Surveys completed	Number satisfied	Satisfaction rate	Normal?	Prediction range
B&G Appliance	9	9	100.0%	No	n/a
Victory Appliance	6	6	100.0%	No	n/a
Appliance Center	38	35	92.1%	Yes	(0.552, 0.849)
AAA Appliances	17	15	88.2%	Yes	(0.478, 0.923)
Harvard Appliances	56	48	85.7%	Yes	(0.578, 0.823)
5MC Appliances	30	25	83.3%	Yes	(0.533, 0.868)
Modern Appliances	53	44	83.0%	Yes	(0.575, 0.826)
P&L Appliances	15	12	80.0%	No	n/a
DNC Appliances	89	71	79.8%	Yes	(0.603, 0.798)
Harris Appliances	94	70	74.5%	Yes	(0.606, 0.795)
John's Appliances	79	56	70.9%	Yes	(0.597, 0.804)
Appliance Town	63	39	61.9%	Yes	(0.585, 0.816)
RUX Appliances	78	45	57.7%	Yes	(0.597, 0.804)
Billings Appliances	44	24	54.5%	Yes	(0.562, 0.839)
Y&A Appliances	28	15	53.6%	Yes	(0.527, 0.874)
Gentry Appliances	34	15	44.1%	Yes	(0.543, 0.858)
ABC Appliances	18	7	38.9%	Yes	(0.485, 0.916)
Pete's Appliances	5	1	20.0%	No	n/a
City Appliances	8	1	12.5%	No	n/a
Edison Appliances	4	0	0.0%	No	n/a

As illustrated in the two examples, a 95% prediction range would need to be determined for each dealer to identify those shown to be higher, consistent, or lower than the benchmark of 70.1%. This analysis can be done only if the dealer's process is stable and their sample size allows for the normality assumption to be made. We will assume that all dealers shown in Table 10.3 have stable P charts. The prediction ranges are shown for those dealers with sample size sufficient to assume normality. For example, the 9 customers completing the survey at B&G Appliance are insufficient to assume normality because $9(1 - 0.701) = 2.7$, which is less than 5.

The following dealers are consistent with the 70.1% benchmark: AAA, 5MC, Harris, John's, Appliance Town, and Y&A. The following dealers are shown to exceed the benchmark: Appliance Center, Harvard, Modern, and DNC. The following dealers are shown to fall below the benchmark: RUX, Billings, Gentry, and ABC. The remainder of the dealers has sample sizes that are too small for a 95% prediction range to be calculated. These include dealers with 100% satisfaction as well as those with 20% satisfaction or lower. Because their sample sizes over one quarter are insufficient, their performance should be analyzed on a less frequent basis.

11 Service reliability and intervention analysis

Introduction

An ideal business process will satisfy the precise needs of every customer completely without unnecessary delay. The likelihood that a process meets this standard is referred to as its reliability. Reliable processes serve customer needs consistently, while unreliable processes should be improved. Many methods are available to improve a service process based on a purposeful process change. These interventions modify an activity that takes place before, during, or after service delivery. The success of an intervention is evaluated using data that are analyzed through statistical methods that account for variation. In some cases, an inspection may be necessary while process improvements are identified or developed.

This chapter introduces key concepts of reliability. It introduces the FMEA methodology for identifying the ways a process can fail, which leads to the creation of risk mitigation strategies. Some basic Lean improvement methods, called 5S and poka-yoke, are detailed. They should be included in a set of standard work procedures to ensure process reliability. Statistical hypothesis testing is introduced so that intervention success can be verified. Although not a desirable long-term solution, the use of inspections when quality is not acceptable is discussed, including a rule for determining when inspections should be considered.

Service reliability concepts

Service process reliability is the probability that a service is performed successfully under a specified set of conditions. The definition includes a description of the service process, the definition of a successful outcome, and a list of conditions so that extraordinary situations are exempted. For example, reliability may be defined as the probability that an accurate price quote is provided within one week to customers buying from a standard list of customizable products. Reliability definitions can be particularly important for services where a failure would cause undue hardship for customers. They include reliability of a Wi-Fi network, a public transportation system, or

DOI: 10.4324/9781003199014-11

open-heart surgery. Every process manager should understand the concept of reliability, and they should seek to maintain reliability at high levels.

An important metric associated with reliability is the mean time between failures (MTBF), which represents the average time from one service failure to the next service failure. For example, a public transportation system could express reliability as the mean miles between breakdowns of a subway. MTBF is often misinterpreted to represent how long a user can expect a process to perform successfully. The cause of this misunderstanding is the term "mean" which is also referred to as the expected value in statistics. To be clear, "mean" is a statistical expectation for the average. Because the distribution of time between failures is usually right-skewed, in most cases the probability that a process will fail before the MTBF is greater than 50% (it could be as high as 68%).

The reliability of a service can be evaluated for a relatively complex service process that consists of many interconnected activities. In these systems, any of the activities can cause a process failure. Reliability can be improved by adding redundancy (e.g., on call physicians or technicians) for some key activities. For example, a price quote may be unsuccessful in providing an accurate quote within one week if there is a delay in the design department's delivery of design cost. If the system includes a backup design function, then only one of these options (the default department or the backup) needs to perform successfully for the quote to be delivered on time.

In general, the reliability of a complex service is the product of the reliability of each activity. For example, if the price quoting service includes 6 key activities with reliabilities 0.99, 0.97, 0.86, 0.92, 0.94, and 0.95, then the reliability of the price quoting system would be 0.678 (the product of the 6 activities reliabilities). Mathematically, and conceptually, the service's reliability can never be higher than the lowest activity's reliability, and reliability will decrease when more activities are added to the service process. If the service's reliability is unacceptable, then the process manager needs to consider improving (or adding redundancy to) the activities with the lowest reliability.

FMEA

FMEA is a popular methodology used by many quality practitioners in conjunction with quality improvement. It was traditionally applied to products and systems, but now FMEA is also applied to service processes. The goal of service process FMEA is to identify the risks associated with service delivery and determine priorities for the risk factors (i.e., failure modes) that are especially problematic. These risks should be avoided or mitigated so that the overall reliability is maximized in the most effective manner. Priority is assigned based on a combination of three parameters: the likelihood of risk occurrence, the chance of detecting the risk before it causes a failure, and the severity of the failure's impact on the firm. High priority exists when a risk factor is more likely to occur, has a more severe impact, or is unlikely to be detected before delivery to a customer. Reliability associated with a failure mode can be enhanced by improving detection, reducing likelihoods, or decreasing impacts.

FMEA should be performed by a project team that, collectively, possesses detailed knowledge about all facets of the service process. It commences with the listing of every failure mode, each of which will cause in one or more effects. The team assigns three values to each effect based on the likelihood of occurrence (O); the chance of detection (D); and the severity of the potential failure (S). Often, an ordinal scale is used to quantify each of the values as follows: S (1 = insignificant to 10 = catastrophic); O (1 = extremely unlikely to 10 = inevitable); and D (1 = certain to detect to 10 = certain not to detect). Overall priority is calculated by multiplying O, S, and D, called the risk priority number (RPN). The failure modes having the highest RPN represents that they should be given the highest priorities.

Consider the operation of a bicycle sharing service. Paid members use a mobile application to unlock a bicycle at a station, then later relock the bicycle at the same or a different station. The FMEA presented is simplified by focusing on the bicycle unlocking activity, which consists of three steps: login to the application, scan the QR code, and unlock the bicycle. The potential failures modes and the complete FMEA analysis are shown in Table 11.1.

Table 11.1 FMEA for ride sharing service (simplified)

Mode	Effect	S	Cause	O	Controls	D	RPN
System login failure	Cannot get bike	7	App crash, network failure	3	Load balancer distributes workload	3	63
User login failure	Delay	5	Update not done, customer confusion	6	Reminder to update	5	150
User scan function failure	Delay	3	Customer camera failure	2	Enter the code directly	1	6
QR code failure	Delay	3	QR code deformed or blocked	5	Periodic inspection	6	90
Unlock failure	Cannot get bike	7	Mechanical lock failure	4	Offer another bike automatically	3	84
Bike damaged	Cannot ride bike	7	Flat tire or chain problem	3	Periodic inspection	3	63
Bike adjustment failure	Ride is unsafe	9	Rust or previous user issue	2	Periodic inspection	7	126

Several failure modes exist, with many of them having more than one cause. Some failure mode severities are high (e.g., ride is unsafe has the highest score), while others are relatively low (e.g., delay caused by QR code failure). The likelihood of some occurrences is greater than others (e.g., QR code deformed or blocked has a higher likelihood than customer camera failure). Finally, some causes are less likely to be detectable than others (e.g., bike adjustment failure is less likely to be detected than user scan function failure). Overall, as shown by the RPN, the highest priority would be given to user login failure because its RPN is the highest at 150. Some project teams will also consider the failure modes with very high severity scores, such as the bike adjustment failure, regardless of their RPN.

Unfortunately, FMEA can suffer from analyst bias and scoring imprecision. Bias is introduced when the project team has imperfect knowledge, and creates S, O, and D ordinal scores on their opinions rather than facts. The resulting RPNs will simply reflect these opinions. Precision is compromised when the 1–10 ordinal scale is implemented. Occurrence is actually based on a probability that (if known) could be input directly. The severity score is actually based on a cost that (if known) could also be input directly. Finally, detection is actually based on a probability that could be input directly. It can be argued that translation of these costs and probabilities to an imprecise 1–10 ordinal scale is unnecessary. If the more accurate values were used, the RPN would reflect expected cost, which makes more sense to a process manager compared to the 1–1,000 ordinal RPN score.

Improving service processes

Every proposed improvement intervention should be evaluated in light of its effect on the BCF service process goals. It is rarely advisable to sacrifice one of the goals for the sake of one or two of the others. For example, adding an inspection when quality is poor is not a desirable intervention because it will add time and cost to the process. Although the better goal is improved, the faster goal would be sacrificed and costs would increase. In fact, adding an inspection should be considered a temporary action of last resort while better approaches are developed.

Many of the process improvement approaches pioneered at Toyota Motors (known as Lean methods) are applicable to services. The aim of Lean is to reduce the time spent on non–value–added (also called wasteful) activities. They focus on the root cause, rather than the symptom, of a problem. For example, rather than add an inspection in response to poor quality, a Lean approach would focus on the cause of the failure so that it can be eliminated (ideally) or so that its likelihood would be reduced.

An interesting perspective on quality improvement can be found in the FMEA methodology. The RPN can be reduced in one of three ways: (1) by reducing the likelihood of the failure; (2) by instituting a control to detect the problem immediately after it occurs; or (3) by reducing the severity of the failure's impact. Generally, the first approach is most effective, but the second approach may be necessary. Three methods used by Lean practitioners are especially helpful for improving a service process: 5S, poka-yoke, and standard work.

5S

The 5S method consists of five principles that ensure an organized workspace. They are intended to make all necessary information, tools, and materials readily available in locations that are intuitively obvious. The 5S method applies equally to physical workplaces and virtual workspaces. The organization of a virtual workspace is often more important to customers and service providers. However, 5S can be difficult to accomplish in these settings due to the intangible nature of information. Many service providers also lack control over how their firm organizes the information used internally by multiple service processes throughout the firm.

Five Japanese terms describe each principle of 5S. Five English terms have been suggested although the principles themselves are more important than their labels. As applied to a service, the 5S principles are defined as follows: *seiri* ("sort" through all information and identify what is needed for the job), *seiton* ("straighten" the workspace by organizing what is needed into self-explanatory locations that are quick to find), *seiso* ("shine" the workspace by removing clutter that interferes with a service provider's ability to find information), *seiketsu* ("standardize" the way all workers use the workspace), and *shitsuke* ("sustain" the 5S system by establishing rules to periodically revisit the other four principles).

The websites and electronic databases used by service providers are among the most obvious workspaces that should be subject to a 5S analysis and improvement. Many websites, for example, lack the intuitive organization that a service provider would require because web site developers organize the sites without knowledge of all user perspectives. Firms often violate the seiso goal when terminology used on websites is inconsistent with terms used by service providers or customers. For example, customers may be confused when different terms have the same meaning inside the firm (e.g., passcode, password, and PIN). Websites also fall short of the seiketsu goal when, for example, rules change within the organization and associated web site updates are not made.

Consider a service provider's computer desktop and folder structure. To be effective, all information not needed to serve a customer (e.g., personal information, company information, benefits information, etc.) would be moved into folders that would be placed in one or more clearly named folders that would not consume desktop space. These folders would never be required during service delivery (seiri). Folders and subfolders for job tasks would be organized by job type (or customer type). They would be labelled using descriptive names (seiton). Files that were temporary or no longer needed, such as old versions of reports, would be deleted promptly (seiso). A time would be scheduled each week to go through the folder structure and clean up any violations of 5S rules (seiketsu). And each service provider would be devoted to following the rules faithfully (shitsuke).

Poka yoke

Poka yoke is often referred to as mistake proofing because it attempts to stop a failure from occurring. Service process failures include mistakes, errors, delays, or other undesirable events that add time or reduce quality. If a failure cannot be prevented, then poka yoke would be used to reduce its likelihood. Poka yoke is grounded in common sense, with interventions that are application specific. For example, giving a colleague your car keys will guarantee that you will remember to take them home from an event.

Technology can facilitate a poka yoke intervention. For example, customers who enter information onto an online form would not be able to submit the form unless all required fields are completed. A project team should be aware that not all service providers or customers will be technologically sophisticated. A manual version of the same form–submittal poka yoke approach could consist of bright colors and large fonts to highlight required sections of an input form. This approach will not eliminate submission of incomplete forms, but should reduce likelihood.

Poka yoke has many applications for processes where failures can be especially harmful. In medical settings, different style connectors can ensure that correct medical gas is flowing to the patient. Similar, many intravenous feeding systems are designed with tubing that can only be connected to the correct syringe. Prescription systems can be augmented with checks for unsafe drug interactions with warnings issued to prescribers. Technology has also been installed in most hospitals to prevent medication from being given to the wrong patient. These same interventions can apply to other services where failures may not be as impactful, such as ensuring that a label is attached to the correct package.

Project teams or analysts who seek to implement an intervention based on poka yoke should recognize that warnings do not constitute a poka yoke solution. Lessons can be learned from occupational safety and health regulations in the United States. These regulations require that physical barriers be erected to prevent injuries while operating dangerous equipment. Therefore, the creation of a warning that service providers or customers remember certain rules is rarely an effective mistake proofing solution. For example, maintaining social distancing during a pandemic is more effective when signage is supplemented with floor markings showing where people should stand while waiting for a service provider to become available.

It is sometimes difficult or impossible to prevent a failure from occurring. In these cases, poka yoke can be used to notify service providers that the failure has occurred as soon as reasonably possible. Many visual controls can assist with this form of intervention. A checklist can be used by a service provider to confirm that each required step has been completed during service delivery. Visual controls that show customers in a virtual queue or whose service is in progress can create a common sense of urgency among service providers across departments. These visual cues reduce the likelihood that one of the providers is the cause of delay when all other activities have been completed.

Standard work

Standard work was pioneered by the American engineer Frederick Taylor (1856–1915). This approach specifies the preferred way that a job should be done and documents these procedures so that all producers or service providers use the same standard procedure. When successful, standard work guarantees that the service is always completed in the best way possible, that the time required is minimized, and that customers will perceive consistency across service providers and over time. Application of standard work also helps to highlight problems. When a deviation from the standard work practice is necessary, the events that precipitated the deviation will be noticeable and identifiable. These issues are often hidden when a job is done haphazardly.

Toyota's production system strictly enforces standard work, with one major difference from Taylor's approach. Although Taylor considered work design to be management's responsibility, Toyota relies on a partnership of managers and workers to create a standard work procedure. Toyota's approach reduces the likelihood of workers' reluctance to follow the standard work guidelines, because workers themselves play a role in standard work development. Service providers know more about customers than their managers; they know the main service delivery challenges, and they understand the process well. Hence, their ideas are typically valid and practical.

Standard work should be applied to service process activities with caution. Differences in customer needs are unlike tasks in manufacturing where consistency is expected among items being produced. Standard work for a service requires flexibility to respond to a diverse set of customer needs. Standard work for a service process often takes the form of customer-specific customization. Although standard work advocates frown upon workarounds (i.e., when a service provider deviates from the normal mode of operation), workarounds offer a glimpse into where and how unusual customer needs should be addressed.

The development of a standard work procedure starts by creating rules by which a service provider distinguishes an ordinary customer from an extraordinary customer. The standard approach for ordinary customers would then be developed. For extraordinary customers, a specific standard work procedure may not be possible because these needs can be broad and dynamic. When serving these customers, service providers should be trained to apply their knowledge within reasonable (i.e., standard) boundaries established by the standard work procedure.

Some general rules for the creation of standard work are as follows: (1) make every activity a one-way customer-supplier relationship whereby each service provider knows who supplies what to whom; and (2) make the flow of activities one-to-one (simple and direct) with no branching unless the standard work rules specify otherwise. A mantra that should be avoided is "if it is everybody's job, it's nobody's job." For example, rather than giving customers the option of whom to contact, one central hub could be used to route each customer to the entity that will solve their issue most effectively.

The standard work approach has value when expanded beyond work processes. Other useful standard work practices apply to many aspects of a firm's operations and work environment. Examples of these standard approaches include (1) documentation (consistent formats); (2) terminology (across the firm); (3) training materials; (4) software applications (and versions); (5) statistical methods (and applications); (6) problem solving approaches (e.g., DMAIC); (7) communication channels; (8) uniforms; (9) safety procedures; and (10) health protocols.

Statistical intervention analysis

Statistical methods should be used to determine if an intervention that seeks to improve a process is successful. The analysis would use data derived from changes in performance metrics, satisfaction survey results, or other outcomes. This coverage will focus on before-after comparisons, where a set of data collected after an intervention is compared to data collected before the intervention. The data could be based on either a prototype test or actual performance after implementation. The statistical methods employed for this purpose are called two-sample hypothesis tests. Although the conceptual underpinnings of every hypothesis test are consistent, the specific calculations depend on the type of data being analyzed.

A hypothesis test ensures that action is taken only after a decision maker has confidence that the action is warranted. Without a hypothesis test, the action may not be prudent and unnecessary costs may be incurred. This happens when decision makers ignore random variation or when they base their decision on a subjective opinion. Every hypothesis test begins with the statement of a "null" hypothesis and an "alternative" hypothesis. The null hypothesis states that the intervention did not improve quality and this statement is assumed to be true (hence, a better term would be "default" hypothesis). The alternative hypothesis states that the intervention did improve quality.

In every hypothesis test, the null hypothesis is rejected (i.e., the alternative hypothesis is accepted as truth) when it is unlikely that the null hypothesis is true. Although the statistical calculations are beyond the scope of this book, templates are provided on the book's companion web site that perform two-sample hypothesis tests. Every hypothesis test generates a p-value, defined as the likelihood that the null hypothesis is true. Simply stated, when the p-value is low (most practitioners use 0.05 as a threshold), it is unlikely that the null hypothesis is true. Therefore, when the p-value is less than 0.05 (5%), the null hypothesis is rejected and we have statistical justification to state that the intervention improved quality. This rule can be phrased as "when p is low, the null must go."

Two-sample hypothesis test for proportion data

A two-sample hypothesis test for proportions is used to compare the likelihood of a success in the "before" data set to the likelihood of success in the "after" data set. The null hypothesis states that there is no difference in these likelihoods. As a result of the analysis, one of two statements will be made: (1) no statistical evidence exists that the samples are drawn from processes with different likelihoods of success; or (2) there is confidence that the likelihoods of success differ between the two data sets. If the p-value is below 0.05, the latter conclusion would have a confidence level of at least 95%.

A template for performing a two-sample hypothesis test for proportion data is provided in the book's companion web site. It requires the following inputs: (1) the proportion of successes in the first sample; (2) the sample size for the first sample; (3) the proportion of successes in the second sample; and (4) the sample size for the second sample. The template provides the p-value (based on a normally distributed Z-statistic – this formula can be found in any basic statistics book). A concluding statement is also provided. This hypothesis test requires that the normality rules associated with the binomial distribution are validated for both data sets.

Consider the following example. A ridesharing firm keeps track of the proportion of no-show customers. Data for the previous three months in a small city indicates that, for 1,254 customers, the no show proportion was 2.79%. An intervention is created to help the driver better locate the customers. After the change, the no show rate for the next 500 customers dropped to 1.4%. Figure 11.1 shows the two-sample hypothesis test inputs and results.

Because the p-value exceeds 0.05, the conclusion is that the null hypothesis cannot be rejected. That is, we cannot state with confidence that the intervention was successful. The hypothesis test takes sample size into

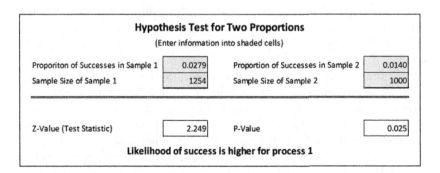

Figure 11.1 Two-sample hypothesis test for proportions.

account. In fact, the p-value would be reduced to 0.025 (and the intervention would be declared successful) if the same 1.4% rate occurred for 1,000 (instead of 500) customers.

Two-sample hypothesis test for count data

A two-sample hypothesis test for counts is used to compare the mean unit count in the "before" data set to the mean unit count in the "after" data set. The null hypothesis states that there is no difference in the mean unit counts. As a result of the analysis, one of two statements will be made: (1) no statistical evidence exists that the samples are drawn from processes with different mean unit counts; or (2) there is confidence that the mean unit counts differ between the two data sets. If the p-value is below 0.05, the latter conclusion would have a confidence level of at least 95%.

A template for performing a two-sample hypothesis test for count data is provided in the book's companion web site. It requires the following inputs: (1) the average unit count in the first sample; (2) the sample size for the first sample; (3) the average unit count in the second sample; and (4) the sample size for the second sample. The template provides the p-value (based on a normally distributed Z-statistic – this formula can be found in any basic statistics book). A concluding statement is also provided. This hypothesis test requires that the normality rule associated with the Poisson distribution is validated for both data sets.

Two-sample hypothesis test for measurement data

A two-sample hypothesis test for measurements is used to compare the process mean in the "before" data set to the process mean in the "after" data set. The null hypothesis states that there is no difference in the process means. As a result of the analysis, one of two statements will be made: (1) no statistical evidence exists that the samples are drawn from processes with different means; or (2) there is confidence that the process means differ between the two data sets. If the p-value is below 0.05, the latter conclusion would have a confidence level of at least 95%.

A template for performing a two-sample hypothesis test for measurement data is provided in the book's companion web site. It requires the following inputs: (1) the sample average for the first sample; (2) the sample standard deviation for the first sample; (3) the sample size for the first sample; (4) the sample average for the second sample; (5) the sample standard deviation for the second sample; (6) the sample size for the second sample. The template provides the p-value (based on a normally distributed normally distributed t-statistic – the formula can be found in any basic statistics book). A concluding statement is also provided. This hypothesis test requires that the processes are both normally distributed unless their sample sizes are both at least 30.

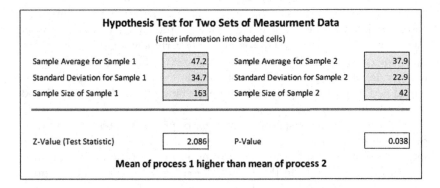

Figure 11.2 Two-sample hypothesis test for measurements.

Consider the following example. A city's public transportation department outsources bus repairs to a vendor. Last year, 163 instances of damage were reported. The waiting time (from damage report to start of repair) was stable, with a right-skewed distribution. The average waiting time for the 163 instances was 47.2 hours and the standard deviation was 34.7 hours. After a project to reduce the waiting time by strategically relocating the vendor's repair vehicles, 42 repairs were performed with an average waiting time of 37.9 hours and a standard deviation was 22.9 hours. As shown in the template (Figure 11.2) we can be at least 95% sure that the intervention to reduce the average waiting time was successful (because the p-value is less than 0.05). Note that the sample sizes both exceed 30, so the processes need not be normally distributed for the analysis to be accurate.

To inspect or not to inspect

An improvement project will usually include a recommended intervention for which the project team will seek approval before implementation. An inspection may be warranted as a short-term course of action during the period between recommendation and implementation. Service process inspections are usually referred to as a review or check. W. Edwards Deming created a rule, called the *kp* rule, for determining when an inspection is warranted. The *kp* rule states that the most cost-effective alternative will be one of the following: (1) inspect all (100%) service output; or (2) inspect no (0%) service output. This determination is based on the values of *p* (the probability of a service failure), k_1 (the cost to inspect a unit of service output), and k_2 (the cost to the firm should a customer notices the service failure).

The *kp* rule states that 100% inspection should be performed when *p* exceeds the ratio of k_1 and k_2. Otherwise, no inspections should be performed. Under no circumstances would sampling be done. For example, consider a legal transcription service that converts an audio file to a written contract.

A data collection effort showed that 2.6% of contracts have errors that would be concerning to the firm's management. Inspecting a contract requires that an expert listen to the audio while reviewing the contract, which costs an estimated $45 per contract. Customers are government regulators who fine firms for contract mistakes. The estimated average fine is $3,600. To apply the kp rule, we have $p = 0.026$, $k_1 = 45$, and $k_2 = 3600$. Accordingly, the firm would perform 100% inspection because the ratio of k_1 and k_2 is 0.0125, and p exceeds this ratio.

There are times when a process manager or project team is not confident that the three parameters of the kp rule can be accurately estimated. The inspection under consideration may also be a short-term action not deemed worthy of careful study. In these cases, the rule creates a sound conceptual awareness. An inspection should be implemented when the failure cost is likely to be high or the inspection cost is likely to be low.

Vendor or server certification

Another approach to consider in the presence of service failures is certifying organizations or service providers as exempt from having their process output inspected. This approach has traditionally been applied to some internal services. For example, some firms inspected the expense reports of new employees, then eliminated the inspections after being assured that the employee understood the expense reporting rules and requirements. The quality function can play a role in these certification systems because they will possess expertise in external certifications such as ISO 9001.

In a service provider certification system, service providers are expected to do high quality work while being responsible for finding root causes and recommending corrective action when problems occur. If effective, overall quality costs are reduced because problems are identified in a timely manner by personnel in a good position to diagnose causes and improve quality. Increased direct labor costs are offset by reductions in inspection costs and quality department overhead. Service delivery can be more reliable in both quality and timeliness.

A suitable structure for certifying a service provider would start with training. Candidates would be required to pass a series of written and hands-on exams. Service providers would then be evaluated with respect to the following: (1) their ability to apply basic quality methodologies; (2) their technical understanding of the job; and (3) their performance during the probationary period during which their work is audited. Candidates satisfying the stated requirements would be certified.

Organizations can also create an informal service provider certification system by encouraging their employees to obtain certification in process improvement methodologies. The most popular of these certifications is Six Sigma (or similarly LSS). There is no single standard for this certification. In almost all cases, certifications are awarded using martial-arts-inspired color schemes based on demonstrated levels of expertise. Black Belt LSS certification is the main standard sought after by many quality practitioners. The quality of these certifications lies with the reputation of the certifying entity and the rigor of their educational programs.

Vendor audits

To ensure that certified service providers continue to operate effectively, random or scheduled audits may be conducted. These audits differ from those performed by external certification or accreditation bodies, whose responsibility is to ensure that their certification standards are met. Service provider audits are internally focused, performed by employees or contractors who are acting on behalf of the firm. Their intention is to ensure that the targeted process delivers services following internal procedures and highlights areas that need improvement. They will be referred to here as quality audits.

The basic steps in a quality audit are: preparation, audit team selection, checklist development, opening meeting, implementation, analysis, exit meeting, reporting and corrective action, follow-up, and closure. It is important to ensure that quality audits are unbiased, and that the auditor(s) include individuals experienced in the procedures evaluated. Auditors need to be firm in their assessments, but somewhat flexible so that they identify unusual circumstances that may affect how certain procedures are implemented. Auditors should understand both the letter and the spirit of each procedure they audit. Although a certain amount of flexibility may be warranted, too much customization of service tasks among the service providers can lead to confusion and misunderstandings.

In some special cases, the auditors may recommend a change to the standard work procedures rather than allow an organization to purposefully violate that procedure. In fact, these situations can have a positive effect on organizational learning and enhance future customer service. For example, a firm may find that many service providers work around unnecessarily complex procedures in ways that fit their special circumstances. In these cases, auditors may find a certain commonality with how service providers are secretly doing a workaround, and perhaps their method is generally applicable.

12 Quality improvement foundations

Introduction

Content thus far has been focused on the tools of quality management – defining customer's needs, creating performance metrics and satisfaction surveys, statistically analyzing outcome data, and evaluating interventions. These tools are often implemented within the context of a quality improvement (QI) project, where teams are mobilized to evaluate a problem's root cause and recommend a course of action. These projects should be chosen and managed within a QI system that ensures effectiveness.

This chapter introduces the foundations of QI. It discusses its origins, which are found in programs such as TQM, Six Sigma, and Lean management. Factors impacting success of a QI program are discussed. Topics include criteria for project choice based on projected financial, quantifiable, and intangible benefits, the selection of a QI project team, and the setting of project performance targets. The importance of informing stakeholders about the firm's QI program is stressed.

Historical background

W. Edwards Deming was the most important influencer in the field of quality management. He argued that improving quality would ultimately decrease costs at a time when most business leaders believed that, to improve quality, costs must increase. Many of Deming's 14 Points for Management deal with continuous improvement, especially #5: "Improve constantly and forever the system of production and service to improve quality and productivity, and thus constantly decrease costs" (Deming, 1986, p. 49). Today, it is generally accepted that every firm should incorporate some form of process improvement into their business practices. The requirements found in important quality certifications and accreditations that include documentation of the firm's QI program.

A successful QI program avoids assigning blame for problems because management appreciates that workers operate within an integrated system. Service providers cannot fully control the resources, tools, and the training provided to them. They have even less control over external factors that

DOI: 10.4324/9781003199014-12

play a role in service quality such as cooperation of other departments within the firm. Finally, they have little or no control over expectation of customers. Therefore, a QI project team should be ready to address root causes that fall anywhere within this integrated system. According to Deming, "I should estimate that in my experience most troubles and most possibilities for improvement add up to proportions something like this: 94% belongs to the system (responsibility of management)" (Deming, 1986, p. 315).

Instituting a formal QI program can serve to consistently reinforce the notion that workers have two important jobs: (1) doing the work; and (2) improving how their work is done. Improvement projects are most effective when they follow a prescribed mandate and structure, so they ensure that important problems are addressed using a sound and consistent methodology. This approach avoids pitfalls common to efforts that focus on symptoms, rather than root causes, of problems. It also enforces the use of data in decision making.

The consistency of approach provided by a QI program can enhance the effectiveness of project teams and the sharing of project results across the organization. Disciplined follow-up ensures that project team recommendations are implemented and tracked. But sustaining these programs requires a culture that actively supports QI in both words and actions. And the active commitment of leadership is critical. Their commitment includes direct participation, so operational nuances are appreciated and required modifications to the QI system are forthcoming.

Over the years, many QI programs have been advocated by business leaders and consultants. Although their names have varied, they have tended to use similar sets of tools. These programs have been called many names such as TQM or continuous quality improvement (CQI). Unfortunately, many consulting organizations argue for their specific version of process improvement as a panacea; often these efforts fail because they do not approach each firm as a unique entity and they fail to ensure true leadership commitment. This tendency has contributed to a "this too shall pass" mentality for employees who see these programs come and go over the course of their employment.

Six Sigma and Lean are popular monikers for process improvement programs, although variations exist in the specific content as they are applied in various environments. Although some firms use one or the other name, most of their principles and tools intersect. Therefore, they will be called LSS in the remainder of this chapter. The implementation guidelines for LSS apply to any other process improvement system. They consist of a disciplined, project-based approach that ensures effectiveness of improvement efforts. They will be useful for administrators responsible for a wide range of organizations that serve customers, including those that are private, public, for-profit, not-for-profit, charitable, and governmental. Their application also applies to business processes for internal customers within any firm.

Six Sigma foundations

Six Sigma was initiated by Bill Smith (1929–93) at Motorola Corporation. The problem Smith addressed stemmed from quality-related returns of products that were significantly more complex than those previously manufactured. Although the Motorola production processes had each been acceptable, the new quality challenges stemmed from the increased number of OFD in newer product offerings. Each OFD represents a potential cause of ultimate product failure. When a product becomes more complex, the number of OFDs increases. To maintain final product quality with many more OFDs, production processes needed to improve by increasing the proportion of output that met performance specifications.

Prior to Six Sigma, a common quality standard was called 3-Sigma quality, which generated 3 defects per 1,000 opportunities. This standard can result in unacceptable final product quality when many hundreds or thousands of OFDs are included in a single product. Smith recognized that a more stringent quality standard was necessary. It was Motorola's responsibility to provide support for these improvements. Six Sigma originated as a set of statistical techniques to reduce manufacturing variations. The number 6 refers to the desire to have specifications that spanned 6-Sigma units on both sides of a target specification (6-Sigma quality corresponds to a defect rate of 3.4 per million OFD).

Six Sigma has evolved to include a project management framework and structured training. Although Six Sigma originated in manufacturing settings, it is routinely applied to services. Its structural elements include a set of techniques, a QI framework, and a structured training regimen. The tools of Six Sigma that apply to services have already been detailed in this book. They are applied within a structured framework called DMAIC, with participants trained to play roles as QI project managers or participants.

The DMAIC structure refers to five stages: define, measure, analyze, improve, and control, which has its origins in Shewhart's PDSA cycle. Although DMAIC is a more contemporary approach, research has shown that any similar approach that is applied consistently will produce effective results. DMAIC is considered by many practitioners to be the reason for Six Sigma's success. It enforces a high degree of discipline and commonality in project organization, problem solving tools, software, and terminology.

Six Sigma implementation would begin with executive education followed by training throughout the organization. Formal training levels would be established with project and mentoring roles often defined by a belt level (e.g., master black belt, black belt, green belt, etc.). The tools of Six Sigma include well-known problem-solving techniques and popular statistical approaches; in addition, a common software platform would usually be integrated to achieve a consistent means of internal communication. Six Sigma black belt certification is becoming a standard by which many quality practitioners are judged.

Lean foundations

Lean seeks to eliminate waste during the production of goods and delivery of services. It is based on the system developed at Toyota Motors in Japan (in fact, Lean is also referred to as the TPS). Its founders are generally accepted to be Toyota manager Taiichi Ohno (1912–90) and engineer Shigeo Shingo (1909–90). Deming, who gave a series of management seminars in Japan in the 1950s, also played a role in the TPS development. Lean has its origins in manufacturing but many of its elements apply to services.

Lean seeks to identify activities that do not add value for customers, which are referred to as non-value-added or wasteful (they were discussed in an earlier chapter). A Lean practitioner understands that the removal of these wasteful activities never ends. Lean needs to be supported by a culture that highlights problems instead of hiding them, such as when a pharmacy prescription is incomplete and needs to be recreated. All employees should be on the lookout for wasteful activities.

Lean Thinking (Womack and Jones, 2003) introduced many practitioners to Lean, and included a five-step application guide: (1) specify value from the customer's perspective; (2) identify the stream of processes used to provide value; (3) remove non-value-added activities from the value stream; (4) create pull by having all work initiated by customer demand; and (5) strive for perfection. These steps would typically be applied during a one- to five-day activity called kaizen, where a project team would be devoted full time to a process improvement project.

Lean will succeed only if the organization's infrastructure reflects a common focus, which can be difficult to achieve in a large bureaucracy. All departments and functions need to be aligned because often wasteful practices result from attempts to optimize "parts" of a system. Many Lean firms use profit sharing as the main financial incentive so that a common metric motivates everyone to focus on system-wide performance. Lean cannot achieve sustained success unless executives, as well as middle managers and their staff, are active participants.

Despite their disparate roots, Six Sigma and Lean encompass common features, such as an emphasis on customers, a culture of process improvement, the search for root causes, and comprehensive employee training and involvement. High degrees of training and education take place, from upper management to all service providers. As such, LSS is now considered management system rather than a collection of techniques.

Quality improvement program development

QI programs have succeeded in some organizations but failed in others. Many similar characteristics have been identified across organizations whose QI programs have been effective. The following success factors that are applicable to all types of organizations were present in organizations that have successfully applied process improvement (Maleyeff, 2007):

1 They have supportive leadership that is sustained over time.
2 They remove organizational barriers that hinder effective implementation.
3 They maintain a consistent conceptual framework and set of tools.
4 They guarantee that no layoffs will occur as the result of an improvement project.
5 They communicate information about the program to stakeholders.
6 They allow the program to grow as the organizational support improves.

A QI program will not be effective without considerable employee involvement, from top leadership to front-line employees. Everyone in the organization (executives, middle managers, front-line employees, etc.) needs to be convinced that they will personally benefit from the program's success. A personal benefit can occur, for example, when a process's effectiveness makes it less likely that an internal function will be outsourced. In a U.S. city that practiced Lean, legislators attempting to cut costs discovered that external private firms were not more efficient than the city's public works department thereby eliminating unionized workers' job security concerns.

Barriers to employee participation take many forms. A middle manager may be reluctant to modify a process if a KPI will suffer, which can happen when attempts are made to improve a service process that spans multiple departments. As such, performance incentives need to be modified in preparation for a QI program implementation. Perhaps the most common fear concerns job security. QI will not be effective if used as a mechanism for cutting payroll costs through layoffs. In these cases, employees are likely to avoid participation, and may even discourage or sabotage efforts of others within the organization.

Project initiation

The planning stage of a QI project is important because it ensures that an impactful problem is addressed, the organization supports the effort, and the most effective project team is built. Typical causes of ineffectiveness include not informing a key stakeholder about the project, not addressing political sensitivities, not employing a skilled facilitator, not considering the needs of key customers, and not ensuring that the problem warrants commitment of the organization's resources. An organization will maximize the chance of success by implementing a structured mechanism for project selection and by carefully populating the project team.

QI project motivation

There are many reasons to initiate a QI project. Projects may be initiated when a process becomes unstable, a stable process is no longer acceptable, or an extraordinary event affects the process or its management. For example, a department may routinely initiate a project when a retirement or transfer from a department occurs. In these cases, the goal may be to determine if the process can be operated effectively by the remaining employees. More intangible motivations exist, such as giving newly trained employees practice working on a QI project or performing a project whose intent is to improve employees' work environment. A project may routinely be created for each QI training course so that trainees can apply what they learn in a just-in-time manner.

An organization may initiate a project when poor performance is noticed in a visible way, including extreme cases such as newspaper or television investigative studies. For example, a transportation firm initiated a process improvement project after a fatal automobile accident that resulted in a United States Department of Labor Occupational Safety and Health Administration (OSHA) inspection and subsequent citation for noncompliance of safety requirements. In this case, it was discovered that no standards existed for pretrip vehicle inspection, which in turn became the focus of the improvement effort. These types of projects benefit by having a project team that possesses a clear and common motivation.

Project justification

Devoting resources to a QI project requires confirmation that the effort will be consistent with the organization's strategic plan and that the anticipated benefits will outweigh the associated costs. Although choosing a project from a group of candidate projects is based on their net benefit to the firm, often the benefits are difficult to quantify in purely financial terms. Therefore, criteria for project selection should be robust; it is ultimately a leadership decision. An effective approach to documenting impacts would include three categories of benefits:

1   Financially quantifiable benefits can be stated in monetary terms. Cost reductions such as labor, equipment, and material would typically be included as well as revenue increases such as sales, interest, and fees.
2   Non-financially-quantifiable benefits cannot be stated monetarily but can be quantified in other ways. The category would include the projected number of customers affected if the process was improved. Quantifying these impacts provides decision makers with a scope of potential impacts.
3   Intangible benefits cannot be quantified precisely either financially or otherwise. They include accreditation impacts, higher employee satisfaction, better chance of customer retention, or more participation from employees in future projects. They should be stated as specifically as possible to be trusted by a decision maker.

The careful delineation of project benefits brings credibility to the project initiator and creates a sense of trust. When uncertainties exist, conservative assumptions regarding projected benefits should be made. In this way, a decision maker will appreciate that the project will be beneficial even under the most conservative assumptions. Intangible impacts alone are insufficient to justify a project because they are somewhat vague and can appear clichéd or exaggerated. They should be consistent with, and supported by, the quantifications included in the other two categories. They should complete the robust list of benefits (so-called icing on the cake).

To illustrate the project justification procedure, consider a firm's EH&S department that is responsible for tabulating and communicating OSHA-recordable accidents and injuries. This department also provides expertise to facilitate safety projects within the firm. The reporting process is likely to include time wasted tracking down late or inaccurate data, dealing with a disorganized IT system, or creating ad hoc reports for specific administrators. If this activity were improved, the benefits would include more time available for the department's engineers to solve important problems within the facility. The benefits might also include OSHA fine reductions and decreased use of outside consultants (both quantifiable as dollars), more technical staff time devoted to safety improvement (quantifiable as time), and greater job satisfaction of technical staff (because their work will be more interesting, create value for the firm, and enhance their career aspirations).

Example 1

The emergency department (ED) of a 200-bed independent community hospital serves about 33,000 patients annually. The average revenue per ED patient is $1,450. Over the past three months, control charts have shown that the patients leaving before treatment completed (LBTC) metric increased beyond limits of expected random variation, which initiated an RCA. An analyst for the hospital's risk management and QA department noticed that waiting times have been increasing during the same period. Data on patient demand was stable, no changes to work schedules had been implemented, and no planned or unplanned disruptions had been reported.

After consultation with the ED's head nurse and the hospital's director of quality, it was agreed that the root cause was likely systemic. Several articles have been appearing in the healthcare literature detailing the effects of more complex treatments, including longer ED stays. What puzzled the group was why a gradual complexity increase would cause waiting times to increase dramatically in recent months. A consultant who worked with the hospital was contacted for an informal consultation.

The consultant who recognized the situation at the ED was typical of queuing systems that operate in the presence of arrival and service time variations. In these systems, changes that cause resources (i.e., doctors, nurses, beds, technology), to increase their utilizations will increase waiting time linearly until a certain threshold utilization is reached. At that point, customer queue lengths and waiting times will increase more profoundly, usually when the utilization of a key resource exceeds about 85%.

The consultant developed a simulation of current ED data, which was calibrated based on the current patient demand, treatment time data, and patient waiting times. The simulation showed that beds had the highest resource utilization and that a 15-minute reduction in treatment times could reduce waiting times by two hours. A scatterplot showed an anticipated decrease in proportion of patients leaving the ED from 4% to 2.5%. The head nurse recognized that the time spent in beds included significant wasted time (e.g., waiting for blood and imaging tests, or waiting for patient discharges to be acted upon). Along with the director of quality, the head nurse decided to ask that a project be initiated to find ways to remove 15 minutes from service times.

For financial benefits, if the current revenue lost annually due to patients leaving the ED is reduced by 1.5% (from 4% to 2.5%), then the annual benefit of the project will be $717,750 (the product of 33,000 patients, 0.015, and $1450 per patient). For other quantifiable benefits, about 495 patients who would have left the ED last year will be treated this year (the product of 33,000 patients and 1.5%). Intangible benefits include improved accreditation status (because accreditation agencies expect each client to show that data were used to make improvements), improved reputation in the community, less frustration among workers who will respond to fewer patient complaints, and some treatments will be more effective because patient needs are addressed sooner.

Example 2

Bill payments at an insurance company are made either online or by check by 155,000 auto insurance customers that pay an average of $1,570 per year, billed semiannually. Payment processing activities cross many departments. The lead time metric (from notice of bill payment to deposit of funds) is stable with an average of 6.0 days. This lead time is known to be dominated by delays and other wasteful activities. In fact, the value-added elements of the processing system consume only about 18 minutes per payment. Two impacts have been noticed because of the excessive lead time: (1) unnecessary calls to the call center; and (2) earned interest decreases while payments remain in progress.

The call enter is affected because a late notice is sent to the customer if the bill is not processed within three days of the due date. With the average six-day lead time, many customers receive the late notice even though their bill was paid, and many of these customers contact the call center for verification. At the call center, 9 employees answer 95,000 calls annually from auto insurance customers, with an average duration of 8.1 minutes. Twelve percent of callers ask questions related to their late bill notice, but almost all of them have paid their bill.

Interest earned decreases because of the missed opportunity to deposit the payments sooner. Funding of the firm's business operations can also be affected by the lack of available moneys. An improvement project needs to be justified that would reduce the average bill processing time from 6.0 to 2.0 days. This change is estimated to reduce the last notice calls arriving at the call center to 3% from the current 12%. The firm makes 5% on money invested in its operations and that "fully loaded" (i.e., with benefits and overhead) call center labor cost is $40 per hour.

The first financial benefit concerns cost savings at the call center. With 95,000 annual calls and a 9% reduction in unnecessary calls due to late notices (to 3% from 12%), the number of employees can be reduced by 0.8 (from 9 to 8.2), which translates to a labor cost savings of $64,800 (the product of 0.09, 9 workers, $40 per hour, and 2,000 hours per year). Although it is not possible to reduce labor costs on a continuous scale, this calculation is appropriate because other changes occur at the same time also affecting labor.

The second financial benefit concerns increased revenue. With a 4.0 day improvement in processing a payment (to 2.0 days from 6.0 days) and a daily 0.0137% rate of return (0.05 divided by 365 days), we can estimate the benefit to be $133,356 annually (the product of 155,000 customers, $1,570 revenue per customer, 4 days, and 0.000137). A nonfinancial quantifiable benefit is that 8,550 fewer unnecessary calls per year will arrive at the call center (the product of 95,000 calls and 0.09).

Intangible benefits include less frustration among call center workers (who will no longer answer the same question repeatedly), better job satisfaction (which is known to correlate with retention which lowers hiring costs), and less frustrated customers (who will no longer be annoyed that the bill was paid although they received a late notice). As a final note, assuming that the company has a no layoff pledge due to an improvement process, the labor savings in the call center would be achieved through natural attrition or transferring an employee to another department.

Example 3

A new general manager at a manufacturing facility with 125 employees wants to get employees involved in QI activities. A supervisor notes that machine operators and other workers have been complaining about the waiting line in the building's cafeteria. An informal week-long data collection effort by the supervisor showed that about 70% of employees eat in the cafeteria and indeed the lines were long. The supervisor suggests that the general manager show their commitment to employee well-being by approving a project to reduce the cafeteria lines. The target reduction in average waiting time would be 6.0 minutes. The general manager likes the idea because it also provides a low-risk opportunity for workers to practice applying QI methods they learned during their green belt training programs that started the previous month.

There is no easily calculated financial justification for this project. If the project is successful, workers' time spent operating machines will be unchanged. A nonfinancial quantifiable benefit is the cafeteria waiting time reduction of 8.75 hours per workday (the product of 125 employees, 0.7, and 0.1 hours). Workers will be able to spend this time chatting with co-workers, relaxing, or exercising. The project has several intangible benefits. They include practice in QI methodologies and showing the management team's commitment to employees' well-being. In addition, a prominently displayed poster of the project results can motivate others to get involved and illustrate how QI projects are performed.

Team selection

The project team should be large enough to encompass key process stakeholders but not too large, which can hamper its effectiveness. The team would typically include front-line service providers, supporting personnel (technology, data, or information providers), and customers if they are internal. Among the group of about 6–10 members, the project team should include the following categories (some team members will belong to more than one category):

1   An experienced facilitator.
2   At least one representative from each department through which the process flows (if practical).
3   Front-line service providers who understand how the process currently operates.
4   An administrator who understands the context within which the process operates but not a supervisor of other team members.
5   Someone from outside the area of focus (to provide perspective and fresh ideas).
6   Someone new to QI (to give practice and help sustain the QI program).
7   A customer if customers are internal.

The project facilitator plays a very important role. Their responsibilities encompass project management tasks, such as keeping the project on schedule (and budget if one exists) and ensuring that documentation is thorough and clear. As such, they are the conduit between the firm's leadership and the project team. Their most important role concerns moderating project team activities. They need to be assertive and impartial, while encouraging participation. Their assertiveness is important for limiting the disruptive impact of strong personalities, including team members who overtly sell their ideas, ignoring those suggested by others. They should mobilize the team to find practical solutions rather than solutions that will not likely be implemented. The importance of the facilitator cannot be overstated.

External customers usually cannot participate in QI project team activities because of the proprietary nature of the discussions. They can, however, be asked to provide input early in the project to ensure that the project team thoroughly understands customer needs. Customers will generally be thankful for the opportunity to participate, which can create enhanced loyalty. It is imperative that participating customers be informed of the project's outcome after the project is completed.

A positive attitude across the entire project team is also critical for success. Even the best facilitator will have difficulty mobilizing a dysfunctional team. Dysfunction can be minimized while forming the project team. Knowledge of incentives that apply to each potential team member should be evaluated to confirm that the goal of the project does not conflict with these incentives. The project originator should ensure the cooperation of any support function, such as IT or human resource management. The following rules constitute intangible characteristics of potential project team members:

1   Never assign blame.
2   Eliminate pressure to agree.
3   Be willing to change.
4   Respect one another.
5   Maintain positive attitude.
6   Seek equality across the team.
7   Generate practical ideas.
8   Consider sustainable solutions.

The facilitator should be aware that many project team members will begin the project with an awareness of the problem. They will likely have considered some potential solutions beforehand. The facilitator needs to avoid the presentation or discussion of these ideas until called for in the project's scheme. This tendency can be especially evident when technology-savvy team members quickly propose IT-based solutions. Ideas should be formed directly in response to the analysis. For example, automating a customer product price quoting process will be ineffective if the main problem is that customers do not understand the definition of inputs that are required to initiate the process (this tendency is referred to as the automation of waste).

Performance targets

Project initiation should include projected impacts on all relevant performance metrics. The project should not be focused on improving one category of performance to the detriment of another category. A project undertaken in response to mistakes should not, for example, add an inspection to the business process. This intervention may improve quality (improve the better goal), but it will increase lead time (i.e., degrade the faster goal) and raise costs (i.e., degrade the cheaper goal).

Some organizations tabulate mistakes, errors, and other quality-related impacts into two categories: (1) turnbacks, defined as a mistake detected internally and addressed prior to customer delivery; and (2) escapes, defined as mistakes identified by a customer. Progressive firms also tabulate near misses (also referred to as close calls). These events occur when a mistake is almost made – they should be of concern because they are an early warning of bigger problems to come. For example, a casual conversation with a colleague that reveals a mistake made by a younger associate should be reported.

The establishment of performance targets is useful to the project team. These targets create a focus on either incremental or substantial performance improvements. But many projects should be considered successful even if the target improvement is not achieved. Therefore, care must be taken to eliminate any sense of punishment or disappointment if targets are not met. Otherwise, to avoid failure, the team may resort to artificial manipulations. In fact, administrators should be careful not to classify any project as a failure as long as the project team worked diligently on the improvement effort.

Project authorization

Every approved QI project should be accompanied by a documented project authorization. These documents ensure that projects are defined and focus on areas that deserve attention. They also assist in maintaining a database of past projects. Although they contain similar elements, each project authorization form should be customized at the firm level. The example in Figure 12.1 would correspond to the billing lead time reduction project discussed earlier in this chapter as Example 2.

Project communication

Information about the firm's QI program should be communicated to stakeholders who need to support the effort, including investors, executives, regulators, customers, and employees. The information disseminated by the firm should be factual, without exaggeration. Each project should include an informal communications plan. The project team needs to play an important role by answering questions about the project to whoever expresses interest. At a minimum, these communications should be targeted at administrators responsible for the service process, to employees affected by the project, and to other administrators indirectly affected by the project. Project results should be communicated in written or video form to make them widely available.

Early in the project, the creation of an elevator speech (of about 30–40 seconds in length) is recommended so that the project team communicates a common message to co-workers and others. It would be a less formalized version of the problem statement, but brief and stated in conversational form. The elevator speech can help serve an internal public relations purpose by exposing other employees to ongoing projects and reinforcing the QI program's usefulness and transparency.

For longer duration projects, occasional briefings are recommended with those affected by the project. These presentations should be targeted at key administrators who are not members of the project team. Keeping all decision makers informed is critical. For example, it eliminates unfortunate

Quality Improvement Project Authorization

Division	Auto Insurance	Contact	Lynn Browning	
Department	Accounts Payable	E-Mail	xxxxxxxxxx@mycompany.com	
Start Date	April 10, XXXX	Duration	30 Days	

Project Title	Payment process lead time reduction
Problem Statement	The current lead time to process an automobile insurance customer's payment averages 6 days and the process has been stable over the past 2 years. Late notices are often received by customers who have already paid their bill, causing customer frustration and unnecessary calls to the call center.
Project Objective(s)	The objective of the project is to reduce delays in payment processing so that the lead time from payment initiation by the customer to deposit of funds is reduced to 2 days from the current 6 days.
Scope (SIPOC)	Supplier: Billing department (bill created); Inputs: Information on bill (sent 21 days before due date), bill payment Process: Bill created, Mailing (bill); Payment (customer); Mailing (if check), Agent (if mistake); Lockbox service, Logging; Contact customer (if mistake), Reminder notice sent. Outputs: Verified payment deposit; Customer: The firm (revenue deposited)
Justification	Financial: $64,800 annuals labor cost savings at the call center & $133,356 annual revenue additions Other quantifiable: 8,550 fewer unnecessary calls to call center annually Intangible: Reduced call center agent frustration, reduced customer frustration (correlated with retention)
Stakeholders	IT department, policy holder, postal service, agents, lockbox, bank, payment processing worker, call center.
Budget	None
KPI's w/Goal	Bill processing lead time: Reduce to 2 day (average) from 6 day (average) Call center call volume: Reduce unnecessary calls to 3% of calls from 12% of calls Turnbacks: Rate improved or kept constant Bill processing worker utilization: Reduced or kept constant

Member 1	Lynn Browning (accounts payable)	Member 5	Aurora Marrero (external manager)
Member 2	Jacob Fister (QA, facilitator)	Member 6	Pat Gillian (bill payment processor)
Member 3	Nate Settle (call center supervisor)	Member 7	Richard Williams (IT)
Member 4	Esther Negron (independent agent)	Member 8	

Approval by	Nicki Harrison	Date	10 March XXXX

Figure 12.1 QI project authorization.

surprises by identifying challenges that the project team has not anticipated. The briefings also help support cultural change within the organization.

Final project results should be delivered to key leaders and affected administrators. It is also helpful to expose each project to a broad set of employees. Communication with external stakeholders may be considered to promote a sense of progressiveness and competency. For example, the Fort Wayne (Indiana, United States) organizes a forum held in the city's conference center for the presentation of improvement projects. Other firms hang posters in their lobby, cafeteria, hallways showcasing their QI efforts.

References

Deming, W.E. (1986). *Out of the Crisis*. Cambridge, MA: MIT Center for Advanced Engineering Study.

Maleyeff, J. (2007). *Improving Service Delivery in Government with Lean Six Sigma*. Washington, DC: IBM Center for The Business of Government.

Womack, J.P. and Jones, D.T. (2003). *Lean Thinking 2/e*. New York: Free Press.

13 Quality improvement project management

Introduction

Project management frameworks for QI can vary from organization to organization, although they have common features. They each employ a well-defined sequence of stages to enforce a discipline that assures comprehensiveness and objectivity. Their training programs introduce workers to the framework when teaching problem solving methodologies. This consistency in approach enhances communication within the team, and between the team and other stakeholders. Perhaps most importantly, an effective QI framework motivates and expects employees to play a role in identifying problems and finding solutions, because without enthusiastic cooperation of all workers (from leadership to service providers), the QI system is doomed to failure.

This chapter begins with a historical perspective that describes an evolution that started with Shewhart's PDCA approach. It then details a popular project management framework known as DMAIC. Each stage of DMAIC is described in detail, and a comprehensive case study is provided to illustrate how each stage is accomplished. Implementation of this chapter's methodologies will be effective only when the organization has a supportive infrastructure and workers are trained effectively.

DMAIC

The first QI project management methodology was plan–do–check act (PDCA), created by Walter Shewhart. Deming was a major proponent of Shewhart's PDCA system but preferred to use study rather than check as the third stage (PDSA). Although PDSA is usually referred to as the Deming cycle, Deming gives credit to Shewhart for its development (Deming, 1986, p. 88). As the name implies, PDSA consists of four discrete stages that are completed as an ongoing cycle. In brief, the four stages of the PDSA Cycle are as follows: plan (define problem, identify objectives and approach, specify data collection requirements), do (carry out the plan), study (analyze data to determine if objective are met), and act (adjust based on analysis of results).

DOI: 10.4324/9781003199014-13

PDSA can apply to QI projects associated with either production or service processes.

DMAIC is an updated version of PDSA. It seeks to create a more intuitive and easier-to-follow set of stages that helps project team apply similar tools in similar ways. It seeks to enhance training, often by utilizing a set of martial-arts-inspired "belts" that signify competency level. And it seeks to make communication of QI efforts transparent across the organization. The DMAIC approach detailed here is meant to be flexible; its steps should be customized to fit the needs of organizations. These differences are often associated with the application of more quantitative versus more qualitative analysis tools.

Project timeline

The planned timeline for completing a QI project would depend on the problem's scope and the project team's availability. The project may follow a Lean kaizen format whereby it is completed in one to several days, with the team devoted full-time to the effort. Or the project may be executed over weeks or months with the team devoted part time to the project. A third alternative, which combines the first two options, would consist of a several hours to one day sessions that are each devoted to one of the five DMAIC stages. This approach allows for the gathering of information between sessions and can maximize the effectiveness of each project stage.

Because employees who produce products and deliver services are closest to the process's customers, they are uniquely positioned to be agents of improvement. The firm's leadership needs to ensure that financial and metrics-driven incentives do not conflict with worker motivation to actively participate. The organization should also be opened to utilizing improvement events to improve work environments.

Comprehensive case study

The following scenario is referred to throughout this chapter. It concerns an existing business process with fictional names to protect privacy of the company and individuals. A division of a large manufacturing conglomerate, called Haibao Engineering (HE), builds products for residential and commercial use. The division outsources their IT needs to another company, called Technology Operational Excellence (TOE). One of the services provided by TOE is called the annual personal computer (PC) refresh.

The PC refresh service is used to keep the electronic computing devices used by each HE engineer, technician, and analyst (about 150 HE devices in total) up to date. These customers (called clients by TOE) work in one of the five core engineering departments within the firm – design, process engineering, manufacturing, support, and administration. The PC refresh service ensures that clients' computing devices all use the same operating systems and applications software. It commences every September and it is usually completed by the end of November.

The PC refresh service was created about 10 years ago because important work was delayed due to poor electronic communications within and across the five departments. The root cause of the delays was found to be incompatible systems that caused confusion and data integration workarounds. By ensuring that all HE clients used the same hardware and software systems, these delays were reduced substantially. It was common knowledge, however, that some individuals were not allowed to use applications that they preferred in favor of standardized applications. HE managers believed that these sacrifices were outweighed by better alignment with business objectives and improved productivity.

Some skeptical or stubborn clients refuse to participate and others take a passive-aggressive attitude during service delivery. These problems are noticeable during the PC refresh appointment scheduling activities. Some clients do not respond to repeated appointment scheduling and repeated requests (TOE stops trying after three attempts, which is referred to as the three strikes rule). Other clients find convenient reasons to miss scheduled refresh appointments when the technicians arrive to perform the system upgraded. These problems are exacerbated because of the general inefficiencies associated with the current appointment scheduling activities.

TOE project managers decide to seek approval for a project to improve the appointment scheduling process. Improvement projects at HE will not proceed until a project authorization is approved, which includes a problem statement, quantification of problem impacts, list of objectives and restrictions, and a timeline. Some of this information will be revised by the project team as they take more of a detailed look at the problem and its impacts.

The approved project authorization form for improvement of the PC refresh appointment scheduling process is shown in Figure 13.1. The DMAIC project framework can now begin with the define (D) stage.

D: Define

The define stage of DMAIC starts by creating a project charter. This document includes verification of the information included in the project authorization, with revisions based on the initial work of the project team. The process activities that are relevant to the project are precisely delineated at this time. The updated problem statement and project objective includes major constraints, key metrics, and improvement targets. The list of stakeholders is updated and, if necessary, the team's composition is modified.

The PC refresh project team looked closely at the data for no shows, appointment reschedules, and three strikes instances to estimate the reliability of the appointment process (defined as the probability that an appointment will be scheduled and that the refresh will be accomplished without changes or other disruptions). The 11% no show rate, 17% three strikes rate, and the 62% reschedule percentage were each translated to reliabilities of 0.89, 0.83,

Quality Improvement Project Authorization

Division	Haibao Engineering	*Contact*	Hanting Lu
Department	Technology Services	*E-Mail*	hlu@haibaoengineering.com
Start Date	June 10, XXXX	*Duration*	45 Days

Project Title: PC Refresh Scheduling Improvement

Problem Statement: The annual PC refresh system, a service provided by TOE, suffers from delays and inefficiencies that are traced to appointment scheduling. The process requires each internal customer (Haibao engineers, technicians, analysts, etc.) to make an appointment months in advance of the refresh visit. Sixty-two percent of appointments are rescheduled (including 11% no shows), and the "three strikes" rule occurs 17% of the time.

Project Objective(s): The objective of the project is to improve the appointment scheduling process within the PC refresh system. Our goal is to reduce appointment changes by 50%, and reduce the no show and three strikes occurrence rate to 5% each from current levels.

Scope (SIPOC):
Supplier: TOE
Inputs: Refresh time requirements, technician's work schedule
Process: Start by contacting client, end at refreshing commencing
Outputs: Instructions to client
Customer: Client at HE

Justification:
Financial: $8,928 per year savings due to more efficient scheduling
$8,640 per year savings due to reduced no shows
Other quantifiable: 970 HE project team members will not include an engineer with outdated software
Intangible: Better reputation of TOE within HE
More secure data
More efficient projects at HE

Stakeholders: Haibao management, internal customers, TOE.

Budget: None

KPI's w/Goal:
Appointment reschedules: Reduce to 31% from 62%
No Show Percentage: Reduce to 5% from 11%
Three strikes percentage: Reduce to 5% from 17%

Member 1	Hanting Lu (Haibao supervising engineer)	*Member 5*	George Terry (HOE hardware technician)
Member 2	Anil Gupta (Haibao engineer)	*Member 6*	Siavash Razavi (HOE software technician)
Member 3	Stanley Boose (Haibao business analyst)	*Member 7*	
Member 4	Daisy Rosa (HOE senior manager)	*Member 8*	

Approval by Gretchen Braun   *Date* 10 May XXXX

Figure 13.1 PC refresh improvement project authorization.

and 0.38. The product of these subsystem reliabilities is 0.281, and therefore the reliability of the appointment scheduling process is 28.1%.

The project charter for addressing appointment scheduling during the PC refresh service is shown in Figure 13.2. If the improvement goals are met, the no show rate will be reduced to 5%, the three strikes rate will be reduced to 5%, and the reschedule percentage will be reduced to 31%. By translating each of these failure modes to a reliability, the reliability of the system should improve to 62.3% (the product of 0.95, 0.95, and 0.69).

Quality Improvement Project Charter	
Project Title	**Project Sponsor (Department)**
PC Refresh Scheduling Improvement	TOE
Problem Statement	**Business Impact (Summary)**
The PC refresh system suffers from delays that are traced to appointment scheduling. Sixty-two percent of appointments are rescheduled (including 11% no shows), and the "three strikes" rule occurs 17% of the time. The reliability of process is 28%.	About $12,500 per year is wasted in labor hours due to reschedules and no shows. The effectiveness of communication within HE project teams is compromised due to three strikes effects.
Project Objectives	**Projected Benefits (Summary)**
Improve the PC refresh appointment scheduling process. Our goal is to reduce appointment changes by 50%, and reduce the no show and 3 strikes occurrence rate to 5% each from each of the current levels.	Reduce appointment reschedules to 31% (from 62%), no shows to 5% (from 11%), and three strikes occurrences to 5% (from 17%). Improve appointment process reliability from 28% to 62%.
Solution Restrictions/Constraints	**Dependencies/Risks**
No new scheduling system software.	Requires cooperation from several HE departments.
Suppliers/Inputs	
Software/hardware refresh technical requirements (man hours required), an assigned technician, and availability of the assigned technician during the refresh time period.	
Process (Activity List)	
E-mail sent to client from TOE requesting appointment with suggested time slots, reminder emails if no response, changes to schedule initiated by either client or technician, TOE travel to client location, start of refresh in client's office or other arranged location.	
Outputs/Customers	
A refreshed PC (ideally), a three strikes event (no refresh), or a no show (may require repeating the appointment process later).	
Team Members/Role (include Supporting Members)	
1 [Project Leader] Hanting Lu	6 Siavash Razavi
2 Anil Gupta	7
3 Fred McNally (replacing Stan Boose)	8
4 Daisy Rosa	9
5 George Terry	10
Timeline: Phase (Add Notes if Needed)	**Target End Date**
Define	June 17
Measure	July 1
Analyze	July 15
Improve	July 22
Control	August 5

Figure 13.2 PC refresh appointment scheduling improvement project charter.

The main customers of the PC refresh appointment scheduling process are the HE clients who should have their devices updated. A list of their performance dimensions was determined earlier in the book. They are listed as follows: (1) clarity; (2) accuracy; (3) usefulness; (4) timeliness; (5) knowledge; and (6) responsiveness. Although not all these dimensions apply directly to appointment scheduling activities, they create a common awareness of clients' expectations as the project commences.

Although not essential, the creation of an elevator speech early in the project should be considered. The elevator speech is communicated to stakeholders verbally in about 45 seconds (approximately 100 words); it need not be spoken verbatim. Among its benefits include getting the team members (especially new ones) excited about the upcoming project. For the PC refresh appointment scheduling improvement project, the following would serve as a useful elevator speech.

> I am working on a project to improve appointment scheduling for the annual PC refresh process. This process is important for HE because using common software versions eliminates miscommunications during collaborative projects, and our professional staff deserve the most up-to-date hardware. Right now, over half of refresh appointments made by HE staff to TOE (our IT vendor) require rescheduling and many no shows occur when TOE technicians go to HE offices to perform the refresh. Also, a good number of HE staff do not participate, which causes miscommunication problems that the refresh process is designed to eliminate.

M: Measure

The measure stage of DMAIC creates a common, detailed understanding of the process under study. It focuses on the process activities located where the problem is evidenced, while maintaining an understanding of where the root cause of those problems may originate. For example, if the problem is known to be affected by late or incorrect information from another department, that department's activities during service delivery should be studied. The measure stage should almost always begin with the creation of one or more displays that depict the process as it currently operates.

The most useful service process map is usually a flowchart. It is imperative that the process map displays how the process actually operates, rather than how it is supposed to operate. It should include activities that are undesirable, such as inefficiencies, mistakes, and delays. The process map needs to be created using a collaborative team effort with all project team perspectives. The inclusion of activities that rarely occur should be avoided so as not to create an overly complex display. The process flowchart for the appointment scheduling activities of the PC refresh process is shown in Figure 13.3.

The creation of a process flowchart will change the focus of a project team from finger-pointing at one another (to assign blame) to finger-pointing at the display (to understand the process). A process flowchart also highlights the interaction among stakeholders during service delivery, which is not always obvious to a worker focused on performing a specific task. The project team will begin to appreciate that they indeed work together and that the service will be enhanced if they work together more effectively.

Multiple maps of the process are often helpful to support the analysis. Typical options for process maps that can supplement a flowchart include: (1) a time value chart that highlights the process lead time and its value-added portion; (2) a spaghetti chart that shows how people or documents move

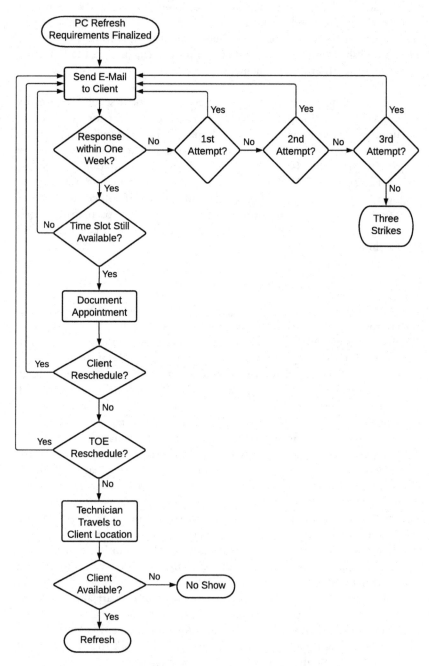

Figure 13.3 Process flowchart of PC refresh appointment scheduling.

through a facility or from location to location; or (3) a fishbone diagram that lists potential root causes of a problem using a hierarchical structure. For the example project, a fishbone diagram (Figure 13.4) can help the team set up a data collection plan for identifying how often various causes negatively impact the appointment making process. It shows 26 potential reasons for a disruption in the appointment scheduling process, including rescheduling events, appointment of no shows, and three strikes occurrences.

Data should be collected to complement the visualization of activities shown in the process maps. Useful data usually includes processing times (average and variation, if available), waiting times at various process steps, and the location and frequency of mistakes. In addition, new data may be collected using quantitative surveys or open-ended interviews with various stakeholders, especially customers. The time required to accumulate useful data sets needs to be managed so that the QI project will maintain its project schedule.

The project team requested data on the frequency of each reason for appointment disruptions. These reasons would encompass the 26 reasons shown in Figure 13.4 and some reasons with which the project team was unaware. To initiate data collection, an email was sent to 147 HE clients asking each client to list reasons that affected them. A list of those reasons documented on the fishbone was included along with a category labelled "other." Hence, the fishbone diagram acted as a check sheet data collection form, along with a convenient visual tool. The clients were asked to respond within one week; a reminder was sent after five days.

The project team also requested that TOE provide data showing the date of the initial appointment email sent to each client as well as the date that the successful refresh process was completed (or when the appointment process was terminated due to a no show or three strikes violation). They also requested information about each client, such as their name, department, years of service, and job title.

A: Analyze

In the analysis stage lies the core of DMAIC because it seeks to ensure that recommended improvements have the greatest impact on the problem being addressed. It also ensures that subjectivity (i.e., opinion) does not determine recommended action plans. The integration of the various DMAIC stages is evident because this stage will not be effective unless useful and comprehensive data collection is initiated during the measure stage.

The analysis tools typically employed dosing the analysis stage are drawn from the entirety of qualitative and quantitative tools described earlier. Because the PC refresh services takes place once per year, control charts will likely not play a role in this project. Control charts are effective when a process operates continuously, so that the requisite number of outcome subgroups can be collected. But other analysis tools can be very useful.

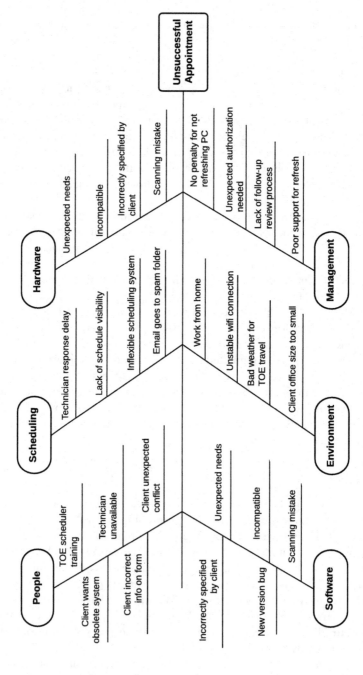

Figure 13.4 Fishbone diagram for PC refresh appointment scheduling.

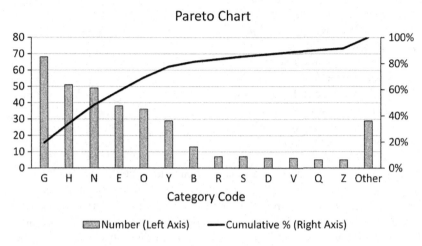

Figure 13.5 Pareto chart for unsuccessful appointments.

The process flowchart, other process maps, and associated data will often highlight areas of concern without excessive analysis. To evaluate the process flowchart (Figure 13.3), it helps to consider how the process would operate under perfect conditions – the initial email is sent, responded to immediately, the time slot does not need to be adjusted by either the client or TOE, the travel time is very short, and the refresh proceeds as planned. All other time spent during the current process would be classified as wasted.

The wasteful activities that currently exist in the appointment scheduling process include the following: (1) waiting for responses from clients because they increase the chance that a currently available time slot will be unavailable; (2) rescheduling initiated by the client; (3) rescheduling initiated by TOE; (4) a three strikes event which causes problems at HE during projects and may require later emergency intervention by TOE; (5) technician travel time from TOE to the client's location; and (6) a client no show that necessitates the need to reschedule and wastes the technician's time.

The Pareto chart in Figure 13.5 shows the analysis of the measure stage data collection concerning reasons for unsuccessful appointments. It shows that 6 of the 26 reasons (23% of the 26 total reasons listed on the fishbone diagram) were the cause of the 78% of the total reasons indicated by clients. Reducing the likelihood of occurrence for any of these six reasons will have a disproportionately positive impact on overall process performance. The Pareto chart uses the following codes (all other reasons fall into the Pareto chart's "other" category):

G: Lack of schedule visibility
H: Inflexible scheduling system
N: Incorrectly specified by client: hardware

E: Client unexpected conflict
O: Incorrectly specified by client: software
Y: Lack of follow-up review process
B: Client wants obsolete system
R: New version bug: software
S: Work from home
D: Client incorrect info on form
V: Client office size too small
Q: Scanning mistake: hardware
Z: Poor support for refresh

The analysis of process data may also include exploratory analyses to determine if certain variables effect process outcomes. For example, a scatter plot was created to determine if there is a relationship between years of employee experience and the time from appointment initiation to resolution (e.g., completion of service, three strikes, or no show). This analysis may be motivated by a hypothesis that more experienced workers would be less likely to cooperate and have longer appointment times, or that less experienced workers may be unfamiliar with the service and therefore take longer to make an appointment. In the scatter plot (Figure 13.6) it is evident that no relationship exists, so there is no need to pursue these hypotheses further.

A contingency table (Table 13.1) was created to study the relationship between the department and the reason for appointment scheduling failure. The contingency table includes some useful insights, including the following: (1) the design department is most likely to experience a problem with no single dominating reason; and (2) the process engineering department reported a disproportionately high proportion of inflexible scheduling failures. Further interviewing of clients and their managers showed that the design department manager, who never supported the refresh service, was

Figure 13.6 Scatter plot of experience versus refresh time.

Table 13.1 Contingency table of department versus reason for appointment failure

Department	Reason for failed appointment code						Total
	G	H	N	E	O	Y	
Design	22	12	18	13	9	14	88
	(25%)	(14%)	(20%)	(15%)	(10%)	(16%)	
Manufacturing	11	5	5	9	10	11	51
	(21%)	(10%)	(10%)	(18%)	(20%)	(21%)	
Process engineering	17	23	11	10	6	4	71
	(24%)	(32%)	(15%)	(14%)	(8%)	(6%)	
Support	7	6	13	1	9	0	36
	(19%)	(17%)	(36%)	(3%)	(25%)	(0%)	
Administration	10	5	2	5	2	0	24
	(42%)	(21%)	(8%)	(21%)	(8%)	(0%)	
Total	67	51	49	38	36	29	270
	(25%)	(19%)	(18%)	(14%)	(13%)	(11%)	

due to retire soon. Process engineers often travel off site on short notice to troubleshoot manufacturing problems.

The available performance metrics (proportion of clients needing rescheduling, proportion of no shows, and proportion of three strikes events) will have limited value in the analysis. These metrics are not collected frequently enough for patterns to emerge, and they already satisfied their role of quantifying the problem with scheduling appointments. The other data whose collection during the measure stage was motivated by this project are more helpful.

The stage should be set for improvement idea generation by looking at the root causes that make the appointment process inflexible, especially those that affect process engineers. A methodology that helps find root cause is referred to as the five whys, which starts with a noticeable problem symptom and iterates until a root cause is uncovered (the number five is arbitrary since the root cause may be found after any number of iterations). Consider the application of the five whys to process engineering clients (in each case, a "why" question is asked followed by a response):

1   Why are there so many no shows and reschedule requests for process engineers? Answer: Because these clients need to change appointments often.
2   Why are appointment changes needed? Answer: Because they require many last-minute trips to troubleshoot manufacturing problems.
3   Why is this a problem? Answer: Because the scheduling system is inflexible and requires a long appointment scheduling lead time.
4   Why is the lead time long? Answer: Because TOE wants to optimize technicians' time and cost.
5   Why is this a concern? Answer: Because HE's contract with TOE requires that TOE highly utilize their technicians to make a profit.

At this point, it would be clear that a potential solution should involve evaluating the contractual relationship between TOE and HE. The intent would be to shorten the lead time between course registration and course delivery. However, shorter lead times require more TOE flexible staffing, which will add TOE labor costs and, therefore, this change would require a contract modification.

I: Improve

The improve stage of DMAIC encompasses the generation and evaluation of interventions (i.e., recommended improvements). The project facilitator plays a critical role in this stage, where their assertiveness is most needed and their value is most apparent. The facilitator needs to stress that intervention recommendations should follow naturally from the previous DMAIC stages. Because humans seek problem solutions naturally, team members will often start thinking about interventions during earlier stages. This tendency needs to be mitigated. The team should avoid documenting intervention ideas until after completion of process and data analyses. The facilitator needs to exude fairness and objectivity when controlling these tendencies, while encouraging enthusiastic participation.

The team should be encouraged to generate ideas using well-known Lean methods (e.g., 5S and poka yoke), as well as more innovative ideas. Lean methods would typically seek to standardize activities, reduce uncertainty, create unambiguous connections, and develop a simple and direct process flow. They attempt to simplify rather than complicate, as they try to improve the value of the information provided during service delivery. The team should consider ways to mistake-proof tasks, especially during information handoffs. Finally, Lean methods should seek to create a system-wide sense of urgency of what's important, ideally using shared and visible communication mechanisms.

At times, so-called "low hanging fruit" will be evident – these are obvious fixes that are easy to implement and obviously beneficial. The only caveat is to avoid simply copying solutions that have been successful in other processes, because they may not address root causes of the problems at hand. It is often tempting to focus interventions on streamlining paperwork flow because a similar approach works well in manufacturing settings. Because services transport intangible information, the project team should be aware that more quickly moving documents that contain mistakes or misunderstood information will not be effective.

Besides Lean methods, innovative ideas are also sought. These interventions tend to have higher impacts, but they are often more difficult to implement. Research on innovation suggests that, contrary to popular belief, the creation of innovative ideas is not a skill that requires a creative mindset. Many innovative thoughts occur when one can think about a situation in new ways. This ability is enhanced using one or more methods that attempt to create an environment where: (1) team members temporarily unlearn what they already know about the process; and (2) seemingly unrelated thoughts can be reshuffled to solve the problem at hand.

It is tempting to consider interventions that involve the implementation of IT, such as handheld devices, PCs, or software modifications. The team should be careful to avoid the automation of waste. If automation is considered, it is imperative that representatives from departments that would be responsible for its creation and maintenance be consulted. Indirect costs, such as training and maintenance, must be considered as well as the capability of the users (especially external customers).

For improving the appointment scheduling activities within the PC refresh process, the project team generated the following intervention ideas based on the application of Lean methods:

A   Self-service scheduling where client accesses technician schedule.
B   HE dashboard to show status of appointment scheduling.
C   Email confirmation with standard terminology (with client acknowledgment).
D   On call part-time TOE technician who creates excess capacity when needed.
E   A tracker to show client where arriving technician is located.
F   TOE modifies clients' mail system to avoid TOE email being categorized as spam.
G   Reword TOE email to eliminate spam-sensitive words.
H   Work with HE client managers for refresh schedule planning.
I   Confirm correct hardware/software just before dispatching technician.

The team also generated the more innovative ideas using a technique called the random word method (random words generators are available online). This method helps team members temporarily unlearn how the current service is offered, which allows them to conceive of new innovative approaches. Because many new ideas can be generated in a short time, the facilitator should allow the free flow of ideas with few restrictions on solution (the ideas will be evaluated later).

The random word method starts with the first random word – the team first discusses its various meanings then associates these meanings with the problem at hand. After some ideas are generated, a new random word is generated, and the procedure continues. The random words (and associated meanings) generated in the project team meeting were fever (associated with illness, slang for strong support with a sports team, etc.), flag (signifying importance, national identity, etc.), and dry (dessert, boring, etc.).

The following intervention ideas were generated using the random word method (the random word that spawned the idea is indicated in parentheses):

J   Client sends computer to TOE when sick or on vacation (fever).
K   Reward those who complete the refresh on time (fever).
L   Complete some refresh remotely (fever).

M   Make extraordinary requirements more visible with checklists (flag).
N   Customer can choose their technician based on published profile (flag).
O   Use same refresh system that TOE uses (flag).
P   Make refresh an exciting time for clients (dry).
Q   Change hiring practice by recruiting people who are collaborative (dry).

The final recommendation (R) followed from the five why exercise performed during the analysis phase. Because their contract with HE motivates TOE to highly utilize their technicians, the project team suggests that the contract terms be considered for revision. The best time for this change would be just before the current contract expires. Hence, the following recommendation is added by the project team:

R   Change TOE contract with HE to promote flexible scheduling using capacity buffers.

The long list of intervention ideas needs to be reduced to a few ideas that will be evaluated more thoroughly, using two criteria. The first criterion concerns projected benefits. The benefits of each idea should be projected for all customers across every dimension of value. The second criterion concerns anticipated costs. The costs of each idea would be associated with implementation time, ease of implementation, risk of creating new problems, required resources, implementation cost, complexity of operation, required training, probability of stakeholder acceptance, and required computer system modifications. As an aside, starting with benefits reduces skepticism regarding an idea because it creates a default desire to make the intervention successful.

The project facilitator needs to ensure that the evaluation process is free of bias. Figure 13.7 shows the project team's evaluation results. Most ideas will tend to fall in the boxes arranged diagonally from bottom left to upper right. This tendency is not especially surprising given the typical correlation between impact and implementation difficulty. Ideas below the diagonal (i.e., B, E, J, M, Q, O, N, and P) are generally not useful ideas because their impacts do not justify implementation concerns. Ideas falling above the diagonal (e.g., H, K, and A) deserve careful consideration because their benefits tend to outweigh costs. For ideas falling on the diagonal, additional information should be generated, including a breakdown of financial costs, details of implementation, implementation time, secondary costs/benefits, maintenance concerns or costs, etc.

At this point, the project team would make their final recommendations. Some recommendations with sufficient benefits and easy implementation can be presented directly to the process manager for consideration (i.e., ideas H and K). Ideas that have good benefits but require moderate or difficult implementation may be recommended to the quality manager, process manager, and the directors at TOE and HE who oversee the PC refresh process activities (i.e., idea A). The project team may also recommend consideration

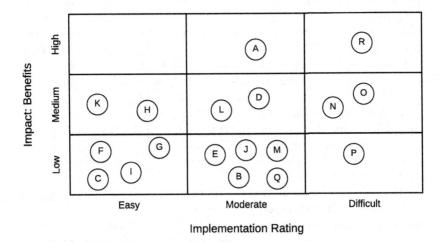

Figure 13.7 Improvement idea evaluation matrix.

of those ideas that have the greatest benefits, regardless of their implementation rating (i.e., idea R).

C: Control

The control stage of DMAIC develops a plan to track implementation progress, collect data on subsequent performance, and mitigate risks. Data on performance may take as many as three forms. First, metrics could be placed within the process to measure targeted activity performance. Second, customer surveys could be created to measure short-term customer perspectives. Third, a feedback mechanism could be initiated to highlight implementation problems.

This DMAIC stage is overlooked by many project teams that mistakenly complete the QI project after recommending interventions to the project sponsor. This stage is critical, however, to ensuring sustainability of improvement implementations. It also enhances the organization's learning about drivers of QI project success. The facilitator needs to ensure that this stage is addressed and that procedures are created for ongoing follow-up. The QI system should include a means to track projects, and QI administrators should periodically evaluate the program's efficacy.

As a component of the control stage, service providers who will implement the new process procedures should document any difficulties, challenges, workarounds, or unanticipated complications. The form of documentation should be quick, easy, and nonjudgmental. For example, employees could write problems they see onto a card or sticky note, which they place onto a centrally located display board. It is important that the note contain an issue rather than an assignment of blame. Periodically, the notes would be retrieved, the issues tabulated, and a subset of the project team could meet to discuss resolutions.

If the goals of the PC refresh appointment scheduling improvement project are met, the reliability of the system should improve to 62.3% from 28.1%. Each year, reliability should be recalculated based on the annual refresh outcomes and metrics. An FMEA could be done to highlight areas of future concern. QI administrators should consider risk mitigation for prioritized failure modes. As a final note, FMEA can play a role in every stage depending on the nature of the project. It can help define goals (D phase), determine key process metrics (M phase), analyze risk for a system (A phase), create a focus for improvement idea generation (I phase), or pinpoint areas of future concern (C phase).

Maintaining discipline for each project should extend to the QI system itself. Because QI projects should result in sustainable changes for the better, the firm needs to avoid projects that do not result in noticeable improvements. Two recommendations should be considered: (1) a standard six-month or one-year project team meeting where recommendations would be revisited, their success analyzed, and modifications considered; and/or (2) a centrally located database or spreadsheet containing information for each project, such as its goals, its results, and its implementation timeframe.

The lead time will usually decrease when waste is removed from a process. Problems that were hidden in the past will become evident in these cases. For example, consider a process having a long lead time where paperwork is routinely returned to the sender for corrections, but these events were unnoticed. This problem will be more noticeable when the lead time is shortened. The analogy often employed to illustrate this phenomenon is the depth of a stream. With high water levels (i.e., significant waste) a boat will have no trouble navigating rocks on the stream's bed. When the water level is reduced (i.e., decreased waste) a boat's progress is likely to be hindered by these rocks. As such, a firm should be aware that generation of new problems is a benefit, rather than a drawback, of the QI system.

Reference

Deming, W.E. (1986). *Out of the Crisis*. Cambridge, MA: MIT Center for Advanced Engineering Study.

14 Quality system creation and deployment

Introduction

Quality strategy refers to how an organization ensures that the quality of its products and services are consistent with its strategic business goals. Although progressive quality management principles and techniques have already been described in this book, some options do exist regarding how they are formalized and implemented. Although flexibility is warranted and desired, some firms inadvertently employ a quality strategy that conflicts with process thinking principles. They can be especially prone to ignoring, sometimes inadvertently, the integration of management practices and quality principles.

This chapter presents a comprehensive quality system that is consistent with a process thinking philosophy. It shows how performance measurement systems, quality analysis methodologies, and QI approaches are integrated within a supportive organizational infrastructure. A quality system can be difficult to deploy because its elements can sometimes appear to conflict with short-term objectives. Its success relies on leadership that appreciates the impact of a supporting culture. If one element of the quality system is missing or misapplied, its entire foundation will be at risk.

Quality system framework

An effective quality system requires the alignment of all incentives, including those that apply to individuals, departments, and the extended enterprise (e.g., suppliers, regulators, and partners). A quality system framework is presented in Figure 14.1. It rests on an organizational foundation having the strength and resiliency to sustain the system. This foundation applies to all departments, functions, processes, and people; it is particularly focused on the ways with which the organization incentivizes behavior.

The framework supports the measurement of performance, which is based on the needs of customer as defined by their lists of performance dimensions. Each process will have a unique set of performance dimensions based on the different needs of their customers, including those that are internal. It contains the determination and collection of performance metrics as well as the creation and dissemination of customer satisfaction surveys.

DOI: 10.4324/9781003199014-14

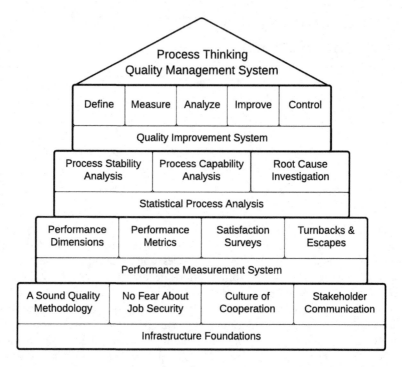

Figure 14.1 Quality system framework.

Ideally, turnbacks (failures found internally) and escapes (failures noticed by customers) would also be tabulated.

The statistical analysis of performance using SPC methods (e.g., process stability analysis and process capability analyses) are also included in the framework. These methods are often associated with the application of other quantitative and qualitative tools, whose main purpose is to identify problems and their root causes. Finally, the QI system should be well defined and disciplined. It should employ a project management construct such as DMAIC or a similar approach.

Infrastructure foundations

Management commitment to a QI program must go beyond slogans, banners, or motivational speeches. Leadership should exude a constancy of purpose, along with discipline and patience to help the program take root. The management team should be made responsible and accountable for both managing the organization and improving its effectiveness. Many methodologies can be employed (e.g., Lean, Six Sigma, or some combination of these or other approaches) as long as the quality system is based on sound principles. Although the methods described in this book are not complex, implementing them effectively often fails because leaders do not appreciate the barriers that can hinder their effectiveness.

The quality system should motivate and expect participation of everyone within the organization. Front-line workers are included because they are closest to customers, know best how processes actually operate, and deal with existing problems on a daily basis. Their managers are needed because they control workers' time and work assignments. They can ensure that time spent improving a process will not interfere with customer service. Manager should encourage the highlighting of problems as a positive aspect of a worker's job. The organization's leadership is needed because hierarchical corporate structures and labor union relations can hinder the ability of a firm to improve business processes. But these challenges can be overcome.

It may seem puzzling that the implementation of a quality system often achieves less success than hoped. Often legacy performance incentives can conflict with achieving an "optimizing the whole" approach. Examples include purchase price reduction goals, bonuses based on the quantity of work completed, and resource utilization targets. An overly assertive approach can also have drawbacks. Moving too quickly to remove inspections or other verifications before substantially eliminating waste can lead to problems that affect customers and discourage continued efforts.

Toyota is well known for its successful production system including the integration of workers ideas, which the firm refers to as "respect for people." They expect workers to participate in process improvement, and workers expect to be acknowledged for their efforts. Workers need to be assured that no job security risk will accompany a QI system. They need to be assured that no punishments will be forthcoming as a result of mistake reporting (even their own mistakes). Toyota acknowledges that individual workers are rarely the root cause of a problem, a concept best stated by W. Edwards Deming, who wrote: "I should estimate that in my experience most troubles and most possibilities for improvement add up to proportions something like this: 94% belongs to the system (responsibility of management)" (Deming, 1986, p. 315).

Changes may be required in an organization that wishes to transform their culture to process thinking. These changes should be initiated slowly and with patience, so that a culture of cooperation is established. A recommended and very visible initial action would be for leadership to make an official statement (and associated policy) that no layoffs would occur as the result of a process improvement project. Indeed, labor cost savings can be achieved, but through reassignments and attrition. This promise would not extend to layoffs necessitated by business downturns or other unexpected disruptions.

A fundamental principle of human behavior is that no one will change unless they envision a personal benefit. A manager cannot expect employees to change their actions for the benefit of the organization if they perceive personal harm. This principle extends to leaders who should not expect managers to change their approach unless they also personally benefit. Finally, the principle extends to groups – like unions – who will cooperate with a

QI program only if its leaders (and members) will benefit. The creation of a sustainable infrastructure requires that attention be given to the four actions that are detailed in the sections that follow.

Choose a sound quality methodology

To be effective, an organization should choose a QI approach that best matches their process types and the employees' skills. The approach should be robust so that the entire organization uses the same set of methodologies, using similar software packages, with a similar project management structure. No internal entity should be allowed to choose their own approach. Differences in terminology, visualizations, and project management constructs will compromise a firm's desire for effective cross-functional cooperation.

Carefully choosing the QI system is critical because it needs to be nurtured over time, which allows its methods to be understood and its philosophies to be engrained. Research has shown that QI systems do not reach their full potential quickly; they require perseverance and time to take root. Mistakes will occur, but they should motivate study to modify the system when warranted. QI methodologies should be easy to understand, and training should be consistent with the chosen methodologies. Just-in-time training, with projects performed by training classes, is effective at creating low-risk projects. The methodologies chosen should be allowed to evolve as circumstances change.

Remove fear associated with job security

Employees often work in an environment of fear, which is usually associated with job insecurity. But workers in successful QI systems need to but are unafraid to ask questions, point out mistakes, or to suggest ways to improve how their service is delivered to customers. Managers can operate in a culture of fear as well. Their concerns may be attributed to missed opportunities for career advancement or poor promotion potential. Managers should be encouraged to suggest changes and not fear being blamed if their suggestions fail. Common management practices can exacerbate fear among managers. For example, monthly quota targets with the dissemination of variance reports showing how the metrics fared relative to the quota can create fear. The end-of-the-month push often prioritizes quantity over quality.

Leadership should ensure that workers and managers do not fear being laid off when a process is improved or being punished for reporting problems. Leaders should address directly the fear that will inevitably accompany a QI program's initiation so that organization-wide support is inevitable. A clear statement should be made by the leadership team guaranteeing that no layoffs will take place because of a process improvement activity. It would also be helpful to create mechanisms for publicizing and celebrating success. These rewards will motivate other employees to participate in future QI projects.

Create a culture of cooperation

Many organizations purport to have workers comprising a team dedicated to a common set of goals. But workers are not always managed in ways that promotes teamwork, especially across departments or functions. On a successful team, each member plays a role and every team member is critical to the team's success. Although there may be a few "all-stars" it is rare that they alone will lead the firm to be successful. Unfortunately, many management structures assume that competition within the team will enable the best performance of each member. They create incentives that work against a successful team approach in favor of an environment where everyone tries to reach all-star status. These structures can work against the team's collective success. They should be replaced by a QI culture that supports cooperation and limits internal competition especially in the presence of cross-functional service process flows.

Gradual but steady implementation is generally preferred over a massive rollout that often produces a "this too shall pass" passive-aggressive reaction. Over time, management at all levels should continuously reinforce a focus on process thinking by avoiding the assignment of blame when problems occur. Supervisors must allow workers to devote attention to improving their work in addition to doing their work. And workers should see that tangible benefits can be derived from their participation in improvement efforts. Gradual implementation also mitigates the effect of mistakes that are likely to occur early in the program's initiation.

Communicate the system to stakeholders

The stakeholders of an organization consist of its suppliers, customers, employees, managers, investors (or shareholders), unions, regulators, accreditors (or certifiers), and the communities within which the firm operates. Although many of these stakeholders would appear to play a passive role in the firm's success, their collective impacts can be great. Their knowledge of, and cooperation with, a QI program is essential. For example, investors and shareholders need to be cognizant of the need to report mistakes, even at the risk of bad publicity. Unions need to be aware that quality improvements will not do harm to their members; they in fact will benefit from the program because of reduced likelihood of their jobs being outsourced to lower cost vendors.

Publicizing the program in early stages helps build support, and publicly communicating project results helps maintain sustainable process improvement. All affected constituencies should be kept abreast of the program's development. This communication should address the tangible benefits that should accrue each stakeholder, while avoiding promises that may not be realized. The leadership team should be involved in a clear, convincing, and vocal way. For example, presenting the results of projects using posters or other visible media, placed predominantly in a common work area or public web site, should be considered.

Turnbacks and escapes

A process manager should understand that although they are best avoided, mistakes represent opportunities to make improvements. Some mistakes are detected before being noticed by a customer, which is referred to as a turnback. Consider a price quoting mistake that is found just before the quote is sent to a customer. This turnback requires that the quote is corrected, which adds time and cost to the process. These consequences would often be hidden from view because the mistake would usually not be tabulated. Therefore, turnbacks are likely to continue in the foreseeable future.

A mistake that does affect a customer is referred to as an escape. For example, an escape would occur when an incorrect price quote is presented to a customer. The cost of this escape depends on many factors. A mistakenly low price quote may force the firm to sell the product at a loss, while a mistakenly high price quote will result in a lost sales opportunity (and perhaps future sales opportunities if the customer removes the firm from future business consideration). Escapes often take the form of customer complaints, although not all complaints are escapes and not all escapes are reported.

The costs of turnbacks and escapes can be tabulated within a COPQ calculation, with turnbacks classified as internal failures and escapes classified as external failures. Both internal and external failure costs could be quantified, although tabulating their occurrences may be sufficient. This tabulation is best when accompanied by a severity rating. The severity rating should be correlated with business impacts and include hidden costs such as correcting mistakes, lost customers, and poor reputation. The importance of tabulating turnbacks and escapes is exemplified by some firms that assume the 1-10-100 rule. This concept states that a single mistake costs 10 times as much to fix when caught immediately after it occurs, and this cost increases to 100 times if noticed by a customer.

Although the cost of making mistakes can be high, they should be leveraged as identifiers of underlying problems. Taking action to quickly eliminate problems or mitigate their impact will improve process performance. It follows that close calls (near mistakes) offer even better opportunities for improvement because no customers are affected and few costs are incurred. In most organizations, however, close calls are not routinely reported.

Some organizations have acknowledged the importance of close call reporting. They make use of systems based on the Aviation Safety Reporting System (ASRS), which is administered by the U.S. Federal Aviation Administration (FAA) and operated by the U.S. National Aeronautics and Space Administration (NASA). This system was first implemented in 1976. All airline personnel (pilots, flight attendants, air traffic controllers, and others) are required to report all "safety incident/situation reports ... Reports submitted to ASRS may describe both unsafe occurrences and hazardous situations." These reports are understood to include both mistakes and close calls. NASA publishes analysis results periodically so that all stakeholders benefit from knowledge gained.

An important aspect of the ASRS is the immunity policy. This policy requires that a report be submitted within 10 days of the incident but

> ensures the confidentiality and anonymity of the reporter, and other parties as appropriate, involved in a reported occurrence or incident. The FAA will not seek, and NASA will not release or make available to the FAA, any report filed with NASA under the ASRS or any other information that might reveal the identity of any party involved in an occurrence or incident reported under the ASRS. There has been no breach of confidentiality in more than 34 years of the ASRS under NASA management.

This immunity extends to punishments for those who submit reports based on their own conduct. Although the conduct will be documented in the reporter's FAA file, no punishment will be forthcoming.

Airline personnel understand that not filing a report in the ASRS can be risky because of the penalties that could result from a reportable incident being discovered later. Some efforts have been made in hospitals to mimic the ASRS; they are often referred to as incident reporting (IR) systems. One hospital (UCSF Medical Center in California) operates an IR system that receives over 20,000 reports annually. Although mistake reporting is generally known to enhance quality, nuances present in many workplaces limit IR. Often, mistake reporting is discouraged either explicitly (e.g., no immunity policy) or implicitly (e.g., a significant paperwork requirement).

Faulty quality management practices

The effectiveness of a quality management framework (e.g., Figure 14.1) will be compromised if some of its elements are ignored. Examples abound. Many firms rely on metrics that are readily available but do not cover all important customer performance dimensions. Some firms overtly focus on KPIs that do not quantify the totality of concerns that should be addressed by their leadership. Similarly, many forms focus on cost-related and highly visible metrics, such as the number of customers served, labor cost, or equipment utilization. In many cases, business needs are given priority over customer needs. A common infrastructure failure is the absence of a "no layoff" policy for improvement efforts. If workers are laid off after a process improvement project, workers will not continue to actively participate and future project success will be compromised.

MBO

Incentive systems constitute a popular management practice that compromises quality system effectiveness. For example, MBO and process thinking form a dysfunctional pair. Even well-intentioned managers will allow MBO schemes to remain when attempting to implement process thinking. Quality systems that incentivize employees based on targeted metrics can lead to gaming or outright fraud and ethical violations. Two well-known cases are educators cheating on high stakes testing systems in Atlanta and employees creating fake customer accounts at Wells Fargo.

In 2009, standardized test results in Atlanta's public schools were falsified. Although teachers and administrators were blamed (in fact, some of them served prison sentences) perverse incentive systems were the root of the fraudulent actions. When explaining why they cheated, guilty parties blamed the pressure to meet unfair test result targets. At Wells Fargo, starting around 2013, sales staff opened millions of accounts for customers without their consent. These actions were a response to sales quotas that rewarded them for cross-selling financial products. This scandal was well-reported in the press, although executives faced fewer criminal penalties than the school teachers in Atlanta.

Performance dashboards

Performance dashboards have become a ubiquitous presence in many forms. They are especially prevalent in executive suites where the firm's KPIs are aggregated in hopes of providing a clear picture of recent performance trends. They are also used when external suppliers are a predominant mechanism for delivery systems (e.g., insurance claims processing, medical image interpretation, call centers, and audio transcription). The dashboard often presents each KPI as a dial or color-coded visualization that compares performance to targets. Usually, green shows that a target is achieved and red that a target is not achieved (sometimes yellow is used to indicate that the target is almost achieved). The dashboard would be updated periodically, usually monthly or quarterly.

With few exceptions, a performance dashboard promotes an MBO approach, and therefore they conflict with the intentions of a process thinking quality system. Fault lies in their inability to provide useful contextual information and their encouragement of rewards and punishments for individuals or departments. A useful example involves how a dashboard would be used to encourage quality improvement. Assume that a KPI that has consistently shown green has its target changed to motivate better performance. The previous month, the target was met (green color) but this month the target was not met (red color), even though the process has not changed. Previous rewarded entities will no longer be rewarded even though their performance has not degraded.

Dashboards provide poor contextual information about quality because they will not tell a manager when: (1) the process achieves a target but its performance has recently degraded; (2) a process does not meet the target but its performance is improving; or (3) random variation causes a target to be met one month but not the next month (or vice versa) — when in fact the process is unchanged. The fear created by a performance dashboard can result in what Deming described as workers shifting from serving customers to serving "the numbers." A dashboard often ignores the role played by the system because they assign responsibility to individuals, which can result in a culture of blame. Like the Atlanta public schools and Wells Fargo cases, they will often cause metrics to be gamed or artificially manipulated. These actions draw attention away from satisfying customer needs and create useless data sets for QI project teams.

Organizing the quality function

Although no standard departmental structure exists within organizations, one function or department should be responsible for maintaining the firm's quality system. Here we will assume that responsibility rests with the QA department. Its specific responsibilities depend on many factors, including the type of business and the size of the firm. Besides quality, its responsibility may extend to the management of accreditation (or certification), risk (or business continuity), and/or compliance (or regulatory affairs). In smaller firms or startups, the quality system may be the responsibility of a single individual or committee.

Regardless of the entity that maintains the quality system, every process manager should be expected to ensure the quality of services they deliver to customers. The QA function provides the tools and systems to allow this responsibility to be implemented successfully. Indeed, the QA function's role includes quality system development and maintenance, and QI system oversight. They provide instructors for training courses and facilitators for improvement projects. The QA function is also responsible for ensuring that process thinking is nurtured throughout the organization. They should inform leadership when they see policies that conflict with a process thinking mindset.

Roles and responsibilities

The QA function should ensure that performance metrics and satisfaction surveys are aligned with customer performance dimensions and that data are collected in unbiased and precise ways. They should be the developers of the satisfaction surveys that are likely to be completed, with unbiased questions and a precise set of response options for each question. Although turnbacks and escapes are best tabulated at the process level, the QA department needs to provide guidance and a common database. They should ensure that training courses employ consistency in approach throughout the firm. This consistency extends to methods, terminology, software, and reporting formats.

The QA function should be responsible for the implementation of statistical process analysis methodologies, which requires an infrastructure that includes IT (e.g., performance data collection, statistical application, and visualization software) as well as statistical analysis expertise (e.g., consultation, training, webinars, and updates). QI system oversight encompasses many of the same elements as statistical process analysis, along with RCA tool training and support and DMAIC training and facilitation.

A larger QA function should be organized around specialties (e.g., product lines or service categories) but only when the process activities vary significantly from one specialty to another. A good application of this approach would be an insurance company that organizes the QA function based on insurance products, such as life, auto, home, and health. This approach works well when products lines are independent of one another where it may be necessary to use different software or analysis methods. It may not be wise to organize the QA function by technical specialty due to the importance of integrating principles, methods, and techniques within the QI system. A liaison should be assigned to each department in the firm, so that every process manager has a single point of contact in the QA function.

Ensure departmental involvement

The QA function should pay close attention to its working relationships with each department within the firm, who are their clients for the quality system. All departments, including those that serve only internal customers, should be included. Each department may wish to appoint a process improvement liaison. The liaison will serve as a communication link with QA while possessing credibility among their peers. The liaison will help present the program as valuable to the department rather than pushed onto the department from "headquarters." One-to-one connections reduce the tendency for "if its everyone's job it's no one's job" syndrome.

Several risks emerge in a firm whose departments do not all participate enthusiastically in quality system activities. External customer quality can suffer because of the cross-functional nature of many service processes. A department may include one or two supporters who participate repeatedly in improvement projects, which decreases the chance of long-term viability. The attitude exuded by skeptical department personnel can sabotage other departments' efforts to motivate participation among their workers.

Focus on an appropriate toolbox

Only the basic tools of QI are necessary during the early stages of a process improvement system implementation, with priority given to tools not requiring application by experts. The tools utilized in projects need to create mutual understanding and transparency. When a worker improves how their work is done, they are motivated to play an active role in future projects. Other employees viewing project results will become less intimidated and often volunteer for membership on project teams. A common toolbox also economizes training and software application costs. A few specialized internal or external experts can be developed or made available when the need arises.

Many project teams need to interact remotely because they are geographically dispersed. Workers may provide a similar service although they are not located in close proximity, which precludes in-person project meetings. For example, a legal firm may outsource audio transcription to multiple firms located in various worldwide locations. Improving these processes should involve all suppliers of the service. Recent increases in WFH, either as a routine work environment or in response to a business disruption, provides motivation for setting up a system of process improvement that does not rely on co-located project teams. A common toolbox of analysis routines and electronic synchronous interfaces would be necessary to maintain cohesiveness.

Develop skilled project facilitators

QI project facilitators are critical to the success of improvement projects, and they help to ensure consistency in project management approaches. Each facilitator needs to be skilled in the techniques of quality management, while also being assertive, competent, and impartial. They should have effective communication skills and be able to work with both management and staff. External consultants can be used as temporary project facilitators especially when the organization is new to QI. But this practice should be considered temporary. Internal facilitators should be chosen carefully because not every technically competent employee will make an effective project facilitator.

The most important task for a facilitator during a QI project concerns team dynamics. When a skeptical worker is forced to join a project team, their lack of enthusiasm or passive aggressive stance can disrupt the mood of cheerfulness that a facilitator needs to establish. Overconfident team members can also cause conflict when they consider themselves "the smartest person in the room." They will not listen well to the thoughts and recommendations of others, thereby causing frustration and loss of team cohesiveness. Perhaps the most challenging personality is one who wants to control the project by having their ideas implemented, usually for egotistical or selfish reasons. They will actively conspire to control the project in explicit and subtle ways. These individuals are especially problematic when organizational politics or reporting structures restrict free and open communication within the project team.

Reference

Deming, W.E. (1986). *Out of the Crisis.* Cambridge, MA: MIT Center for Advanced Engineering Study.

15 Quality improvement with remote collaboration

Introduction

The COVID-19 pandemic forced most organizations to quickly create and manage WFH environments for their professional employees. The need for WFH was not new (e.g., WFH was common in the northern United States during winter storms), but the breadth of its application across jobs were unprecedented, as was the duration of WFH in many firms. A parallel phenomenon has existed in QI project teams for multinational firms. What used to be informal and sporadic remote QI projects now need to be managed more comprehensively. Projects can no longer be routinely undertaken with participants traveling to a common location where the problem existed. The reduction or elimination of travel has motivated the need for a more robust QI project management approach.

This chapter details the operation of a system whereby QI projects are completed in virtual settings with participants who are geographically dispersed and culturally diverse. It describes challenges associated with distance, culture, skills, and workplace, while making recommendations for operating a QI project that overcomes these challenges. It makes suggestions on how to manage remote meetings that include data visualization interpretation, improvement of idea generation, and implementation planning. The intent is to leverage the opportunities afforded by newer technologies so that a QI project's success is consistent with (or potentially better than) a traditional in-person project.

Challenges and opportunities

The evolution to remote working environments for QI project teams has paralleled other technology-enabled modifications to product and service delivery. Shoppers now expect to use technology that eliminates the need for travel to purchase goods, execute financial transactions, or consult with healthcare providers, among others. Although many of these service offerings have been improved, they required time and customer education to overcome challenges when transitioning from brick-and-mortar services.

DOI: 10.4324/9781003199014-15

QI project teams can be enhanced when transitioning from in-person to remote meetings by utilizing state-of-the-start technology with new project paradigms. For example, the ability to reach out to experts outside of the project team is enhanced when meetings are held virtually. Internal or external expertise can be quickly and temporarily called upon during specific project stages like problem definition, metric identification, data collection, and FMEA development. This ability enhances the accuracy of project information without unnecessarily delaying a project's timeline.

Many challenges need to be overcome when managing a remote project. Participants can more easily be distracted by other tasks or commitments at home or in their workspace. Unenthusiastic team members can more easily maintain a passive attitude about the project than they could at an in-person meeting location. The inability to see a problem first-hand or visit the area affected by a problem can compromise its understanding. Technology failures can stop the progress of a project, including when some team members' technologies or technical abilities are insufficient.

Many new capabilities can be leveraged to the benefit of a remote QI project team. Project costs can be reduced substantially when team members no longer travel to a common location. These savings include direct costs such as transportation, food, and beverage, as well as indirect costs such as facility cleaning and maintenance. Time management can be simplified because logistical obstacles are reduced. A meeting's progress can be enhanced when team members have faster access to information during discussions. The ability to record meetings allows all team members to be privy to all discussions, even when they miss all or part of a team meeting. In addition, recordings can be revisited as more project-related knowledge is gained; for example, discussions with customers or service providers may be better understood after the teams know more about the process being analyzed.

The remainder of this section includes a discussion on important factors that should be considered when developing a QI project management system with remote collaboration. The discussion is followed by a list of recommendations that circumvent challenges and improve QI project effectiveness.

Impact of distance

Many challenges of remote collaboration concern a form of distance: geographical, linguistical, and cultural. Geographical distance requires participants to use technology to collaborate, a topic that is discussed in detail here. Often, the most difficult challenge for geographically dispersed project teams concerns time zone differences, which impacts the scheduling of synchronous meetings. Enterprises that operate global supply chains have traditionally dealt with this challenge by relocating liaisons and adjusting work schedules (although supply chain managers will often be required to hold meetings at inconvenient times and nonworking hours).

Most traditional approaches that enterprises with global supply chains employ will be ineffective for QI project teams. For example, relocations and work schedule adjustments are usually not possible. Widely available calendar applications help by allowing team members to choose available time slots that adjust for local time zones. For lengthy (e.g., 10–12 hours) time zone differences, workers may need to sacrifice personal time for the sake of the project. Moving some of the work to an asynchronous format can reduce the need for inconvenient meetings, although this approach sacrifices the ability to collaborate on important parts of the project. Asynchronous approaches should be undertaken with caution because many decisions (e.g., analysis results) become individualized rather than collaborative.

The necessity for remote communication can make it difficult to appreciate various forms of nuance, although video-enabled communication helps in this regard. In fact, "camera on" expectations should be observed when privacy is not compromised. Team members should also be aware that presenting on video makes it more difficult to infer enthusiasm. Giving presentations with a "laid back" attitude can be conceived as apathy. Therefore, presenters should use facial expressions as the primary means to project enthusiasm.

The limited informal times spent together (e.g., a coffee chat or water cooler conversation) can also hamper idea exchange and reduce the likelihood of inspiration offered by peers and managers within the firm. A famous example is Dr. Katalin Karikó, a co-developer of the mRNA vaccine, who met her most important collaborator (Dr. Drew Weissman) at a photocopying machine where she conversed with him about cooperation in vaccine development. Differences in laws and regulations that apply in each team member's location should be identified and addressed. They may impact information-sensitive projects or government-sensitive businesses, although intra-enterprise collaboration will usually not be affected.

Impact of language and culture

Another challenge for remote collaboration concerns linguistics, including spoken languages, idioms, jargon, and slang expressions. In most professional settings around the world, English has become the primary second language. Therefore, the spoken language itself is typically not a major barrier for QI project teams. For team members who are employed within a specialized industry, jargon is usually well understood (although some jargon is discipline-specific). The use of unknown expressions (e.g., idioms and slang) by some team members can lead to embarrassment, confusion, or a team member feeling neglected or isolated. For example, "ballpark figure" has been interpreted as a sporting participant rather than a numerical estimate. Other examples of misunderstood U.S.-based expressions include piece of cake, dead in the water, hard and fast rule, and circle back. Unnecessarily complex wording can also be problematic, even for some native speakers.

Cultural differences exist among members of many remote project teams. It is important to distinguish culture from stereotype, where often negative characteristics are attributed to groups of people based on unsubstantiated beliefs. Culture is a defining characteristic of human beings; it results from geography, education system, history, political systems, and other objectively determined causes. Culture impacts one's values, beliefs, traditions, attitudes, and behaviors. Tolerance of other cultures, and their approaches to life and business, provide a critical foundation for understanding people and building relationships. It is important for all team members to be cognizant of culture. Ideally, they will be interested in learning from their culturally diverse teammates. Otherwise, teams can suffer from hurt feelings and miscommunications (e.g., some jokes may be interpreted as insulting by some team members).

Impact of technology skills

Most remote interactions require participants to operate technology-enabled communication systems without real-time support. The firm should provide technology and training to all potential contributors. A QI project facilitator needs to ensure that every team member can participate prior to the project's kick-off session. To avoid project timeline delays, it may be necessary to modify the team's configuration while the required skills are obtained. A precise checklist of team members' skill requirements would be warranted.

Employers should enforce a common remote collaboration platform to ensure compatibility and technology integration. Some remote communication applications do not support Windows and OS operating systems equally well. The information and data analysis software used by the team should be available for all team members, and the version employed should be consistent across the team. The firm needs to keep instructions up to date and provide training in a consistent manner. Technology support can be difficult in WFH environments, but risks can be mitigated by providing company-supplied laptops with preinstalled software to all team members.

Impact of workspace

Few locations around the world pose a physical or technological barrier to remote collaboration. WFH has become commonplace, either as a temporary measure during disruptive events (e.g., flood, fire, pandemic), or as a routine work plan that many employees utilize periodically. Some workers are unable to adapt easily to these WFH settings, especially those with child or elder care responsibilities. Team members are generally sympathetic and even enjoy the occasional child or pet intrusion into a remote meeting. At times, however, these distractions can prevent meaningful work from taking place.

The sense of common mission can be compromised when workers are not located in a common physical meeting space. This effect is mitigated when team members already work together or know each other well. It is up to the facilitator to create a sense of common purpose in the QI project team. A game or other social event can be employed before the project begins to foster comfort across the team. Remote project teams may also encounter difficulty accessing certain documents, especially those not electronically enabled. Concerns regarding sensitive information that are stored in locked offices or behind firewalls need to be considered. In some projects, laboratory or other work-related equipment are not available at home.

Impact of work tasks

Remote project team coordination requires a new set of management skills. These new skills include allocating tasks to enhance collaboration among different teams, setting priorities to achieve common goals within a company, ensuring work efficiency with less direct supervision, encouraging new employees to contribute, and avoiding negative emotional impacts. These emotional impacts include implicit biases, multitask conflicts, disproportionate work-life balance, and mental health issues. A greater focus on fostering team spirit would be warranted in virtual meeting settings.

WFH requires precautions concerning the potential for hacking and the protection of sensitive information. Web security is a concern for remote project teams that operate in multiple regions around the world. The inability to explicitly monitor workers or provide direct mentorship of new or inexperienced workers can be concerning. Remote workers should be self-motivated and assertive, asking questions when needed but otherwise working autonomously. The team needs to be aware that sensitive conversations can be heard by others when work is done in quasi-public settings or places where people gather. And the project team needs to be careful when they store information to ensure privacy and information security.

Recommended approach

The most important goals when creating a remote QI system are enthusiastic participation and effective engagement. Not only does today's technology make remote collaboration possible, but when used effectively it creates a work environment that is superior to in-person settings. These advantages will not be experienced unless organizers take many of the actions recommended in this section. Project organizers should be cognizant of both the advantages and risks of remote collaboration. The firm needs to ensure that the technology they employ is easy to use but capable, although there is no need to implement technology that is laden with features that project teams are unlikely to employ.

The important role of facilitators is expanded when the QI project team works remotely. They should possess the technical skills to set up and manage remote sessions. Facilitators should be experienced working with remote teams because they need to ensure that all team members are engaged in the project's activities. Facilitators should understand the impact of language differences to ensure that communications within the team is effective. And they should appreciate the nuance that cultural differences introduce, while ensuring that interactions are professional and respectful.

Remote project teams with diverse membership can suffer from subtle forms of confusion and misunderstandings. Certain words and expressions may not be understood by every team member. The facilitator should attempt to impose a standard set of terms corresponding to the problem statement and project objectives that are maintained throughout the project. For example, if the project seeks to reduce mistakes, synonyms of mistake such as lapse or blunder be avoided. An informal game can be introduced whereby uses of slang or idioms are flagged with the identifying team members awarded a small prize. Simply making team members aware when they use these terms is helpful; they will begin to self-identify them as the project proceeds. Finally, when recommending process interventions, simple terms should be used such as "pick up the form" instead of "retrieve the form."

Concerted action should be taken in response to cultural differences. Devoting time to informal activities that allow team members to exchange personal stories and anecdotes can be an effective approach. Consider the National Basketball Association that includes players from over 40 countries. The Philadelphia franchise had a starting line-up consisting of a Croat, an Australian, a Caucasian American from the southern United States, an African American from Chicago, and a native of Cameroon. A recent head coach, Brett Brown, organized breakfasts where informal talks were given by players and coaches, with topics that included pet snakes, tattoos, experiences in the Balkan conflict, and Australian wildlife. Culture should also be considered when making recommendations for improvement. Although most improvement concepts are universal, implementation plans should be tailored to the prominent culture at the targeted process location.

The mission of a QI project team with technology-enabled remote collaboration can be enhanced by creating a secondary (i.e., ancillary) project team. This team will not fully participate in all stages of the project, but they possess specialized process or customer knowledge that may be helpful to the project team. They will know details regarding marketing, IT, regulations, and other topics that may become important as the project progresses. A secondary team member can be asked to attend part of a meeting to address a specific issue. For example, if the project team is completing an FMEA, a secondary team member from manufacturing can be asked to attend. Their contribution would consist of identifying production-related failure occurrence probabilities and explaining failure detection mechanisms.

Project teams should avoid asynchronous activities to a reasonable extent. Asynchronous work tasks seem appealing because of the flexibility they afford. Team members can work independently, then meet to consolidate results. But this approach rarely works well in QI projects, whose activities need to be tightly integrated. It is especially ineffective during idea generation, data interpretation, root cause identification, and other interactive tasks. For example, when one team member is given the responsibility to interpret the results of a data analysis, their interpretation can be biased or inaccurate. There will be a tendency for other team members to trust the interpretation because they have not been directly involved, or they may keep quiet to avoid embarrassing their teammate. Many project tasks are dependent on other tasks, and asynchronous work can delay project timelines while a team member waits for their colleague to complete a prerequisite analysis.

Software application recommendations

Software applications enable remote QI project teams to complete their work effectively without creating an unnecessarily complex work environment. Applications should be powerful and robust. But they should also be intuitive so that advanced training is unnecessary. Applications designed for technology professionals and those that are ladened with many advanced features should be avoided. Many of today's software applications are appropriate for QI project teams. In most cases, firms already use these systems to support WFH and other forms of remote meetings.

This section makes recommendations for the features that should be considered when choosing software applications for a QI project team. It also includes guidelines concerning how to leverage these features. The recommendations cover four perspectives: teleconferencing, collaborative software, social networking, and project dissemination. In each case, features are classified as "must have" or "nice to have" based on a typical project framework. The section ends with a summary of the recommendations (Table 15.1).

Teleconferencing applications

Teleconferencing software enables members of project teams in dispersed locations to meet synchronously. Various teleconferencing applications have many features in common that can enhance project success. Some of the must have features common to teleconferencing applications include participants' ability to see and hear presenters (and their presentation materials), participant audio feed that can be muted by the participant or the meeting host, and host ability to restrict attendance to invited individuals. When used intelligently, these features can help facilitate meetings that are more effective than their in-person counterparts.

The ability of team members to engage a video feed is a must have feature. Video feeds enable a facilitator and the project team to judge participants' emotions during project deliberations. They highlight a team member's enthusiasm, confusion, or uncertainty. Screen sharing initiated by every team member is another must have feature because it enhances collaboration and information exchange. A team member can share their screen to solicit feedback and participant reactions. They can also show the team documents, websites, or other visualizations to enhance understanding of the problem at hand or its solution.

Teleconference breakout rooms are very helpful during multiple QI project stages – this feature is a must have. The combination of large group deliberations and breakout rooms can amplify engagement of both extroverted and introverted personalities. Extroverted participants tend to thrive in a larger group environment while introverted thinkers often feel intimidated in large groups. Breakout rooms can vary in size and create a more collaborative environment for introverted thinkers. They are also effective at data interpretation and idea generation where every team member input is sought. The small groups can contrast their results after returning to the full team session. Examples where breakout rooms can enhance team success include SIPOC development, interpretation of data visualizations, root cause investigation (e.g., five whys), idea generation for QI, and FMEA development.

The ability to record meetings is a final must have for a QI project teleconferencing application. Absent team members can watch the recording later, while others who were distracted during the meeting or misunderstood a portion of the deliberations can view a targeted section. Recordings are especially helpful when the team interviews stakeholders (e.g., customers, service providers, and others), because some nuances will be appreciated only after more is known. Videos should be firewall or password protected to restrict access by unauthorized individuals. The facilitator should be aware that participants will easily forget a meeting is being recorded. A team member may state embarrassing or sensitive information. Editing capability can be employed if allowing this information to remain in the recording is a concern.

Allowing participants to send short chat messages to the group or a subset of team members is useful and should be considered a nice to have feature. Some applications allow participants to send web links or documents using the chat feature, which can be especially helpful for quick information exchange (thereby precluding the need to send information by email). The chat feature can also be helpful for cross-language or cross-disciplinary project teams because unknown words or phrases can be typed into the chat and quickly defined.

Other features that are nice to have in teleconferencing applications depend on the nature of the project. Audio transcriptions act as detailed meeting minutes and they can help some participants understand unknown words of phrases including cases where pronunciations were not clear. The ability to remotely control another participant's screen can be a help to troubleshoot minor technical glitches or confusion. Icons that show reactions by participants (such as thumbs up, raising hand, or applause) are effective for larger meetings when the facilitator seeks opinions. Finally, a white board (during screen sharing) for ad hoc communication of ideas can be helpful, especially when participants' devices employ touch screen technology.

Collaborative software applications

A QI project team will hold highly interactive synchronous meetings during all phases of an improvement project. Typically, software applications (e.g., spreadsheets, word processing, and presentation) will likely be employed; all team members should be familiar with their use. Other applications specifically designed for team collaboration should also be made available. These applications include affinity diagramming, flowcharting, and SIPOC documentation. Some collaborative software applications include templates that are nice to have, although they often cause users to compromise their needs for the sake of the template. Analytical software that applies statistical or modeling methods will likely be used by a subset of the team's membership.

A QI project will find more than one collaborative software application useful. Popular spreadsheet, presentation, and word processing packages are generally able to exist within a collaborative structure. They would be used, for example, during FMEA development, report writing, and presentation creation. Statistical software and other specialized analysis tools (including programming languages) need not be included among the collaborative applications because not all team members will possess the expertise to use them. But the presentation of results from these applications should be visually intuitive so that the entire team can participate in interpretation discussions.

File sharing using cloud storage is a must have for effective remote collaboration. The organization should ensure that access to documents can be restricted, especially when information is private, or the team is not ready (or is not inclined) to make their deliberations public. Simultaneous document editing is required without the creation of conflicting documents. This capability eliminates confusion or later reediting. Facilitators need to be aware that some team members who lack confidence will not want drafts of their work made available to the team. They may, for example, wish to have the facilitator approve files before they are posted. It is up to the facilitator to handle this situation while being aware that delays in making certain documents available can hamper team progress.

Scheduling meetings when participants span time zones has always been a significant challenge, especially when meeting schedules are created by more than one participant. A must have for remote collaboration is a calendar application that automatically adjusts meeting times based on each individual's time zone. With participants using a variety of smart phone and laptop calendar applications, conflicts can arise when their integration is unsuccessful. Hence, a good calendar application should include reminders for each participant, which have increased importance when meetings are scheduled during usual time periods (e.g., evening hours) or when participants WFH.

Network stability is important for all team members. The firm should ensure that remotely located employees have a reliable information infrastructure. A virtual private network (VPN), firewall, and other cyber security precautions are also the responsibility of the firm; they should be considered a must have collaborative application. These systems ensure that documents and information are secure and hacking potential is minimized.

Social networking applications

Although any form of social networking for QI project teams should be classified nice to have, some potentially significant benefits can result from informal interactions within the project team. This social networking suggestion does not replace the teleconferencing application described earlier, or the use of company email to communication formally between meetings. The social networking application can facilitate informal communications while enhancing and maintaining a healthy team atmosphere. The application would typically allow for nonintrusive communication that team members can quickly consider and react to (or not react to) that maintain awareness of the topics addressed.

The choice of application should consider the locations of team members, because some applications are not available worldwide. With any social networking application, individual team members would be able to chat with individual colleagues or send a message to the entire team. Simple tasks, such as meeting confirmation, location, and agenda can be quickly accomplished, ensuring that participants are fully prepared for scheduled group meetings. Issues that become apparent to one or more team members between meetings can quickly be communicated to the team without the risk of team members wasting time when errors or misunderstandings exist. The application should also allow for voice calls and, optionally, video calls for more nuanced or vital communications.

The social networking application should be able to communicate photos and videos. These visuals should be related to the project, even tangentially or in a humorous way. Team spirit can be enhanced while maintaining an environment that leads to innovative idea generation later in the project. For example, consider a project that seeks to improve the waiting time for customers of a virtual help desk. Team members who spend time in line for any number of different services (doctor's office, retail store, restaurant, etc.) can send a photo and make a comment about the queue. They can include information about how the queue is managed (good and bad elements). This type of interaction keeps team members engaged, reminds them of the project at hand, and generates thoughts regarding what methods may apply to the process under study.

Project dissemination applications

A QI project team should inform all stakeholders about the project. These stakeholders include employees who deliver the service under study and employees in other departments who interact with the process. These communications can help motivate worker participation in future QI projects. The team could also communicate information about the project to internal customers, regulators, IT personnel, and other internal stakeholders. These communications can generate useful feedback from individuals with insight into the problem being studied. It helps to break down barriers between

Table 15.1 Recommendations for remote applications (X = must have, /= nice to have)

Teleconferencing

Video–audio	Maintain ability to see and hear presenter	X
Invitation only	Maintain confidentiality	X
Video feed	Observe team members' emotions	X
Screen share	Enhance multisource information exchange	X
Breakout rooms	Engage introverted personalities	X
Recording	Maintain archival meeting information	X
Chat	Quickly confirm meanings and context	/
Audio transcription	Help with language issues if viewing later	/
Remote control	Help troubleshoot problems	/
Reactions	Signify comprehension or voting	/
White board	Demonstrate ideas in ad hoc ways	/

Collaborative working

Document creation	Allow all team members to create files	X
File sharing	Allow all team members access	X
Cloud storage	Permit access to files from anywhere	X
Editing	Facilitate simultaneous editing without conflicts	X
VPN	Maintain data privacy	X
Calendar and reminders	Arrange meetings across time zones	X
Firewall	Restrict file access	X

Social networking

Individual chat	Enable quick information exchange	/
Group chat	Engage all members in real-time	/
Photo/video share	Build team spirit and show relevant visuals	/
Audio calls	Enable one-on-one quick conversations	/
Video calls	Create intimate interactions	/

Dissemination

Word processing app	Create reports and other documents	X
Presentation app	Create slide shows or posters	X
E-distribution	Place documents on stakeholder websites	X
Video creation	Create demonstrations and tutorials	X
Video editing	Edit online tutorials and presentations	/
Screen recorder	Create tutorials and demonstrations	/

departments and exposes key stakeholders to the QI program. Optionally, by including external stakeholders, the QI project team can promote a sense of progressiveness and competency for the firm.

The project team should pay close attention to the content of the information it disseminates, along with its format. Accurate information should be generated in the context of confidential or privacy concerns, while maintaining awareness of internal sensitivities. Information should be communicated in standard ways to promote understanding across the organization and over time. A standard reporting format plays a secondary role of exposing future project team members to the QI methodology used by the firm.

Standard word processing and presentation software will suffice for a primary communication tool. Templates that create project charters, one-page executive summaries, and posters should be made available to all project teams. Saving the files so that they cannot be edited is critical to avoid unauthorized changes. Information dissemination will need to be electronic when project teams are dispersed; this ability should be considered a must have. Electronic versions may be placed on a shared drive or company web site, while printed materials can be posted in areas visited by target stakeholders. These locations include the facility's lobby, high traffic hallways, and company cafeterias or break rooms.

Videos are effective at disseminating important presentations, or to create and distribute excerpts from more lengthy presentations. An application to generate videos is a must have. Videos can also demonstrate how new service delivery approaches would operate, both the physical activities (e.g., where customers should wait in line) and cognitive activities (e.g., how to run a software application). Presentations made and recorded at professional conferences are ideal for distribution – they showcase the QI project and highlight the firm's professional exposure. Knowledge workers who deliver these presentations will personally benefit from making the presentations more widely viewed.

Creating more professional videos requires editing software, which should be considered nice to have. Many video editing applications are inexpensive and easy to use. Only basic video editing capabilities are necessary for the editing of QI videos. This software will likely include screen capture for demonstrating software applications or new electronic service approaches.

Index

Printed in the United States
by Baker & Taylor Publisher Services